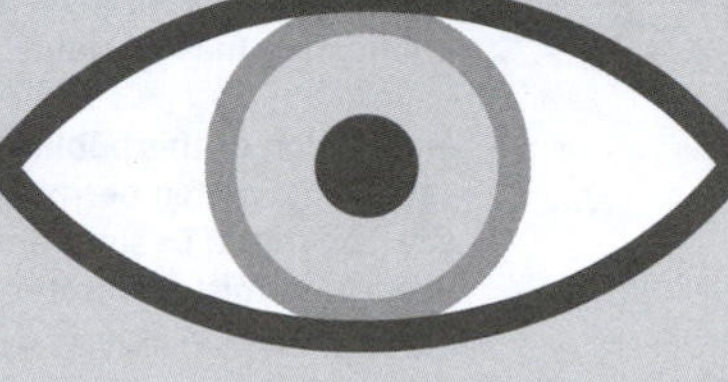

Obsessive Compulsive Disorder

Graham Davey,
Suzanne Dash and
Frances Meeten

PALGRAVE INSIGHTS IN PSYCHOLOGY

SERIES EDITORS:
NIGEL HOLT
& ROB LEWIS

palgrave
macmillan

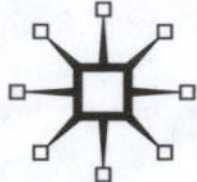

First published 2014 by
PALGRAVE MACMILLAN

Palgrave Macmillan in the UK is an imprint of Macmillan Publishers Limited, registered in England, company number 785998, of Houndmills, Basingstoke, Hampshire RG21 6XS.

Palgrave Macmillan in the US is a division of St Martin's Press LLC, 175 Fifth Avenue, New York, NY 10010.

Palgrave Macmillan is the global academic imprint of the above companies and has companies and representatives throughout the world.

Palgrave® and Macmillan® are registered trademarks in the United States, the United Kingdom, Europe and other countries.

ISBN 978–1–137–30868–9

This book is printed on paper suitable for recycling and made from fully managed and sustained forest sources. Logging, pulping and manufacturing processes are expected to conform to the environmental regulations of the country of origin.

A catalogue record for this book is available from the British Library.

A catalog record for this book is available from the Library of Congress.

Typeset by MPS Limited, Chennai, India.

Printed in China

Contents

List of Figures and Tables

Figures

Tables

Acknowledgements

Graham Davey

For my mother, Betty. Also, I would like to acknowledge the dedication and professionalism of my two co-authors during the production of this book – two great colleagues and friends.

Suzanne Dash

This book would not have been possible without the support of Paul Stevens and Jenny Hindley at Palgrave Macmillan, and I thank them for their interest in this addition to the Psychology Insights collection. I am deeply indebted to my co-authors, Graham Davey and Frances Meeten. Graham - thank you for inviting me to join the project and for your expert guidance along the way, and Fran, thank you for sharing the journey and providing the chocolate biscuits. Finally, for enduring yet another summer of writing, a special thank you to my family. Mum and Dad – this is for you.

Frances Meeten

I am grateful to my co-authors Graham Davey and Suzanne Dash for being great company and providing lots of encouragement during the writing of this book. I would also like to thank Palgrave Macmillan for giving us the opportunity to write this book and the many researchers and clinicians whose work has informed the writing of this book. Last but not least, I would like to dedicate this book to my parents.

Publisher's Acknowledgements

The publisher and authors would like to thank the organizations and people listed below for permission to reproduce material from their publications:

Table 2.2 reprinted from *Journal of Affective Disorders*, 124 (3), Fullana, M. A., Vilagut, G., Rojas-Farreras, S., Mataix-Cols, D., de Graaf, R., Demyttenaere, K., Haro, J. M., de Girolamo, G., Lépine, J. P., Matschinger, H. & Alonso, J., Obsessive compulsive symptom dimensions in the general population: Results from an epidemiological study in six European countries, 291–299, copyright 2010, with permission from Elsevier.

Case History 2.2 reprinted from *Journal of Autism and Developmental Disorders*, 38 (5), Lehmkuhl, H. D., Brief report: Exposure and response prevention for obsessive compulsive disorder in a 12-year old with autism, copyright 2007, with permission from Springer.

Case History 2.3 reprinted from *Psychosomatics*, 46 (5), Morris, D. R., Meighen, K. G. & McDougle, C. J., Acute onset of obsessive-compulsive disorder in an adolescent with acute lymphoblastic leukemia, 458–460, copyright 2005, with permission from Elsevier.

Case History 3.6 reprinted from *Psychopathology: Research, Assessment and Treatment in Clinical Psychology*, Davey, G., copyright 2008, with permission from Wiley-Blackwell.

Box 4.1 and Figure 4.1 reprinted from *Behaviour Research and Therapy*, 38 (4), Salkovskis, P. M., Wroe, A., Gledhill, A., Morrison, N., Forrester, E., Richards, C., Reynolds, M. & Thorpe, S., Responsibility attitudes and interpretations are characteristic of obsessive compulsive disorder, 347–372, copyright 2000, with permission from Elsevier.

About the Authors

Graham Davey is Professor of Psychology at the University of Sussex, UK. His research interests are in the areas of anxiety disorders and pathological worrying, and he has published over 140 scientific articles and written or edited 18 books. His publications include *Psychopathology: Research, Assessment & Treatment in Clinical Psychology* (2008), *Clinical Psychology* (2008), *Complete Psychology (2008)*, *Applied Psychology* (2011) and *Managing Anxiety with CBT for Dummies* (2012) with Kate Cavanagh, Fergal Jones, Adrian Whittington and Lydia Turner. He is a former President of the British Psychological Society and is currently editor-in-chief of *Journal of Experimental Psychopathology*.

Suzanne Dash began her psychology career at the University of Oxford, UK, before moving to the University of Sussex to complete a PhD in mechanisms of worry. Following a post-doctoral position in parental transmission of anxiety disorders, Suzanne returned to the University of Oxford where she is now studying Graduate-Entry Medicine.

Frances Meeten is a Research Fellow at Brighton and Sussex Medical School, UK. Since completing her DPhil in 2010 at the University of Sussex, Dr Meeten has specialized in anxiety research and currently works on projects examining the brain/body relationship in anxiety and perseverative cognition.

Note from Series Editors

Many of us will know the term Obsessive Compulsive Disorder (OCD) from the many reports and articles in the press that very often abuse and misuse it. In this book the authors have provided a clear and eloquent description and discussion of this both fascinating and to some very difficult topic. The text provides a clear, up-to-date, concise cover of OCD for both students and practitioners.

We approached Professor Davey to write this book because of his reputation and great skill in explaining otherwise tricky psychological topics to students, and fellow lecturers in the subject. We were delighted that he agreed with the proviso that he were allowed to write with a handpicked team. The result is this very clear and very straight-forward text that does not over-simplify any of the relevant issues, but explains them carefully, accessibly and clearly. Davey, Dash and Meeten write extremely well together with great passion and enthusiasm. This is a fascinating book that will certainly inform and enthuse many a reader.

- *This book may form part of your pre-university preparation or as general reading.* It may be that you are considering or preparing for a place at university to read psychology or a related subject. *Obsessive Compulsive Disorder* will fit within the psychopathology or 'abnormal' psychology component of your course and this book will certainly be invaluable preparation. If reading for general interest, you cannot do better than this as a clear, well-constructed, instructive and very readable introduction to OCD.
- *This book may form part of your university reading list.* If directed to read this book as part of your reading at university it will no doubt

be part of a wider selection of texts. It will have been chosen because it is the most useful partner to this particular part of your course. We have read a good number of textbooks, both professionally as authors, and as students and learners ourselves, and have no doubt that this is one of the clearest, most useful in its class.

- *You may be using this book while studying for a pre-university course, such as A-level.* Whether studying for A-level, the International or Welsh Baccalaureate or any number of other pre-university qualifications, where OCD is on your specification, this book will provide the required information to allow you to really stretch and challenge yourself.

The *Insights* series is unique. The coverage is designed to be useful for a range of readers and we are very pleased to see that the authors of this, and the other books in the series have taken the spirit and original aims of the series to heart. The language is accessible, and the material covered in such a way as to develop a burgeoning understanding of the topic or augment an already whetted appetite to know more. We are absolutely delighted to introduce this book into the series and thank the authors greatly for their efforts here.

NIGEL HOLT AND ROB LEWIS
Series Editors

Reading Guide

This is one of the books in the *Insights in Psychology* series. There are a range of topics covered in the books, and these have been chosen to carefully reflect the subjects being studied in psychology at a number of levels.

Whether reading for interest, for your degree study or for pre-university courses, such as A-level or other courses where you may find psychology, the material in these books will help you reach the very best of your potential.

The authors of these books have written their books to include material from the specifications of all relevant A-level examination boards in the United Kingdom, these include:

- The Assessment and Qualifications Alliance (AQA)
- The Welsh Joint Education Committee (WJEC)
- Oxford, Cambridge and RSA (OCR)
- EDEXCEL

To keep the qualifications fresh and focussed on the workplace and further education destinations, and to respond to the very latest research and trends in our subject, the examination boards regularly update their curricula. To ensure you have the very latest information we have chosen to include a reading guide online at: www.palgrave.com/insights.

Preface

Obsessive-compulsive disorder (OCD) is a disabling and distressing mental health problem. It is characterized by the presence of obsessions and/or compulsions. **Obsessions** are recurrent and persistent thoughts that are often distressing and uncontrollable, and **compulsions** are repetitive behaviours or mental acts that an individual feels driven to perform, and often take the form of elaborate rituals that are both excessive and time consuming. Now, we all recognize some of these types of symptoms in ourselves, and there is growing evidence that obsessions and compulsions are on a dimension from mild and common to severe and distressing. However, these symptoms become clinically significant when the individual feels that they cannot control their thoughts or compulsions, they become highly distressed by their symptoms, and their symptoms interfere significantly with their daily functioning – including interfering with work life, social life and family responsibilities. It is at this point that a clinical diagnosis of OCD is likely to be made, and the sufferer referred for treatment. Common forms in which OCD manifests itself include compulsive washing (in response to contamination fears or fear of disease or illness), compulsive checking (in the form of checking that appliances are switched off or doors and windows are locked), repetitive mental acts such as repetitive counting, praying or repeating words silently (in an attempt to prevent bad things happening), or compulsive ordering of items (e.g. making sure that all items on a bookshelf are symmetrical and in the correct order). In their lifetime, the likelihood that someone will exhibit symptoms severe enough for a clinical diagnosis is around 2.3 per cent. This means that in the United Kingdom alone, with a current population of 63 million people nearly one-and-a-half million people will suffer debilitating OCD symptoms at some point in their lifetime.

This book is an attempt to provide the reader with a comprehensive and detailed account of OCD as a clinical phenomenon, describe the current status of knowledge about the causes of OCD, and introduce the reader to the most popular and efficacious methods of treatment for OCD symptoms. The book is divided into three sections. Section One describes in detail the characteristics of OCD, its diagnosis, prevalence, cultural differences, and describes a broad range of OCD-related mental health problems. Section Two discusses the aetiology and causes of OCD symptoms, and evaluates contemporary theories of OCD, including psychological, behavioural and biological theories. Section Three then covers methods of treatment and intervention, describing many of these in detail, and providing information about the relative effectiveness of these interventions. Throughout the book we have included numerous examples of symptoms in the form of Case Histories, which we hope will provide the reader with an insight into personal experiences of OCD as well as detailed descriptions of how symptoms can manifest themselves.

We hope you enjoy reading the book, either in an academic, clinical or scientific context or as an interested layperson wishing to find out more about OCD.

Graham Davey, Suzanne Dash and Frances Meeten
University of Sussex, Brighton, January 2014

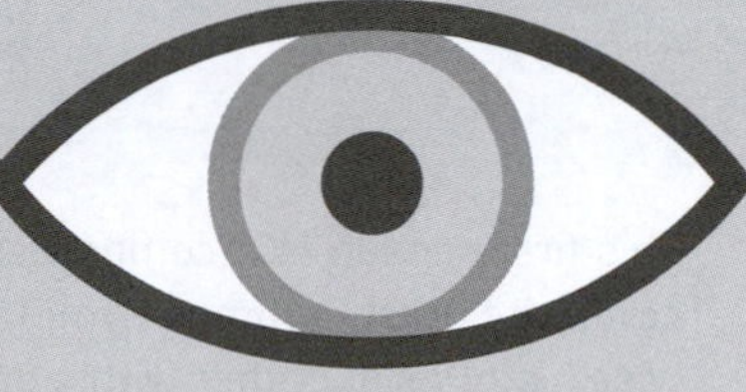

Section One

What is OCD?

Preface

This first section is a comprehensive introduction to OCD. Chapter 1 covers its most common symptoms – illustrated with some example case histories, together with a description and discussion of the latest **Diagnostic & Statistical Manual** (DSM-5) diagnostic criteria for OCD. Chapter 2 is devoted to the prevalence and epidemiology of OCD and considers differences in OCD symptoms that manifest as a result of culture and ethnicity. OCD is also a mental health problem that rarely occurs alone, and is often comorbid with other common mental health problems such as anxiety and depression. This comorbidity is discussed in Chapter 2 along with OCD throughout the lifespan – an insight into how OCD can manifest in childhood, adulthood and old age. Most recent developments in the study of OCD have recognized that there are many other mental health problems that resemble OCD or share characteristics in common with OCD. These are discussed in Chapter 3 and include Body Dysmorphic Disorder, Hoarding Disorder, Trichotillomania (Hair-Pulling Disorder), Excoriation (Skin Picking) Disorder, Onychophagia (Nail Biting), Mental Contamination, Tourette's and Tic Related Disorders, and Obsessive-Compulsive Personality Disorder.

Chapter 1

OCD: Symptoms and Diagnosis

Catherine was twenty-eight years old. It was a week before her wedding. The alarm went off at 7.00am as usual. She turned to switch it off, and was immediately overwhelmed by the feeling of dread that had been her constant companion for the past six months.

She went to the bathroom and washed her hands. She stepped inside the shower and started to wash herself, washing her hands repeatedly between washing different parts of her body. Three quarters of an hour later she emerged, gathered up her nightwear and towel and dumped them in the washing machine. Her hands felt dirty again so she returned to the bathroom to clean them. By now her hands were washed red raw so she rubbed in some moisturizer. They didn't feel as clean and she felt a strong urge to wash them once more. She looked at her reflection in the mirror and told herself not to be so stupid, that she would be late for work again if she didn't get a move on. But she couldn't resist the urge. She quickly washed her hands and hurried into the kitchen, kicking the door open to avoid contact with the germ-ridden doorknob.

After breakfast – and several more hand washes – she systematically went from room to room locking and checking all the doors and windows. Finally she stepped outside the house. By now she was already late for work but thought she'd better go back inside and check everything one more time, just to be sure. When this was done, she got into her car and drove down the street. Before she reached the end of the road she wondered if she had locked the front door properly. Back she went and checked the handle five more times.

She had almost reached her workplace when she was suddenly plagued by the idea that she might have accidentally hit a cyclist. She mentally retraced her steps. She remembered driving past a few cyclists but certainly didn't notice that she had hit any of them at the time. However, just to be on the safe side, she decided to drive round the block again. It came as no surprise when she didn't see any injured cyclists lying on the road and she cursed herself for giving into such an irrational idea.

When she finally pulled up outside her place of work she looked at her watch and saw that, yet again, she was unacceptably late. Work started at 8.30am not 10.30am.

Catherine was diagnosed as having Obsessive Compulsive Disorder in 2012. Her diagnosis came as a relief. At least now she knew she wasn't going crazy and that the behaviour that had inexplicably taken over her life had a name and was treatable. While her family was generally supportive she said the majority of people didn't understand. "A lot of people around me were shocked but felt I should just get over it, they couldn't see any logical reason for the behaviour or the distress."

Catherine's Story
http://www.ocd.org.nz/personal_story.htm
(Adapted from Davey, 2014)

We have all done something in the past that we have felt is a little obsessive or even compulsive – like returning to check whether a door is locked, or a window is shut, or we really did turn the gas off on the cooker. It is also quite common for us to experience intrusive thoughts that seem to enter our heads spontaneously – usually these are quite mundane thoughts, such as a craving for chocolate or a random thought about a friend or relative. However, for the individual with a diagnosis of obsessive-compulsive disorder (OCD) these thoughts and actions can become distressing and disabling and are driven by intense feelings of anxiety. *Catherine's Story* at the beginning of this chapter illustrates a number of the prominent features of OCD as a significant mental health problem. She wakes up with feelings of dread and anxiety, she feels compelled to undertake certain activities – in this case washing her hands; she has intrusive thoughts about catastrophic events that may have happened, and begins doubting that she has done things like lock the house which triggers a lengthy checking ritual. Equally importantly, these compulsions and anxieties have a significant negative effect on Catherine's daily functioning – she is regularly late for work, and although her family were supportive, it is likely that her rituals and compulsions will put strain on her relationships with family and friends. OCD symptoms become a cause for concern when they inflict undue distress or anxiety on the sufferer, and when the symptoms cause significant impairment to daily living in the form of adversely affecting occupational, social, or educational functioning – and later on we will see these characteristics as important components of the diagnostic criteria for OCD.

OCD has two important and sometimes independent characteristics. These are known as obsessions and compulsions, and it may be that some sufferers only experience obsessive thoughts, but others may experience both obsessive thoughts and compulsive actions such as checking and washing that are triggered by the obsessive thoughts. **Obsessions** are intrusive and recurring thoughts that the individual finds disturbing and uncontrollable. These obsessive thoughts frequently take the form of causing some harm or distress to oneself or to some important other person (such as a partner or offspring). Common obsessions also take the form of fear of contamination (i.e. contaminating oneself or important others), thoughts about harm, accidents, and unacceptable sex (Rowa & Purdon, 2005; Berry & Laskey, 2012). Obsessive thoughts can also take the form of pathological doubting and indecision, and this may lead to sufferers developing repetitive behaviour patterns such as **compulsive checking** or *compulsive washing*. Very often, obsessive thoughts can be 'autogenous' – that seem uncontrollable and 'come out of the blue', and it is this autogenous characteristic that helps to make obsessive thoughts distressing. **Compulsions** represent repetitive or ritualized behaviour patterns that the individual feels driven to perform in order to prevent some negative outcome happening. This can take the form of ritualized and persistent checking of doors and windows (to ensure that the house is safe), or ritualized washing activities designed to prevent infection and contamination. Ritualized compulsions such as these also act to reduce the stress and anxiety caused by the sufferer's obsessive fears. While the main compulsions are usually related to checking or washing, compulsions can also manifest less regularly as compulsive hoarding (Steketee, Frost & Kyrios, 2003), compulsive hair-pulling (known as trichotillomania) or skin picking (known as dermatillomania), the systematic arranging of objects (Radomsky & Rachman, 2004) (see Case History 1.1), or superstitious ritualized movements. In most cases, compulsions are clearly excessive, and are usually recognized as so by the sufferer. *Compulsive rituals* can become rigid, stereotyped sequences of behaviours which the individual is driven to perform as a result of cognitive triggers such as intrusive thoughts related to the individual's specific fears. These compulsions are

Case History 1.1

The celebrity footballer, David Beckham, admitted in a television interview that he suffered from obsessive-compulsive disorder. His compulsions included rearranging hotel rooms and lining up cans of soft drinks so that 'everything looked perfect'. Asked if he wanted to stop his obsessive-compulsive behaviour, he said 'I would like to. I've tried and can't stop.

usually intended to either neutralize the thought or reduce the anxiety caused by the thought. For example, individuals distressed by unwanted immoral or blasphemous thoughts can attempt to suppress the thought and reduce anxiety by indulging in compulsive acts such as counting backwards from a number until the thought has gone. In other cases, thoughts about being contaminated by germs or dirt can be neutralized by persistent and ritualized washing and cleaning strategies.

Obsessive thoughts

OCD tends to begin with the individual experiencing obsessive thoughts that they find both distressing and difficult to control. Obsessive and intrusive thoughts themselves are not uncommon, and around 90 per cent of people report having unwanted or intrusive thoughts during an individual day (Rachman & de Silva, 1978). However, one factor that can trigger distress is the theme of the thought. Nonclinical populations rate thoughts about harm, accidents, unacceptable sex, and contamination as most upsetting (Clark, Purdon & Byers, 2000; Belloch et al., 2004; Rowa & Purdon, 2005) and these also tend to be the types of obsessive thought content regularly endorsed by clinical populations (Rachman & de Silva, 1978; Garcia-Soriano, Belloch, Morillo & Clark, 2011). A further factor facilitating thought-related distress is the apparent autogenous (a thought that seems to come 'out of the blue') or uncontrollable nature of the thought (Lee & Kwon, 2003; Lee, Kwon, Kwon & Telch, 2005), and **autogenous thoughts** are more frequently reported by patients with a diagnosis of OCD than individuals without an anxiety disorder (Julien, O'Connor & Aardema, 2009).

Obsessive thoughts in OCD are often distressing not just because of their violent or sexual nature, but because they involve the thought of harming someone vulnerable (such as a child) or someone close to the sufferer (their partner or own child). Some common examples of obsessive thoughts in OCD include fear of becoming ill or contracting a disease, thinking about hurting a loved one or a stranger, indulging in a sexual act with someone you know or a stranger, or the need for organization or symmetry. Because these thoughts are so distressing, the sufferer will either try to actively suppress them or will begin to develop strategies to ensure that any possible outcomes associated with the thought will not happen (e.g. intensely washing to remove germs, or a mother will take all knives out of the kitchen drawer to ensure she will not be able to harm her child as her intrusive thoughts keep indicating). These actions can then often turn into compulsive rituals designed to alleviate the distress and anxiety caused by the intrusive thoughts, and result in a clinical diagnosis of OCD.

Compulsive washing

Washing and cleaning rituals are probably the best-known symptoms of OCD and these are closely linked to an exaggerated **fear of contamination**. Contamination fear is based on fear of disease, illness, or infection and can often lead to the development of complex cleaning rituals in which the individual attempts to rid themselves of any possible germs or other forms of perceived contamination. Some individuals will view their entire world as being contaminated except for a small 'safe zone' (e.g. a bedroom or a personal washing area) that they attempt to keep as clean and uncontaminated as they can. The following case history provides you with an example of the effect that fear of contamination and the ensuing washing rituals can have:

> A 28-year-old man visits his GP (General Practitioner) and describes having an intense fear of germs and contamination. He has thoughts about getting an illness because of becoming contaminated with germs from touching things in public places such as door handles and seats. This has given rise to regular, repetitive hand washing. He claims to get relief from his fears for a short time after hand washing, but intrusive thoughts about

contamination keep returning. He finds himself washing his hands many times a day until his hands are red, raw and cracked. Eventually he had to give up his job because his hand washing and his fears significantly interfered with his ability to do his job effectively.

Because fear of contamination is related to the spread of disease, OCD sufferers who develop washing and cleaning rituals will often be as concerned about contaminating others as much as being contaminated themselves. This is often a source of tension between the sufferer and other family members – especially when the sufferer continually insists that other family members should themselves avoid all possible forms of contamination that might additionally lead to contamination of their 'safe zone'. In some cases, contamination fears manifest as fear of individual diseases such as cancer, HIV, or swine flu, but in other cases it is associated with heightened levels of disgust sensitivity (Olatunji & Armstrong, 2009; Olatunji, 2010). Disgust is an emotion that has evolved to help prevent the transmission of disease and illness, and people with heightened disgust sensitivity will have a particular dislike for disgust- and disease-relevant stimuli such as faeces, mucus, vomit etc., which are all vehicles for the transmission of disease and illness (Davey, 2011). This gives rise to anxieties surrounding activities that involve bodily waste or secretions, in particular, fears of blood, faeces, semen, saliva, etc. But individuals with high disgust sensitivity will also develop fear of substances that possess the properties of disgust-relevant stimuli, and these properties include stickiness and sliminess, meaning that many individuals with fear of contamination will generalize their fears to all things sticky or slimy, including glue, butter, or cooking oil – a fear that will make it difficult to conduct many normal daily tasks like cooking or washing clothes. Interestingly, increased disgust sensitivity is also associated with fear of animals or insects – and especially fear of contamination from animals (Davey, 1994), as a result many OCD sufferers will develop extreme fear of being in close proximity to animals and insects, and will ensure they are not contaminated either by a lick or stray hair from a dog, or by insects such as flies. This usually means banning all animals from their home and taking extreme measures to ensure that insects such as flies cannot contaminate any 'safe zones'. OCD sufferers may often create a set of firmly held beliefs surrounding contamination that will maintain their avoidance of potential contaminants and maintain washing and cleaning behaviours. Examples include the belief that going out in the rain will expose them to contamination, that many types of harmless food are carcinogenic, or walking past a building that may have asbestos in it means that they may be contaminated with asbestos. While there is a small risk of harm to most daily activities, the individual with OCD greatly exaggerates these risks to a point where they cannot tolerate any form of uncertainty about potential harm, and this leads to the extreme responses that such individuals develop in order to try to 'protect' themselves.

Compulsive checking

OCD compulsions are usually associated with exaggerated beliefs about harm (such as becoming ill through contact with germs) or about bad things happening (such as someone being harmed or adversely affected by something the sufferer has, or has not, done). This will frequently lead to checking rituals, so that the sufferer persistently checks that they have done the things they need to do in order to prevent harm happening (e.g. eradicating germs by washing, or ensuring that doors and windows are locked to prevent a burglary). Different types of checking include (1) checking locks on doors and windows; this can occur after someone has experienced a trauma such as a burglary or sexual assault, and the individual will often feel that they are responsible for ensuring that others are safe as well as themselves. What is distinctive about this type of compulsive checking is not that the sufferer may go back to check once or twice, but that they will have developed a fixed, ritualized chain of behaviours that has to be completed before the sufferer will begin to feel less anxious. Here's a case history that gives you an indication of how fixed and important checking rituals may become to the OCD sufferer:

> Leonie was 23-years old and lived with her parents. To everyone outside the family she appeared normal. But when she got home from work her life was taken over by her obsessions and compulsions. Her home life was divided between her compulsions – which took up to 80% of her time – and sleeping, and this pattern had existed for the last 5 years, getting worse and worse year-by-year. She was compelled to check and then recheck everything in the house, make sure everything was in a certain order, and when this was finished she'd simply start over again.

(2) Checking stoves, cookers, and switches is another form of compulsive ritual, developed to ensure that no appliances are left on and could cause harm to anyone. This may generalize to many different forms of electrical appliance, including hair dryers or curling tongs, toasters or television sets, and include beliefs that wiring may also be faulty and should be checked; (3) Checking related to harming others is a common form of OCD. In the introduction to this chapter we read how Catherine became concerned that she may have hit a cyclist while driving to work, and to be sure that this hadn't occurred she would have to retrace her steps and drive around the block to make sure there was no evidence of an accident. In extreme cases, this form of OCD manifests as the sufferer being concerned that they may be responsible for disasters or catastrophes that may harm others (such as a train crash), and they may have caused a disaster of this kind simply by thinking about it (known as thought-action fusion – see Chapter 4). They then need to thoroughly check newspapers, news bulletins, and even obituaries to be sure that no disaster has happened and no one has been killed as a result; (4) This summary of compulsive checking has already shown how sufferers become intensely concerned about having done something wrong or made a mistake that will result in harmful or bad consequences, so checking for mistakes is another common form of OCD compulsions. This may include checking and rechecking schoolwork, completed forms, re-reading important letters, etc., and may extend to the ritualized opening of letters that the sufferer has already sealed in order to ensure that the contents have been completed correctly.

What is interesting about checking compulsions is that it often looks as if compulsive checkers conduct their checking rituals because they lack confidence in recalling whether they have checked properly or not. However, recent research suggests that doubting is in fact a *consequence* of compulsive checking rather than a cause of it (van den Hout & Kindt, 2003; Radomsky & Alcolado, 2010). In effect, the more someone checks, the less confident they will be about what they have checked!

Systematic behaviours and the arranging of objects

Another form of compulsion in OCD is the need to arrange objects in a systematic and ordered way, or to repeat behaviours or mental acts according to a rigidly applied set of rules (e.g. praying, counting, repeating words silently). Frequently, these types of rituals develop out of a fear or belief that if the ritual is not completed according to the rules, then something bad will happen. The following case history provides a particularly vivid example of how such rituals are acquired and how complex and disabling such rituals can become:

> Rosa was now 40 years old, and remembered her obsessions and compulsions starting around 10 years of age, soon after the death of her mother. Immediately after this traumatic event, Rosa's father moved the family from a small town near Cambridge to Manchester. Adjusting to life in a big city was difficult and anxiety provoking, and she soon acquired a number of specific fears and anxieties, including a fear of being run over by a car in the streets as she crossed over the road, and that any new friends she made would be kidnapped by criminals. This led to the development of her rituals. These included an elaborate prayer routine every single night that developed into a long ritual with lots of rules that needed to be followed. Rosa also believed she needed to repeat each family members name up to 20 times in her prayers, otherwise they would not be safe. She also had to kneel down and stand up 8 times during this whole process. If she made even the slightest mistake, she would have to begin the lengthy routine again from the very beginning. If she didn't, something bad would happen to her siblings or her friends.

Some other people may often feel uncomfortable when confronted with situations where objects are misaligned or untidy, and this is often a form in which anxiety is expressed in children and younger adolescents (Geller, Biederman, Faraone, Agranat et al., 2001). This type of compulsion is associated with perfectionism, and is often a sign that an individual may be suffering other anxiety disorders or have an **obsessive-compulsive personality disorder** – a personality disorder involving an overwhelming need for organization, order and perfection (Radomsky & Rachman, 2004; Coles, Pinto, Mancebo, Rasmussen & Eisen, 2008; see Chapter 3). People with a diagnosis of obsessive-compulsive personality disorder tend to be preoccupied with details, rules, lists, order, organization, or schedules to the extent that the major point of the activity will be lost. They may also be unable to complete a task because they are unable to meet their own overly strict perfectionist standards (DSM-5, 2013).

Summary

So far we have discussed some of the main symptoms of OCD. While these are the most common, there are also many more types of symptoms that have obsessional or compulsive characteristics, and we will describe some of these in Chapter 3. Also, it is important to be aware that OCD symptoms develop unique characteristics in each sufferer – largely because everyone's life circumstances are different and often complex, and these will impact on the way that OCD symptoms manifest themselves.

Having described the various characteristics of OCD, the next section looks specifically at the criteria for clinical diagnosis of OCD. Recent research has suggested that OCD symptoms have dimensional rather than categorical characteristics – that is OCD is not a disorder that you either have or you do not have, but the symptoms exist on a continuum from very mild to very severe spanning both nonclinical and clinical populations (Haslam, 2003; Haslam, Williams, Kyrios et al. 2005; Olatunji, Williams, Haslam et al., 2008). This means that clinical psychologists and psychiatrists must make a decision about when symptoms have become severe enough to require some intervention and treatment. They would normally do this according to the diagnostic criteria laid down in the most commonly used diagnostic manuals for mental health problems.

Diagnosing OCD

The most commonly used manuals for diagnosing OCD as a clinically relevant mental health problem are the **International List of Causes of Death** (ICD) and the American Psychiatric Association (APA) *Diagnostic and Statistical Manual (DSM)*. In this book we will primarily use the most recent diagnostic criteria found in DSM-5, which was published in 2013. The ICD system is currently in its tenth edition (ICD-10) with ICD-11 under development and due to be published in 2015, and most revisions of the DSM have been coordinated with the ICD to ensure some consistency of diagnosis across systems. DSM defines what is a mental health problem primarily in terms of the distress and disability caused by the symptoms. Distress relates to the chronic experience of pain or distressing emotions, and disability refers to the fact that distress can lead to impairment in one or more important areas of functioning, such as education, employment, and dealing with family and social responsibilities. As we will see, these overriding criteria are ones to be found when diagnosing OCD as a clinically relevant mental health problem.

When the DSM-5 revision was published in 2013, the significance of OCD as an important mental health problem was recognized by giving OCD its own chapter in the manual, and dividing OCD into a number of separate diagnostic categories. This implied that OCD was not just another anxiety disorder, but an important disorder in its own right. The obsessive-compulsive and related disorders category includes obsessive-compulsive disorder (OCD), body dysmorphic disorder, **hoarding disorder**, trichotillomania (hair-pulling disorder), and **excoriation (skin-picking)** disorder, and we will be discussing most of these latter disorders in Chapter 3. Meanwhile, we will focus in this section on the criteria for the main OCD diagnosis.

Table 1.1 shows the DSM-5 diagnostic criteria for obsessive-compulsive disorder. This provides some basic definitions of both obsessions and compulsions, and the disorder can be diagnosed if an individual exhibits either obsessions or compulsions, or both. However, what makes the DSM-5 clinically relevant is the criteria or measures stating that the

- There should be evidence of obsessions, compulsions or both.
- Obsessions are defined as recurrent persistent thoughts that cause anxiety and which the individual tries to suppress.
- Compulsions are defined as repetitive behaviours (e.g. hand washing) or mental acts (e.g. praying) that the person feels driven to perform, and these acts are aimed at preventing distress or some undesirable outcome (e.g. contamination).
- The obsessions and compulsions must be time-consuming, cause distress, or affect daily functioning.
- The obsessions and compulsions should not be due to the effects of a drug or medication.

Table 1.1 Summary of the main DSM-5 diagnostic criteria for obsessive-compulsive disorder

obsessions and compulsions must be time-consuming, cause distress, or affect daily functioning.

Typical characteristics of an individual with diagnosable OCD would be that (1) obsessions would be repetitive and persistent, and often experienced in the form of uncontrollable urges (e.g. to stab someone). The individual would also attempt to suppress these thoughts (e.g. by avoiding the kinds of things that would trigger the thoughts, or simply by trying to distract or suppress thoughts) (2) compulsions are acts which the individual feels *driven* to perform either as a consequence of an obsessive thought (e.g. washing in response to thoughts about contamination) or according to rules that should be rigidly applied (e.g. counting up to a certain number for proceeding with an action). In addition, compulsions usually have to be performed until everything feels "just right" and anxiety has subsided (Coles, Frost, Heimberg & Rheaume, 2003), and compulsions are usually clearly excessive and out of proportion to the reality of the threat to which the individual is exposed. As DSM-5 notes, compulsions are not done for pleasure, but they can sometimes provide relief from anxiety.

DSM-5 stresses that the compulsions or obsessive thoughts must occur for more than one hour per day, and this helps to distinguish clinically relevant activities from occasional intrusive thoughts or repetitive behaviours found in the general population. The severity of symptoms may vary, with some individuals diagnosed with OCD spending as few as 1–3 hours a day in obsessional behaviours, while for others these activities may be more or less constant throughout the day.

Some individuals suffering diagnosed OCD may also experience other anxiety-related symptoms such as panic attacks when they encounter a trigger for obsessions or compulsions, while others may experience disgust – especially if their symptoms revolve around contamination fears.

In the US, the mean age of onset of OCD is 19.5 years (DSM-5, 2013), but as mentioned earlier it is a common way in which childhood anxiety may manifest itself (25% of cases start by the age of 14 years) (Garcia, Freeman, Himle, Berman, Ogata et al., 2009). Males have an earlier age of onset than females, and more than 25 per cent of males exhibit onset of symptoms before the age of ten years.

Finally, OCD is a very resilient disorder. Its onset is gradual, which means that it is often hard to detect as a problem until the symptoms have become well established. Without treatment, remission rates are low (only 20% of those with diagnosable OCD have recovered from the disorder when followed up later) (Bloch, Green, Kichuk et al., 2013).

Chapter summary

This chapter has described the major characteristics of OCD, including the nature of obsessive thoughts and the different types of compulsions that are experienced by sufferers. Finally we discussed the DSM-5 diagnostic criteria that are relevant to identifying clinically relevant OCD symptoms, and described some of the features that accompany clinically diagnosed OCD.

If you'd like to try out a self-report measure of OCD symptoms you can complete the Obsessive-Compulsive Inventory-Revised (Foa, Huppert, Leiberg et al., 2002) at http://www.ocdtypes.com/oci-r-test.php. This is sometimes used as a diagnostic screening tool for individuals with OCD symptoms.

You can also complete the Y-Bocs Symptom report form (Goodman, Price, Rasmussen et al., 1989) at http://www.ocdtypes.com/ybocs_checklist.php. You can use this to list and print out symptoms.

Chapter 2

OCD: Prevalence and Epidemiology

Interest in OCD has grown considerably since the early days of research on this disorder in the early 1980s. Research began to show that obsessions and compulsions were widely experienced symptoms that were often severely disabling for many sufferers. These findings raised a number of interesting questions about this type of psychological problem. First, how prevalent were obsessions and compulsions in the general population? Secondly, how many people suffered symptoms severe enough to interfere with their normal daily living? Thirdly, which obsessions and compulsions were most common? Fourthly, did OCD afflict some types of people rather than others (e.g. was it more common in certain socio-economic groups)? And fifthly, were there cultural differences in the way that OCD symptoms manifested themselves? These are some of the questions we will try to answer in this chapter.

Prevalence and epidemiology

Epidemiology is the study of the frequency and distribution of disorders within specific populations over a specified period of time. Because of this, epidemiological research usually takes the form of a large-scale survey, and tends to be descriptive in the sense that it attempts to provide details primarily about the prevalence of psychological disorders. However, it can also be used to gather information about the factors that correlate with psychological disorders, and this can provide information about how a specific disorder affects people, whether it is more prevalent in young people or old people, men or women, etc. It can also help us to understand what some of the risk factors are for a specific psychological disorder, and whether the incidence of a disorder is increasing or decreasing over time. Epidemiological studies are usually large scale ones, and need to have enough respondents in the survey to ensure that the sample is representative of all types of persons in the population being studied. One of the largest epidemiological studies in the world is in the US, and is called the NIMH (National Institute of Mental Health) Epidemiological Catchment Area Study (Regier, Myers, Kramer, Robins et al., 1984; Narrow, Rae, Robins & Regier, 2002). This survey has interviewed over 20,000 respondents and has collected data on the prevalence rates of an extensive range of mental health problems. In the UK, epidemiological studies of this kind are often carried out by the Office for National Statistics (ONS) (http://www.statistics.gov.uk/hub/health-social-care/specialist-health-services/mental-health-services/index.html provides information on epidemiological and longitudinal studies of mental health problems in the UK).

One of the main uses of epidemiological studies is to determine the prevalence rates of various mental health problems, and **prevalence rates** can be described in a number of different ways. For example, respondents in an epidemiological study can be asked: (1) "Have you ever experienced symptoms of a specific psychopathology in your lifetime?" (Providing information on the **lifetime prevalence** rate of a disorder), (2) "Have you experienced symptoms of a specific psychopathology in the last year?" (Providing information on the **12-month** or **one-year prevalence** rate of a disorder, e.g. Regier, Farmer, Rae, Myers et al., 1993), or (3) "Are you experiencing symptoms of a specific psychopathology at the present time?" (Providing information on what is known as the **point prevalence** of a disorder, i.e. the frequency of a disorder in the population at any one point in time). You can see from these examples that prevalence rates represent *incidence x duration*, and it is important to view prevalence in this way because some disorders are of high incidence but low duration (e.g. bouts of depression), and some others are of low incidence but long duration, and OCD is probably a good example of this latter category. DSM-5 also usually provides information on either the lifetime prevalence rates of a disorder or its point prevalence.

The benefits of epidemiological studies are that they provide information about the frequency of mental health problems that can be used for planning health care services. They may also provide information about the risk factors for various psychological disorders, which will help health service providers to identify those who may be at risk of developing a mental health problem and so introduce programmes designed to help prevent those problems.

However, like all research approaches, there are some limitations to epidemiological studies. For example, to provide valid descriptions of the prevalence rates of psychological disorders in a particular population, the sample used must be truly representative of that population. This is often difficult to achieve because such studies will never attain a 100 per cent response rate, and many respondents will often refuse to take part. Studies suggest that those who are most likely to refuse to take part in an epidemiological survey are men, individuals of low socio-economic status, and individuals from ethnic minority populations (Fischer, Dornelas & Goethe, 2001), and this is likely to mean that the samples used in most epidemiological studies are not fully representative of the population being studied.

The prevalence and epidemiology of OCD

Epidemiological studies have been fairly consistent in the prevalence rates they have reported for OCD. Using a sample from the US National Comorbidity Survey, Ruscio, Stein, Chiu & Kessler (2010) found a lifetime prevalence rate for DSM-diagnosed OCD of 2.3 per cent, and a **12-month prevalence** rate of 1.2 per cent. Table 2.1 shows the point-prevalence and the lifetime prevalence rates of various OCD symptoms in the survey sample. Ruscio et al. also asked respondents whether they had any OCD symptoms at the time of the survey (whether they met the criteria for clinically diagnosable OCD or not), and 28.2 per cent claimed to be currently experiencing either obsessive or compulsive symptoms, the most common symptoms being checking and hoarding (see column 1 of Table 2.1). The second column of Table 2.1 shows the lifetime prevalence rates of diagnosable OCD calculated from this survey sample. This shows that the lifetime prevalence rate for diagnosable OCD (of all types) was 2.3 per cent, with the most common types of OCD being checking, ordering, hoarding and moral obsessions (all with lifetime prevalence rates of >1.0%).

While only a small percentage of individuals reach impairment levels that meet the criteria for a DSM-5 diagnosis of OCD, OCD symptoms are relatively common in the general population. Using a cross-sectional household survey of adults in Belgium, France, Germany, Italy, The Netherlands and Spain (21,425 respondents in all), Fullana, Vilagut,

	Prevalence of each O/C symptom in the subsample assessed		Lifetime prevalence of OCD	
	%	se	%	se
Types of OCD				
Contamination	2.9	(0.5)	0.6	(0.2)
Checking	15.4	(1.0)	1.8	(0.3)
Ordering	9.1	(0.8)	1.3	(0.2)
Hoarding	14.4	(1.1)	1.4	(0.2)
Sexual/Religious	2.3	(0.4)	0.7	(0.2)
Moral	4.2	(0.6)	1.0	(0.2)
Harming	1.7	(0.3)	0.6	(0.1)
Illness	1.8	(0.3)	0.3	(0.1)
Other O/C	1.1	(0.2)	0.4	(0.1)
Any of the above	28.2	(1.5)	2.3	(0.3)
Number of O/C				
Exactly 1 O/C	15.3	(1.2)	0.4	(0.1)
Exactly 2 O/C	6.7	(0.7)	0.3	(0.1)
Exactly 3 O/C	2.9	(0.5)	0.2	(0.1)
Exactly 4 O/C	1.9	(0.4)	0.7	(0.2)
5 or more O/C	1.4	(0.3)	0.6	(0.1)

Table 2.1 Prevalence of each obsessive or compulsive type in the general population and the lifetime prevalence rates of OCD diagnosis involving each symptom type (reprinted with permission from Ruscio, Stein, Chiu & Kessler, 2010)
se = standard error

Rojas-Ferreras, Mataix-Cols et al. (2010) found a lifetime prevalence rate for all obsessive-compulsive symptoms of 13 per cent, with the most common being harm/checking (8%), followed by somatic obsessions (5%) and symmetry/ordering (3%) (see Table 2.2 for definitions of the different symptom types). They also found that females were more likely to have contamination/cleaning or somatic obsession symptoms than males. There were also some slight differences between respondents from the different European countries. For example, respondents from France and Italy had an increased risk of OCD symptoms, whereas respondents from The Netherlands had a slightly lower risk of OCD symptoms than the average. Respondents in France also had an increased risk of harm/checking, while respondents from Italy had an increased risk of somatic obsessions.

What is interesting about these general population studies is that they suggest that the distribution of obsessive-compulsive symptoms is rather

OCD *Symptom Dimension*	
Contamination/Cleaning	A recurrent concern about dirt, germs, contamination, or feeling compelled to repeatedly wash, clean, or decontaminate things
Harm/Checking	A recurrent impulse either to check things like locks or stoves, or to go back over things in your mind to make sure that a mistake was not made or impulses to do terrible things to people or recurrent concerns that you might do something terrible
Symmetry/Ordering	A recurrent impulse either to line things up, to order or arrange things, to touch things, to count things, or to do things in an exactly defined order
Sexual/Religious Obsessions	Recurrent sexual or religious thoughts, images, or impulses that you found unpleasant, intrusive, and disturbing
Hoarding	A compulsion to save or hoard things
Moral Issues	Recurrent unpleasant thoughts about right and wrong, or a compulsion to pray over and over to ask forgiveness
Somatic Obsessions	A recurrent concern that you or someone close to you had a terrible illness that hadn't yet caused any symptoms

Table 2.2 Definition of the symptom types (reprinted with permission from Fullana, Vilagut, Rojas-Ferreras, Mataix-Cols et al., 2010)

different in the non-clinical population than it is in those more severe cases that are eventually diagnosed as OCD. General population studies show that checking and hoarding are two of the most common nonclinical symptoms (Fullana, Vilagut, Rojas-Ferreras, Mataix-Cols et al., 2010; Ruscio, Stein, Chiu & Kessler, 2010), whereas contamination/cleaning and sexual/religious obsessions are more prevalent in clinical samples (Mataix-Cols, Rosario-Campos & Leckman, 2005), and, indeed, the rarer types of symptom in the general population (e.g. contamination/cleaning) are associated with higher risk of subsequent OCD diagnosis, suggesting that these rarer types of symptoms make people particularly vulnerable to full-blown, diagnosable OCD (Ruscio, Stein, Chiu & Kessler, 2010). Diagnosable OCD is also more likely in those who exhibit both OCD symptoms and have other pre-existing mental health problems (such as anxiety or depression), and also those who have what is known as 'poor insight' into their symptoms. That is, they rarely or never consider their obsessions or compulsions to be excessive or unreasonable (Ruscio, Stein, Chiu & Kessler, 2010).

In a UK population using the British National Psychiatric Morbidity Survey of 2000, Torres, Prince, Bebbington, Bhugra et al. (2006) report a 1-month prevalence rate for ICD-10 diagnosable OCD as 1.1 per cent – a very similar point prevalence rate to that reported by Ruscio et al. (2010) in their American sample. Torres et al.'s (2006) study also highlighted a number of other features of individuals diagnosed with OCD, including a high prevalence in lower age groups (Karno, Golding, Sorensen & Burnam, 1988) and in women (Weissman, Bland, Canino, Greenwald et al., 1994). They conclude that although OCD is a relatively rare condition, it is usually associated with a high degree of impairment. When compared with individuals with other types of anxiety disorder, people with OCD are less likely to be married, more likely to be unemployed, more likely to have very low income levels, and more likely to have low occupational status – all of which is consistent with the severe disabling effects that OCD symptoms can have. Finally, the Torres et al. (2006) study also highlighted the fact that 26 per cent of those exhibiting a diagnosable form of OCD reported at least one suicide attempt in their lifetime – a rate ten times higher than that in a nonclinical population, and further testament to the severity of OCD as a disabling and distressing mental health problem.

Cultural differences

Studies investigating the effect of cultural factors on the prevalence and manifestation of OCD symptoms are increasing – but largely without reporting any substantial cultural differences. For example, a cross-cultural study reported by Fontenelle, Mendlowicz, Marques & Versiani (2004) concluded that universal characteristics of sufferers regardless of cultural background included a predominance of females, a relatively early age of onset, and a preponderance of mixed obsessions and compulsions. Certainly, the prevalence rates of diagnosable OCD are very similar across different cultures and racial groups. Washington, Norton & Temple (2008) examined two measures of obsessive-compulsive symptoms across a large sample of African Americans, white Hispanic/Latino, Southeast Asian and South Asian/East Indian students. They found very similar and reliable symptom rates across the respondents from this variety of ethnic/racial backgrounds, the only exception being the slightly higher rate of symptoms reported by South Asian/East Indian participants.

While there appear to be few cultural influences on symptom severity and prevalence rates, there is some evidence that the nature of OCD symptoms themselves may be influenced by culture and ethnicity. This is especially the case with obsessions, where cultural practices may determine the type of obsessive thoughts that an individual may develop, and also determine how aversive or distressing they find the thought. For example, in cultures where religious beliefs are prevalent and play an important role in regulating everyday behaviour, experiencing intrusive thoughts that may be contrary to these religious beliefs may be particularly distressing. In support of this view, Rasmussen & Tsang (1986) reported that strictly religious OCD sufferers often had religious themes to their obsessional thoughts and compulsive rituals. Sufferers with religious obsessions and compulsions were found to be more religious than individuals without these symptoms (Steketee, Quay & White, 1991). More specifically, Khanna & Channabasavanna (1988) reported a large proportion of symptoms related to contamination and washing among Hindus with OCD – a finding that is consistent with the emphasis in Indian culture on purity and cleanliness. In a study comparing highly religious and moderately religious Protestants with atheist/agnostic participants, Abramowitz, Deacon, Woods & Tolin (2004) found that highly religious Protestants reported greater obsessional symptoms, compulsive washing and beliefs about the importance of thoughts.

Studies such as these attest to the relationship between religiosity and certain types of obsessions and compulsions (e.g. contamination fears/washing compulsions in cultures that emphasis purity and cleanliness) (Abramowitz, Deacon, Woods & Tolin, 2004; Siev & Cohen, 2007), and the distress that certain types of intrusive thoughts might cause (e.g. the thought of having sex with a stranger would be highly distressing to a person who's culture or religion puts great emphasis on monogamy and being faithful to your spouse). However, this relationship doesn't necessarily mean that religiosity causes these types of OCD symptoms it could equally be the case that certain personality characteristics (e.g. perfectionism, inflated responsibility) may cause a person to be both religious and develop OCD symptoms.

In addition to this, certain religions may espouse everyday customs or rituals that may represent risk factors for compulsive behaviour or

Case History 2.1

Burt & Rudolph (2000) report the case history of Ana. When she was age 7, Ana first recalled being uncertain about adhering to many of the religious rituals normally associated with her community's religious beliefs. For example, Orthodox Jews require a waiting period of 6 hours between eating meat and dairy foods. Ana carefully counted the hours between eating a meat meal and a dairy meal, but would later doubt whether or not she had waited the allowed number of hours. Such self-doubt extended into other religious regulations, but mainly she was able to refrain from any ritualistic behaviors. At the age of 18, Ana attended a girls' school in Israel and began developing chronic checking rituals. If she stopped at restaurants that served nonkosher food, she compulsively washed her hands repeatedly because she feared that she might have unintentionally touched some forbidden food, utensils, table, or countertop. She became so frightened of contaminating her own food with nonkosher food products that she began to skip meals.

Ana met her husband-to-be in an arranged meeting. However, after 2 months, her obsessions and compulsions returned and began to trouble her more than ever. She could not prepare any meals because of increasing self-doubt about contaminating utensils.

After marriage, Orthodox Jewish men are prohibited from touching their wives during the time of menstruation or for 7 days thereafter. According to ritual, Orthodox Jewish wives are responsible for ensuring that they no longer exhibit vaginal bleeding by swabbing themselves with a linen cloth for 7 days following the end of menstruation. It is only then, after a ritual bath (the Mikvah), that she and her husband are allowed to physically touch one another. Ana obsessed about whether there was a tinge of pink on her linen cloths, and checked them repetitively, but was unable to decide definitively that the menstrual flow had ceased. Finally, she consulted with her rabbi, who agreed to check the linen on a regular basis and make the decision for her about whether or not she was free of blood.

obsessive thoughts. Huppert, Siev & Kushner (2007) point out that Orthodox Judaism emphasizes cleanliness related to dietary restrictions, family purity, praying correctly, or studying correctly, and normal religious rituals include washing, checking, cancelling vows, consulting rabbis, mentally reassuring oneself, washing hands, checking for blood and praying. The importance of these activities is emphasized by the fact that non-adherence may lead to being condemned in the world to come, or to spreading sin throughout the world, which will increase the anxiety or distress experienced if these rules and rituals are broken. Case History 2.1 provides an example of how strict religious beliefs can lead to diagnosable OCD symptoms based on the ritualized activities required by those religious beliefs.

In summary, there do not appear to be any significant differences in OCD prevalence rates based on ethnicity or culture, but there do appear to be ethnic, cultural and religious factors that can influence the form that OCD symptoms may take – either by determining the types of obsessive thoughts and compulsive rituals that are likely to be developed, or by introducing ritualized patterns of behaviour that might form a basis for later OCD symptoms. Furthermore, the tendency for highly religious Christians, Muslims and Jews to experience greater obsessionality is related to their heightened sense of personal guilt and beliefs that they are responsible for controlling unwanted, threatening intrusive thoughts (Inozu, Kranci & Clark, 2012).

The comorbidity of OCD

Comorbidity is the term used when an individual is diagnosed with more than one recognized mental health problem, and OCD is a particularly comorbid disorder. In Ruscio, Stein, Chiu & Kessler's (2010) epidemiological study 90 per cent of those respondents with a diagnosis of OCD met criteria for at least one other DSM mental health problem. The most common disorders that are comorbid with OCD are other anxiety disorders (75.8%), mood disorders such as major depression (63.3%), impulse-control disorders (55.9%), and substance use disorders (38.6%). Table 2.3 shows the rates of OCD comorbidity with a full range of other mental health problems taken from the Ruscio et al. (2010) study. OCD symptoms often emerge out of a background of pre-existing mental health problems, so most comorbid disorders usually pre-date the onset of OCD symptoms. This is particularly true of impulse control disorders and substance use disorders, both of which begin at an earlier age than OCD, and more specifically, diagnoses of bipolar disorder, agoraphobia, panic disorder and alcohol dependence all predict the subsequent first onset of OCD (Ruscio et al., 2010).

Per cent of OCD cases with a comorbid disorder		
	%	**(se)**
Any anxiety disorder	***75.8***	***(97.6)***
Panic disorder	20.0	(4.5)
Agoraphobia without panic	7.8	(3.5)
Specific phobia	42.7	(7.2)
Social phobia	43.5	(7.4)
Generalized anxiety disorder	8.3	(2.6)
Posttraumatic stress disorder	19.1	(4.4)
Separation anxiety disorder	37.1	(7.9)
Any mood disorder	***63.3***	***(7.8)***
Major depressive disorder	40.7	(6.2)
Dysthymic disorder	13.1	(4.1)
Bipolar disorder	23.4	(5.8)
Any impulse control disorder	***55.9***	***(9.0)***
Oppositional-defiant disorder	27.7	(5.2)
Conduct disorder	14.2	(4.5)
Attention-deficit/hyperactivity disorder	18.8	(6.6)
Intermittent explosive disorder	18.6	(5.1)
Any substance use disorder	***38.6***	***(5.5)***
Alcohol use/dependence	38.6	(5.5)
Alcohol dependence	23.7	(5.0)
Drug abuse/dependence	21.7	(4.8)
Drug dependence	13.9	(4.1)
Any disorder	***90.0***	***(6.6)***

Table 2.3 Lifetime comorbidity of OCD with other DSM disorders (reprinted with permission from Ruscio, Stein, Chiu & Kessler, 2010)
se = standard error

Another group of individuals who appear to suffer OCD symptoms at above normal rates are those individuals with an autism spectrum disorder (ASD). Apart from being associated with social and communication deficits (see Davey, 2014, chapter 14), repetitive behaviours are also a diagnostic feature of autism spectrum disorder. Studies suggest that around 37 per cent of children with ASD also suffer diagnosable OCD symptoms (Leyfer, Folstein, Bacalman, Davis et al., 2006; de Bruin, Ferdinand, Meester, Nijs & Verheij, 2007), and there are moderate correlations between measures of autism (the AQ – Autistic-Spectrum Quotient) and measures of OCD (the Padua Inventory) (Wakabayashi,

Baron-Cohen & Ashwin, 2012). However, there are differences between the types of symptoms exhibited by individuals with autism and those with a single diagnosis of OCD. Individuals with ASD tend to exhibit higher levels of touching/tapping/rubbing, repetitive self-injury, hoarding, ordering, and repeating compulsions, and significantly lower levels of checking and counting (McDougle, Kresch, Goodman, Naylor et al., 1995; Ruta, Mugno, D'Arrigo, Vitiello & Mazzone, 2010). This relationship between symptoms in OCD and ASD has led some researchers to suggest that there may be a symptoms overlap between ASD and OCD (Wakabayashi, Baron-Cohen & Ashwin, 2012) or that ASD may be a clinically important feature of many people diagnosed with OCD (Bejerot, 2007). Interestingly, both individuals with ASD and OCD tend to exhibit executive function deficits and a preference for local rather than global information processing, with the possibility that these characteristics may represent a risk factor for OCD symptoms in both groups (Ozonoff, Pennington & Rogers, 1991; Savage, Baer & Keuthen, 1999). Case History 2.2 provides an example of OCD symptoms in a 12-year-old boy with high functioning autism.

Finally, that OCD is such a comorbid condition suggests that it is a complex disorder associated more generally with severe anxiety and in some cases depression, and it may often arise through pre-existing mental health problems that probably contribute some of the risk factors for developing subsequent OCD symptoms.

OCD through the lifespan

OCD is a mental health problem that can afflict individuals throughout a lifetime, frequently beginning in childhood and extending into adult life. OCD also occurs with some regularity in late life, but is perhaps less frequent than in early or mid-life (Grant, Mancebo, Pinto, Williams et al., 2007; Calamari, Pontarelli & Armstrong, 2012). The chronic nature of OCD cannot be underestimated, and studies suggest that the long term outcome for individuals with a diagnosis of OCD is not particularly optimistic, with Bloch, Green, Kichuk, Dombrowski et al. (2013) reporting that only 20 per cent of a sample of OCD sufferers had recovered from their symptoms 20 years after first being diagnosed with the disorder. Other research has indicated that there is typically a mean interval of 11 years between meeting diagnostic criteria for OCD and

Case History 2.2

Jason, a 12-year-old white male, was evaluated at the age of 2 years due to a loss of expressive language functioning, presences of echolalia, preoccupation with household items (rather than toys), repetitive play, and poor social relationships. Jason was diagnosed with High Functioning Autism by an independent psychologist according to DSM-IV at the age of 2 years.

At the age of 11 years, 9 months, Jason began exhibiting a significant number of ritualistic and avoidance behaviours. It is not unusual for a child to develop symptoms of OCD at this age. Specifically, Jason experienced contamination fears, hand washing rituals, excessive use of hand sanitizer, avoidance of contaminated items (e.g. door knobs, library books, bathroom), contamination related checking behaviours (i.e. repeatedly checking food expiration dates), not sitting in chairs, not using sheets or pillows, and not touching other items (e.g. public benches) due to concerns that they were dirty. Jason reported significant levels of anxiety when prevented from completing his rituals. His symptoms began interfering with his academic, social, and family functioning around his twelfth birthday. His teachers noted that he was not able to turn pages with his hands, touch papers that other children had touched, or sit comfortably in his chair.

(Adapted from Lehmkuhl, Storch, Bodfish & Geffken, 2008)

receiving treatment (Pinto, Mancebo, Eisen, Pagano & Rasmussen, 2006). These facts testify to the chronicity of OCD as well as the relatively poor success rates of both psychological and pharmacological treatments for OCD (see Chapters 7 and 8).

Often beginning in childhood, OCD is now recognized as a relatively common disorder and its phenomenology in childhood is very similar to adult OCD, with the main features of the disorder in children manifesting as intrusive, repetitive thoughts, obsessions and compulsions. The most common obsession themes in children are contamination, aggression (harm or death), symmetry and exactness, and in adolescence religious and sexual obsessions also become common (Geller, Biederman, Faraone, Agranat et al., 2001). Common compulsive behaviours in children and adolescents include washing, checking, ordering, touching, repeating, and reassurance seeking, as well as covert behaviours such as reviewing or cancelling thoughts, silent prayers or counting (Franklin, Kozak, Cashman, Coles et al., 1998). In adults, compulsions (e.g. behavioural rituals) are rarely found without accompanying obsessions (e.g. intrusive thoughts), but in children compulsions without obsessions can be quite common, and these are frequently tactile (e.g. touching, tapping or rubbing rituals) and may be accompanied by behavioural tics (Leckman, Grice, Barr, de Vries et al., 1995). While the range of obsessions and compulsions in childhood and adolescence is very similar to that seen in adults, there are some differences between boys and girls, with boys having an earlier age of onset than girls (Garcia, Freeman, Himle et al., 2009), girls exhibiting more hoarding compulsions than boys, but boys being more likely to have sexual obsessions than girls (Mataix-Cols, Nakatani, Micali & Heyman, 2008). Case History 2.3 provides a typical example of the development of OCD in a 13-year-old adolescent boy, and demonstrates how rapidly OCD symptoms can manifest and establish themselves in childhood, which is in some contrast to the gradual acquisition found in adulthood.

Age of onset for childhood OCD can be as early as 3–4 years of age, but the mean age of onset is more likely to be around 10 years (Swedo, Rapoport, Leonard, Lenane et al., 1989). Childhood OCD is regularly found to be comorbid with a range of other disorders, including **tic disorders**, **Tourette's Syndrome**, other anxiety disorders and eating disorders (Geller, Biederman, Griffin, Jones et al., 1996). Specifically, over 60 per cent of children seeking treatment for OCD symptoms also have a lifetime history of tics or Tourette's Syndrome (Leonard, Lenane, Swedo, Rettew et al., 1992), and 50 per cent of children with Tourette's Syndrome subsequently develop OCD (Leckman, 1993). This suggests that childhood OCD and tic disorder may be different manifestations of the same underlying disorder (Swedo & Leonard, 1994).

The commonest age of onset of OCD is young adulthood, with a mean age of onset between 18–20 years (Pinto, Mancebo, Eisen, Pagano & Rasmussen, 2006), and as we described earlier, OCD is frequently experienced with other comorbid mental health problems – notably anxiety disorders, mood disorders and substance use disorders.

Relatively little is known about OCD symptoms in later life (>65 years), and OCD can be difficult to diagnose in this age group because comorbidity with other anxiety and mood disorders is very common (Bryant, Jackson & Ames, 2008). Estimates of the prevalence of

Case History 2.3

Childhood and Adolescent OCD

Andy was a 13-year-old boy diagnosed with isolated testicular relapse of acute lymphoblastic leukemia 40 days before coming to psychiatric attention. He was first diagnosed with acute lymphoblastic leukemia at age 10. After his initial diagnosis, he experienced remission at the end of chemotherapy induction and finished his treatment for acute lymphoblastic leukemia.

Three years later he began further drug treatment for his leukemia, and the psychiatric consultation-liaison service evaluated him after he expressed bothersome obsessive thoughts, compulsive behaviors, and insomnia beginning 24–36 hours after he had completed a 28-day course of steroid drug treatment. Andy had no history of psychiatric illness or treatment.

At his initial interview, Andy described increasingly bothersome obsessions over the previous 2 days. He felt that he was 'going crazy' and feared that he would forget how to talk and lose his cognitive abilities. He repeated mantras, reassuring himself that if he remained calm, these bothersome thoughts would pass. He sought reassurance from his mother and the interviewers, and he repeated the 'ABCs' to reassure himself that he could think clearly. His mood was dysphoric, which he attributed both to insomnia and worry surrounding his constant bombardment of unwanted thoughts. He reported no depressive symptoms, perceptual disturbances, or suicidal thoughts. He displayed no manic symptoms.

Andy's symptoms rapidly worsened within 24 hours. His thoughts became dominated by fears that he would be condemned to hell and that he deserved this fate. He noted images in his mind of self-harm and harming family members. He struggled against these thoughts and images, as well as guilt from having them, by repeatedly telling family members that he loved them. He continued to deteriorate and struck himself in the head with the blunt end of an axe. He stated that he had no desire to die but had become convinced of the validity of the emerging thoughts that he should harm himself. Although he did not sustain serious injury, he was admitted to a child and adolescent psychiatric inpatient unit for safety.

Clinical Commentary: *Andy's symptoms are typical of many adolescents suffering OCD. In his case, these are obsessive thoughts about going mad and harming himself and others. In an attempt to try and prevent his obsessive thoughts entering consciousness, he indulges in protective behaviours, such as repeating mantras, seeking reassurances from adults, and reciting the alphabet. The symptoms appear to be precipitated by a stressful illness, and such stressors are common precursors of OCD symptoms in both children and adults. OCD symptoms would normally appear very slowly and have a gradual onset, unlike Andy's which appeared very rapidly over a period of a few weeks. Such rapid acquisition may have been facilitated by the abrupt cessation of steroid drugs that he was receiving as part of his treatment for leukaemia (Morris, Meighen & McDougle, 2005).*

(Adapted from Morris, Meighen & McDougle, 2005, first published in Davey, 2008)

OCD in older adults continue to be low in epidemiological studies (Kessler, Berglund, Demler, Jin et al., 2005), but Calamari, Pontarelli & Armstrong (2012) argue that this may well be an underestimate because the epidemiological studies have only focussed on community dwelling older adults and have not included the many older adults living in supported settings or nursing homes where rates of OCD may be significantly higher (Junginger, Phelan, Cherry & Levy, 1993). In terms of symptoms, older adults show a very similar range of OCD symptoms to those seen in general adult samples, including religious scrupulosity, harming and checking, doubting and checking, contamination concerns, and hoarding (Calamari, Pontarelli & Armstrong, 2012). In particular, hoarding difficulties are frequently identified with older adults. Samuels, Bienvenu, Grados, Cullen et al. (2008) found that pathological hoarding was present in 3.7 per cent of their community sample of adults, but rose to 6.2 per cent of adults aged 55 to 94 years. Clinical hoarding can be most prevalent in older women, who often live alone and are unmarried (Kim, Steketee & Frost, 2001), and this often goes untreated because those who indulge in pathological hoarding have poor insight (believe their behaviour is reasonable and not excessive) and have limited motivation to change.

Case History 2.4

Calamari, Pontarelli & Armstrong (2012) report the case of Mr. Rossi, who was an 87 year old when he presented to an OCD specialty clinic.

Mr. Rossi's core symptoms focused on a need to remember names (e.g. past acquaintances; celebrities, including professional baseball players; current associates at his work). His compulsive behaviours included checking how accurate his recollection of names was and asking others to help him recall names. For example, he frequently contacted the employees at his business at all hours of the day or night asking them to help him remember names.

Mr. Rossi reported that his current episode of OCD began during the previous year after a heart attack. Late-onset OCD is known to be regularly associated with neurological injuries in old age (Carmin, Calamari & Ownby, 2013), and the resultant limitations in physical functioning might have led to increased depressed mood, which is also known to be associated with an exacerbation of OCD symptoms.

Finally, because old age is a time of cognitive and physical decline, the problems this decline brings with it may also be a source of risk for OCD symptoms. Case History 2.4 provides an example of an 87-year-old man who became concerned at being able to remember names, and this worry gave rise to a variety of obsessive and compulsive symptoms designed to ensure he did not forget them. While old age almost certainly brings with it its own unique risk factors for OCD, little research has been conducted on these risks to date.

Chapter summary

This chapter has provided you with a description of the epidemiology of OCD and some estimates of its prevalence. While cultural differences in OCD prevalence rates are small (usually a lifetime prevalence rate of around 2.1%), there are some interesting cultural and ethnic factors that can influence how OCD symptoms might manifest, and there are also some cultural/ethnicity factors that might increase the risk of developing OCD symptoms (e.g. religiosity). OCD is a highly comorbid disorder, with anxiety disorders, mood disorders, impulse disorders and substance use disorders being the most common comorbid conditions. OCD is also more prevalent in some groups of individuals, and one such group is those individuals with a diagnosis of autistic spectrum disorder (ASD). Finally we looked at OCD throughout the lifespan. OCD can often be a way in which anxiety in childhood manifests itself, but onset of OCD is most common in early adulthood (18–20 years). There is relatively little research as yet on OCD in later life, but when it is observed in seniors it is often comorbid with other mental health problems.

Chapter 3

OCD Related Mental Health Problems

From what has been described so far, it is clear that obsessive-compulsive disorder (OCD) can manifest itself in many different forms. This diversity in symptoms, and the importance and severity of the disorder has led to OCD being given its own chapter in the recently published diagnostic manual DSM-5. As well as describing the diagnostic criteria for OCD, this new chapter in DSM-5 also lists a number of related disorders, and grouping them together with OCD reflects increasing evidence that these disorders are related or have overlapping symptoms that include ritualized repetitive behaviours or intrusive obsessive thoughts. The related diagnostic categories included in DSM-5 are Body Dysmorphic Disorder, Hoarding Disorder, Trichotillomania (Hair-Pulling Disorder) and Excoriation (Skin Picking) Disorder. We will discuss each of these in this chapter as well as some further related disorders which exhibit OCD-like symptoms; this latter group include Tourettes and tic-related problems, onychophagia, mental contagion, and Obsessive-Compulsive Personality Disorder.

Body Dysmorphic Disorder

The diagnostic category called **Body Dysmorphic Disorder** (BDD) is a preoccupation with assumed defects in appearance. The defect is usually imagined, but if there is a physical anomaly present, those suffering from BDD will greatly exaggerate its importance. In diagnosing this disorder, these preoccupations with defects in appearance must cause significant distress or impairment in social, occupational or other functioning, and the DSM-5 diagnostic criteria for BDD are shown in Table 3.1. Common complaints include flaws in facial features or facial asymmetry, hair thinning, acne, wrinkles, scars, vascular markings, irregular complexions or excessive facial hair. Other common preoccupations include body shape generally (e.g. preoccupations with being obese or overweight), and dissatisfaction with specific body parts, such as breasts, genitals, buttocks, etc. Sufferers will often be so embarrassed about their supposed appearance defects that they will often only talk about them in general terms, and may simply refer to themselves as being 'ugly'. The way in which BDD overlaps with OCD is in the obsessive thoughts that sufferers have about their appearance, and sufferers can also develop ritualistic compulsions around their defects, spending many hours a day viewing themselves in mirrors or attempting to deal with their problems with excessive grooming behaviour (e.g. skin picking, hair combing, applying cosmetics, dieting, etc.), with such behaviours usually adding to the distress that is experienced. Case History 3.1 provides an account of what it feels like to suffer BDD with a description of some of the factors that led to the development of the disorder. Concerns about appearance in BDD are frequently accompanied by a host of repetitive and time-consuming behaviours, aimed at verifying, camouflaging or enhancing the person's appearance, and one particular repetitive behaviour is known as 'mirror gazing' (Windheim, Veale & Anson, 2011). Studies have shown that about 80 per cent of individuals with BDD will repetitively check their appearance in mirrors – often for considerable periods of time. Interestingly, the remaining 20 per cent tend to avoid mirrors altogether (Veale & Riley, 2001). Mirror gazing can be construed as a 'safety seeking behaviour' which briefly acts to reduce distress. However, for

- A fixation with supposed flaws in physical appearance that may seem negligible to others
- This obsession with physical appearance has resulted in repetitive behaviours during the disorder (e.g. continual checking or appearance in the mirror)
- This preoccupation with physical appearance disrupts normal daily functioning or causes the individual distress
- This fixation on physical appearance is not better explained by worries about body weight or body shape that might be symptomatic of an eating disorder

Table 3.1 Summary of DSM-5 diagnostic criteria for body dysmorphic disorder (BDD)

Case History 3.1

Body Dysmorphic Disorder

Schmidt & Harrington (1995) report the case of a 24-year-old patient in his senior year of college. He claimed he had a physical deformity (small hands) which made him feel uncomfortable around women – especially if they had bigger hands than him.

He reported that his body dysmorphic disorder-concerns began when he was 18 years old and was working as a landscaper with a large company. After receiving instructions to plant some shrubs three hand-widths apart, he reported that his boss reviewed his work angrily, saying 'You have the smallest hands I've ever seen! You need to replant the shrubs five hand-widths apart!' After this incident, he began to compare his hand size with others and also became anxious when exposing his hands to others. He spent considerable time researching hand sizes for different populations and pointed out that his middle finger was one and one-fourth inches smaller than the average size for a male in the United States.

He saw his small hands as a sign of weakness and inferiority, and recalled being worried that women might believe that small hands are indicative of having a small penis. The patient began worrying about negative evaluation of his hands throughout most of the day. He began to avoid social gatherings and meetings and began to suffer depression.

Clinical Commentary: *In this example, the patient has catastrophized what was originally an off-the-cuff remark by an employer to proportions where it affects also every sphere of his life. He is constantly obsessed by what he believes to be the small size of his hands, and sought information to confirm his belief that hands were unusually small. He also developed other dysfunctional beliefs about his hands that had a significant effect on his day-to-day living; he believed that hand-size was indicative of penis size, and that women would think he had a small penis. As a consequence he stopped dating women. His negative beliefs about his hand size eventually led to a range of avoidance behaviours, including quitting work and avoiding relationships generally.*

individuals with low body-image satisfaction mirror gazing for more than 3.5 min results in a more negative opinion about their attractiveness (Mulken & Jansen, 2009), and mirror gazing behaviour in the longer term increases distress, maintains negative beliefs about appearance and reinforces repetitive appearance-checking behaviours (Veale & Riley, 2001).

Individuals with BDD also develop dysfunctional beliefs about their appearance, and are quite convinced that their own perceptions are correct and undistorted. As a result they may regularly seek cosmetic surgery in order to correct their 'defects'. In a study of individuals seeking cosmetic surgery, Aouizerate, Pujol, Grabot, Paytout et al. (2003) found that 9.1 per cent of applicants were diagnosable with BDD. In fact, in those applicants who had no defects or only a slight physical defect, 40 per cent were diagnosable with BDD. Body Dysmorphic Disorder can also occur in those who are preoccupied with their musculature, and it is often associated with excessive weight training and the use of body-building anabolic steroids (Olivardia, Pope & Hudson, 2000). Such an obsession with a muscular appearance is often called **muscle dysmorphia**.

A preoccupation with apparent physical defects often leads to the catastrophizing of these characteristics, and sufferers will frequently comment on their appearance to others in negative ways (e.g. 'I am ugly', 'I am fat'). Nevertheless, regular reassurance from others fails to change these views, and the sufferer can slip into a negative decline which incurs further psychopathology such as major depression, anxiety, social phobia, deliberate self-harm and suicide attempts (Phillips, 2001). In addition, adolescents with BDD experience high levels of impairment in school and work functioning, with studies reporting attempted suicide rates of around 45 per cent (Phillips, Didie, Menard, Pagano et al., 2006).

The exact prevalence rates of BDD are unclear, although a nationwide German study suggested that the point prevalence of BDD was 1.8 per cent (Buhlmann, Glaesmer, Mewes, Fama et al., 2010). This study also indicated that those diagnosable with BDD had high rates of previous cosmetic surgery (15.6%), and higher rates of suicidal ideation (31%). BDD is also relatively common in individuals who already have a diagnosis of OCD, with lifetime prevalence rate for BDD of 12.1 per cent in individuals with OCD (Costa, Assuncao, Ferrao, Conrado et al., 2012) – reinforcing the view that OCD and BDD may be related disorders. BDD can begin in early adolescence and even childhood – sometimes as a result of teasing about one's appearance or as a result of parental neglect (Cororve & Gleaves, 2001; Phillips, 2001). Like many other somatoform (mental health problems that manifest as physical problems such as chest pain, tiredness, etc.) disorders it is highly comorbid with other disorders, particularly eating disorders (Ruffolo, Phillips, Menard et al., 2006) and obsessive-compulsive disorder, social phobia and impulse control disorders (Frare, Perugi, Ruffalo & Toni, 2004).

Hoarding Disorder

Hoarding Disorder is a new diagnostic category included in DSM-5 (Pertusa, Frost, Fullana et al., 2010; Frost, Steketee & Tolin, 2012), and the diagnostic criteria are listed in Table 3.2. It is a complex problem made up of three specific attributes: (1) collecting too many items (some sufferers will actually actively collect or steal more items to hoard), (2) difficulty parting with or getting rid of hoarded items and (3) general problems with organizing possessions, probably as a result of problems with more fundamental cognitive processes such as information processing, attention, categorization and decision-making (e.g. Tolin & Villavicencio, 2011). The result of this hoarding is large piles of clutter that make living spaces impassable, home utilities (such as a toilet) unusable, and this can pose both health and safety risks. Initial epidemiology studies suggest that Hoarding Disorder afflicts around 5.8 per cent of the current population, and affects men and women equally (Timpano, Exner, Glaesmer et al., 2011). Hoarding Disorder has high comorbidity rates with major depressive disorder (MDD) as well as acquisition-related

- Long-term difficulty discarding items, even if they have little or no value
- This is associated with distress that is experienced when items are thrown away
- Problems throwing away items results in possessions cluttering the individuals living areas to the point where these areas cannot be used as they were originally intended (e.g. toilets, bathrooms)
- The hoarding of items causes the individual significant distress and impairs normal daily functioning.
- Hoarding is not the result of a medical condition such as brain injury, etc.
- The hoarding cannot better be explained by another mental health problem such as OCD obsessions, depression, etc.

Table 3.2 Summary of DSM-5 diagnostic criteria for hoarding disorder (HD)

impulse control disorders (compulsive buying, kleptomania and acquiring free things). However, fewer than 20 per cent of Hoarding Disorder sufferers meet the criteria for OCD, but the rate of OCD in Hoarding Disorder is higher for men than women (Frost, Steketee & Tolin, 2011).

Individuals with Hoarding Disorder may often try to organize their possessions, but their lack of organizational skills simply makes the chaos worse. The disorder is particularly associated with an inability to throw

Case History 3.2

Animal Hoarding

Reinisch (2009) reports the case of a middle-aged woman employed full time in a personal care home. She lived with her elderly mother in a small house in which the only usable space was the kitchen. There were routes through the remainder of the house, which was filled with boxes of belongings. Although the house was very cluttered with belongings, there were also many cats present, and the woman did not know the actual number. She admitted she did not feel comfortable allowing others to adopt her cats as she felt others would not be able to care for them as well as she could.

The local vet was alerted to the animal welfare problems at the woman's house when he received 3 different cats on separate occasions, each requiring front limb amputation. The vet reported treating many cats owned by the woman, but seldom was the same cat presented more than once.

Some cats were found in confined areas that did not permit adequate exercise or ventilation, and many were kept in crates while others lived primarily in the basement in semi-feral conditions. The basement was littered with debris and cat excrement. A group of 4 cats was housed in a bedroom in darkness at all times. Few were spayed or neutered and appeared to have derived from just a few original individuals. In addition, neighbours reported that the woman was actively trapping free roaming cats in the community.

The woman agreed that the cat population had exceeded her ability to provide care, and 61 free roaming cats were voluntarily surrendered and removed from the premises, and three days after the initial removal, 17 additional cats had emerged from the refuse stored in the house.

away even normally disposable items such as food and sweet wrappings. If the individual has other, more classic, OCD symptoms this can compound the problem. For example, fear of contamination and superstitious thoughts (e.g. 'throwing something away will result in a catastrophe of some kind') may prevent the sufferer from touching or throwing away items. However, the accumulation of clutter in Hoarding Disorder is not simply something that is tolerated by the individual, the hoarding causes clinically significant distress and has a significant impact on social and occupational functioning.

Hoarding appears to begin in childhood or adolescence, with a chronic and progressive course throughout the lifespan. This means that many sufferers of Hoarding Disorder are elderly, and it is often comorbid with dementia and other psychiatric diagnoses such as Major Depression, social phobia and inattentive ADHD (Attention Deficit Hyperactivity Disorder) (Frost, Steketee & Tolin, 2011). Hoarding Disorder can also be restricted to collecting and hoarding individual types of items. **Animal Hoarding** is one recently identified example that can lead to considerable animal suffering and neglect (Patronek, 1999; Frost, Patronek & Rosenfield, 2011), and a case history is provided in Case History 3.2 (Reinisch, 2009).

Trichotillomania (hair-pulling disorder)

The cardinal feature of **trichotillomania** is the recurrent pulling out of one's own hair, particularly from the scalp, eyebrows and eyelids. Less common sites are facial, pubic and peri-rectal regions. This behaviour will frequently lead to hair loss to the extent that the individual will attempt to conceal this with makeup, scarves or wigs. Hair pulling is often accompanied by feelings of loss of control, embarrassment and shame, and sufferers will often have made numerous unsuccessful attempts to stop the compulsion. Hair pulling can also be associated with a range of rituals, including pulling out only certain types of hair (e.g. certain textures or colours), or closely examining or playing with the hair after it has been pulled. These rituals are thought to provide stimulation to the brain's visual, tactile and oral processing centres, and oral manipulation of hair occurs in around 48 per cent of sufferers, and as many as 18 per cent of sufferers will frequently ingest hair, adding to the risk of creating hair balls (Christenson, Mackenzie & Mitchell, 1991). As with other forms of compulsion, hair pulling is usually preceded by negative mood states such as anxiety or boredom, and the act of hair pulling may be reinforced with a sense of gratification or relief when the hair is pulled out. The DSM-5 diagnostic criteria for trichotillomania are provided in Table 3.3.

Historically, trichotillomania was considered a relatively rare disorder, but research on college students has indicated a lifetime prevalence rate of 0.6 per cent (Christenson, Mackenzie & Mitchell, 1991). Prevalence rates for hair pulling that does not meet diagnostic criteria are higher – ranging from 1 per cent to 13.3 per cent (Graber & Arndt, 1993; Woods & Miltenberger, 1996). While hair pulling in nonclinical populations is about equal for both genders, diagnosed trichotillomania is predominantly a disorder that affects women (Christenson & Crow, 1996).

Trichotillomania typically has two patterns, an *automatic pattern* – where hair pulling occurs without awareness while the individual is absorbed in another task – such as reading or studying (Chistenson, Ristvedt & Mackenzie, 1993; Mansueto, Townsley-Sternberger, McCombs-Thomas & Goldfinger-Golomb, 1997), and *focused hair pulling*, which is an activity that is the centre of attention, associated with intense urges, anxiety and uncontrollable thoughts about hair pulling. It has been estimated that around 75 per cent of hair pullers adopt the automatic pattern (Christenson, Mackenzie & Mitchell, 1994).

There are many similarities between trichotillomania and OCD compulsions insofar as the behaviour is in response to urges and can be anxiety relieving, and is driven and repetitive. However, differences between trichotillomania and OCD include gender distribution, where trichotillomania is predominantly seen in females whereas OCD is equally distributed in gender, and age of onset of trichotillomania is usually early adolescence, whereas OCD can frequently start in childhood.

- Hair loss as a result of regularly pulling out of hair
- The individual is unable to stop hair pulling, despite regular attempts to quit
- Hair pulling causes significant distress or impairment of daily functioning
- The hair pulling cannot be explained by another medical condition and cannot be explained by another mental health problem (e.g. depression).

Table 3.3 Summary of DSM-5 diagnostic criteria for trichotillomania (hair-pulling disorder)

Furthermore, the frequency of OCD sufferers also being diagnosed with trichotillomania is relatively low, and not that different from levels in other anxiety disorders (Richter, Summerfeldt, Antony et al., 2003), which suggests only a weak link to OCD.

Excoriation (skin picking) disorder

Skin picking disorder is characterized by the repetitive and compulsive picking of skin leading to tissue damage. The most commonly picked sites are the face, arms and hands. Sufferers may pick at healthy skin, minor skin irregularities, pimples, calluses or scabs from previous picking. Most people pick with their hands, but some use tweezers, pins, etc. (DSM-5, p. 254). Sufferers may spend significant amounts of time per day picking, and it can endure for months or years. Skin picking is also referred to as neurotic excoriation, dermatillomania or psychogenic excoriation. Skin picking can be preceded by negative mood states, such as stress, anxiety or boredom, and various rituals may also accompany skin picking, such as examining or playing with the skin. Case History 3.3

Case History 3.3

Compulsive Skin Picking

Grant, Odlaug, Chamberlain, Keuthen et al., (2012) report the case of 'Ms. B', a 24-year-old single female who picks at her face, arms and legs on a daily basis. She began skin picking around 13 years of age and in the past 2 years the picking has become a daily routine. Ms. B often picks her skin for 2 to 3 hours each day especially during times of boredom or just before bed. She will check her body to find some bump or inconsistency in the skin, and when she finds one, she begins picking with her fingernails and stops only when she starts to bleed or when she feels that the bump has been removed. The irresistible 'need' or 'urge' to pick immediately precedes or is simultaneous with touching the skin. Each episode of picking ends with a sense of accomplishment, but this quickly changes into shame and embarrassment. Ms. B is often late for work or unable to work because of the embarrassment caused to her by the open wounds on her face. At the time of her referral she had not dated or socialized with friends for a year.

provides the clinical example of a young woman with compulsive skin picking.

Epidemiological studies suggest that skin picking is relatively common in the general population, with up to 63 per cent of people in a community sample engaging in some form of skin picking, and 10 per cent of respondents reported picking to the point of skin damage. When the full set of diagnostic criteria were included, 1.4 per cent of the sample met the criteria for skin picking disorder as described in DSM-5 (Keuthen, Koran, Aboujaoude, Large et al., 2010) (see Table 3.4). Skin picking seems to be fairly universal, with the clinical characteristics being similar across different cultures in Europe, Africa, North America, South America and the Middle East (e.g. Bohne, Wilhelm, Keuthen, Baer et al., 2002; Calikusu, Kucukgoncu, Tecer & Bestepe, 2012). However, age of onset varies considerably, and it can begin in childhood, adolescence or later adult life (Keuthen, Koran, Aboujaoude, Large et al., 2010). Picking often begins unconsciously but becomes conscious after a period of time.

Skin picking is comorbid with a variety of other mental health problems, including major depressive disorder (12.5%–48%), anxiety disorders (8%–23%), body dysmorphic disorder (44%), and substance use disorders (14%–36%). Furthermore, rates of co-occurring OCD are significantly higher in skin picking disorder sufferers than the general population (6%–52%) suggesting a further link between these two related types of disorder (Grant, Odlaug, Chamberlain, Keuthen et al., 2012). Other grooming disorders are common in individuals with skin picking disorder, including trichotillomania (Christenson & Mansueto, 1999).

Onychophagia (nail biting)

Onychophagia is compulsive nail biting. Habitual nail biting is a common behaviour among children and young adults (onset can be as young as 3–4 years). This stabilizes from age 7 to 10 years, but incidence increases again substantially during adolescence (Pennington, 1945; Sassouni & Forrest, 1971). The need to bite off and even eat fingernails is linked to anxiety (Massler & Malone, 1950), and case studies have suggested that onychophagia may be related to OCD and even part of an OCD spectrum disorder (Pacan, Grzesiak, Reich & Szepietowski, 2009), but as yet onychophagia has not been included as a specific disorder in DSM-5.

Mental contamination

While there are a significant number of OCD sufferers who fear actual contamination (e.g. by contact with dirt, germs, etc.), there is also another group for whom comparable feelings of dirtiness can be provoked without any physical contact with a contaminant, and this has come to be called *mental contamination* (Rachman, 2004, 2006). Mental contamination can be caused by images, thoughts and memories, and tends to be caused by either thinking about contamination or contaminating substances, or even by a violation of some kind by another person, e.g. degradation, betrayal, emotional abuse, physical abuse or humiliation which give rise to feelings of dirtiness or pollution, and in many cases may be associated with compulsive washing or cleansing (Rachman, 2010; Zhong & Liljenquist, 2006). Case History 3.4 provides you with two examples of mental contamination, one from a woman who felt contaminated by just thinking about dirt and pollution, and a second from a 20-year-old male who developed mental contamination following a 'betrayal' experience. In addition to these feelings of contamination, individuals also experience anxiety, disgust, shame, anger, guilt and sadness (Rachman, Radomsky, Elliott & Zysk, 2012). While mental contamination seems to represent a very specific form of OCD contamination fear that is caused by quite specific experiences, it is possible to ameliorate the symptoms using adaptations of standard CBT (Cognitive Behaviour Therapy) interventions (Warnock-Parkes, Salkovskis & Rachman, 2012).

Mental contamination seems to be relatively common amongst people suffering from OCD, with 46 per cent of those with a diagnosis of OCD reporting experiencing mental contamination (Coughtrey, Shafran, Knibbs & Rachman, 2012). Mental contamination is believe to be associated with thought-action fusion (TAF) (see Chapter 4) – the belief that thinking about an unacceptable or aversive event is more likely to make it happen, and having a thought about an unacceptable action is the moral equivalent of carrying out that action. In addition, the feelings of guilt, anxiety and low mood that result from TAF can be misinterpreted as feelings of dirtiness and pollution, and the mislabelling of mood states in this way may be a significant contributor to experiencing mental contamination (Coughtrey, Shafran & Lee, 2013).

Case History 3.4

Mental Contamination

Below are two examples of mental contamination. The first illustrates how compulsive washing rituals can be triggered solely by the thought of being contaminated, and the second describes how experiences of betrayal can lead to washing rituals associated with any reminders of the betrayal (in this case, letters in brown envelopes sent by government agencies).

Coughtrey, Shafran & Lee (2013) report the case of a 43-year-old Asian female with an 18-year history of OCD symptoms related to a fear of contamination associated with feces. Even imagining feces would cause her to feel dirty and wash compulsively. At the beginning of treatment, she reported using two bottles of shower gel a day, and double washing all her clothes using five washing tablets per wash. She had not slept in her own bed for over 10 years for fear of spreading contamination. As well as her contamination fears, she also reported low mood, low self-esteem, and frequent panic attacks.

Warnock-Parkes, Salkovskis & Rachman (2012) report the case of David whose difficulties started following a series of events that had left him feeling betrayed, angry and distressed. Immediately before his OCD symptoms began, David's wife had left him and he discovered that she had been having affairs with other men. David described the 'deceit and lies' he experienced as being distressing 'emotional traumas' and 'betrayals'. He reported losing his home and his children, and he was served divorce papers in a brown envelope in a manner that made him feel as though he had been treated 'like rubbish'. He felt 'pure rage' at what he saw as immoral treatment and described how endless letters in brown envelopes from governmental agencies arrived in his home 'like an invasion'. Very soon after this he started to feel 'disgusted' when he saw any brown envelopes or anything related to the government and started to think these items were contaminated. Subsequently he began engaging in hours of washing to try to cleanse himself after being faced with a reminder, such as a brown envelope.

Tourette's & Tic Related disorders

Tic Related disorders can be found under Neurodevelopmental Disorders in DSM-5, but they are relevant here because they are repetitive behavioural responses that are often associated with, and comorbid with OCD symptoms (Geller, Biederman, Griffin, Jones et al., 1996).

Tic disorders comprise three basic diagnostic categories, namely Tourette's disorder, persistent (chronic) motor or vocal tic disorder and provisional tic disorder, and the DSM-5 diagnostic criteria for these are shown in Table 3.4. Tics are sudden, rapid, recurrent, nonrythmic motor movements or vocalizations. They are generally experienced as involuntary and can include almost any muscle group, but are most usually manifested as eye blinking or throat clearing. Tics can be either simple or complex. **Simple tics** are of short duration and may include eye blinks, shoulder shrugging, sniffing, grunting or extensions of the extremities. *Complex motor tics* are of longer duration and can consist of combinations of simple tics (e.g. head turning plus shoulder shrugging). They can often

Tourette's disorder

- The occurrence of motor and vocal tics that have persisted for some time
- The frequency of these tics may fluctuate but will have been around for more than 1 year since the first onset of symptoms
- The symptoms occurred before age 18 years
- The symptoms are not due to the effects of a drug or another medical condition

Persistent (chronic) motor or vocal tic disorder

- The occurrence of motor or vocal tics, but not both
- The frequency of these tics may fluctuate but will have been around for more than 1 year since the first onset of symptoms
- The symptoms occurred before age 18 years
- The symptoms are not due to the effects of a drug or another medical condition

Provisional tic disorder

- Motor and/or vocal tics that occur singly or together
- Tics are present for at least 1 year
- The symptoms occurred before age 18 years
- The symptoms are not due to the effects of a drug or another medical condition
- A diagnosis of Tourette's Disorder or Persistent Motor or Vocal Tic Disorder has never been made

Table 3.4 Summary of DSM-5 diagnostic criteria for tic disorders

appear purposeful when the tic consists of imitating another person's movements, making tic-like obscene or sexual gestures, or uttering socially unacceptable words. For Tourette's disorder, both motor and vocal tics must be present. Tic disorders are more common in children than in adults, in special education populations than in general populations of children, and among boys more than among girls (Knight, Steeves, Day, Lowerison et al., 2012). Tic disorders are relatively common in children, with a point prevalence of transient tic disorder of 2.99 per cent. Tourette's disorder is less common, with a point prevalence of only 0.77 per cent (Knight, Steeves, Day, Lowerison et al., 2012).

The onset of tics is typically between 4–6 years of age (DSM-5, p. 83) with peak severity between 10 and 12 years, and symptoms decreasing towards the end of adolescence. The severity of tics can wax and wane over time, and the sufferer may have tic-free periods of months at a time. The first symptoms are usually facial tics such as rapid blinking or twitches of the mouth, but Tourette's Disorder may start with sounds such as throat clearing and sniffing, or even with multiple tics of movements and sounds. Tourette's Disorder and behavioural tics are often comorbid with a diagnosis of OCD in childhood and adolescence, and the relationship between OCD and tic disorder seems to be bidirectional, affecting 20–60 per cent of individuals with each disorder (Lewin, Chang, McCracken, McQueen & Piacentini, 2010). Studies suggest that up to 60 per cent of children seeking treatment for OCD have a lifetime history of tics (Leonard, Lenane, Swedo, Rettew et al., 1992), and some theorists believe that OCD is a heterogeneous disorder with an inherited component that can manifest either as OCD obsessions or compulsions, or as behavioural or vocal tics (Pauls, Alsobrook, Goodman, Rasmussen et al., 1995).

OCD symptoms and behavioural and vocal tics can cause obvious problems for a child, with them being a source of anxiety and fear for the sufferer, and provoking ridicule and victimization by peers (Storch, Ledley, Lewin, Murphy et al., 2006). The severity of behavioural and vocal tics is usually directly related to levels of stress, so learning how to control stress can greatly reduce symptoms (e.g. by learning relaxation techniques). In some cases, a less socially acceptable tic can be replaced with a more socially acceptable one using behaviour therapy methods, and medication can also be used to help control the condition. Treatments normally used with OCD symptoms (such as exposure with response prevention or CBT – see Chapter 7) can also be effective with behavioural tics (Verdellen, Keijsers, Cath & Hoogduin, 2004; Turner, 2006).

 Obsessive-compulsive personality disorder (OCPD)

Obsessive-compulsive personality disorder (OCPD) differs from OCD in that it is not so much a severe mental health problem with distressing and disability consequences, but an obsessive-compulsive personality style that is an enduring feature of the way an individual behaves and organizes their lives. The essential feature of OCPD is a preoccupation with orderliness, perfectionism and mental and interpersonal control at the expense of flexibility, openness and efficiency (DSM-5, p. 679), and Table 3.5 shows the DSM-5 diagnostic criteria for OCPD. Individuals diagnosed with OCPD will stick to rules, work schedules and prearranged procedures to such a degree that the overall purpose of the activity is often lost. Diverging from a pre-set schedule causes them significant distress, as does failing to achieve the highest of standards in the things they do, and their attention to detail and their inflexibility will often annoy other people because of the delays and inconvenience that this may cause. For example, they may hold up a work project by insisting that their component of the project has to be completed meticulously and in the way in which it was originally specified. Individuals with

A long-time history of need for orderliness, mental and personal control, and general perfectionism – all at the expense of flexibility – Begins in early adulthood and can be found in a range of different contexts (e.g. four or more of the following):

1. Concerned with detail, the deployment of rules in everyday behaviour, the use of lists, often to the point where the original purpose of the task is lost.
2. Exhibits perfectionism to the point where this will often prevent task completion.
3. Shows excessive commitment to work and productivity to the detriment of friendships and leisure.
4. Over-concerned with issues of morality, ethics and values.
5. Cannot throw away old items even when they have no sentimental value.
6. Cannot delegate tasks easily to others or work with others unless things are done their way
7. Has an excessive tendency to save rather than spend money
8. Frequently exhibits rigid and stubborn behaviour.

Table 3.5 Summary of DSM-5 diagnostic criteria for obsessive-compulsive personality disorder (OCPD)

OCPD nearly always plan ahead meticulously and are unwilling to contemplate changes to their plan. This means that even hobbies and recreational activities are approached as serious tasks requiring organization and scheduling. For example, they will need to plan a visit to a restaurant well in advance, the menu needs to be checked to ensure that everyone will be happy with what is on offer, and the quality of the restaurant's service must be checked with friends who have been there or by consulting dining reviews. If this planning is disrupted (e.g. if the restaurant is closed when the party arrives), this will cause the individual considerable distress and a spontaneous alternative will be difficult for them to consider. If things are not done 'their way' this also causes distress, and this may be taken to unnecessary extremes (such as asking a child to ride its bike in a straight line or telling people that there is only one way to wash the dishes, etc.), and they will then become upset or angry if people do not comply, although the anger is rarely expressed directly. Because of this they will rarely delegate tasks, but insist on doing them themselves, and often become viewed as 'workaholics'. Their perfectionist tendencies also mean that they often end up hoarding things rather than throwing them away, and will adopt a miserly attitude to spending, believing that money should not be wasted. Because of this, they often end up living at a standard well below what they can afford. OCPD is one of the most prevalent of the personality disorders, with a recent large-scale epidemiological study recording a lifetime prevalence rate of 7.8 per cent, with rates being very similar between males and females (Grant, Mooney & Kushner, 2012).

While the characteristics of OCPD may seem very similar to the symptoms of OCD, there is relatively little overlap between the two. OCD is distinguished by the presence of true obsessions and compulsions that are clearly extreme, ritualistic and maladaptive (e.g. hoarding things until it is impossible to walk through the house, or ritualistically checking that the house is secure to a point where this severely impairs normal daily functioning). In contrast OCPD causes an individual stress and anxiety when things are not done in the meticulous and ordered way that the sufferer wants, and as Case History 3.5 shows, the orderliness with which someone with OCPD requires things to be done can cause friction with other people such as family, friends and workmates.

The exact relationship between OCPD and OCD has been the subject of debate for some time. Some clinicians have argued that OCPD is a precursor for the development of OCD (Krockmalik & Menzies, 2003).

Case History 3.5

Obsessive-compulsive personality disorder (OCPD)

Jane likes to describe herself as a perfect mother. She takes pride in keeping an orderly household and attending all of her daughters' horse-riding events, while being office manager in an insurance company. She knows the schedules of each family member and follows rigid routines to make sure everyone gets to work or school on time. Jane gets very upset when her teenage daughters want to go out with friends at weekends or in the evenings. She says it takes away from their family time and all of her efforts and planning are wasted. She refuses to go out for the evening if this interferes with her planned weekly activities in the house. Her husband doesn't mind Jane planning his schedule but he does complain when he helps out with the household chores because she consistently complains that he hasn't followed her instructions properly. For example, if he does the shopping but does not get the right discounted items, Jane gets upset and accuses him of being careless and extravagant. Jane continually tells everyone that if she wants something doing properly, she has to do it herself, and she will religiously clean the house in exactly the same way every week – whether things are dirty and untidy or not.

Clinical Commentary: *Jane exhibits many of the symptoms of OCPD and probably has the minimum four symptoms required for a DSM-5 diagnosis. These are a pre-occupation with details, rules, lists, order, organization, or schedules to the extent that the major point of the activity is lost (e.g. she will do the housework each week in exactly the same way regardless of whether this is necessary), she is excessively devoted to work and productivity to the exclusion of leisure activities, she is reluctant to delegate tasks or to work with others unless they submit to exactly her way of doing things, she shows rigidity and stubbornness, and adopts a miserly spending style. From this brief case description you can see that Jane frequently gets upset and anxious about family life because of her rigid perfectionism (and this may well lead to a comorbid diagnosis of generalized anxiety disorder), and her rigid and inflexible behaviour also puts severe strains on family relationships.*

(From Davey, 2008)

However, OCPD is not a necessary precursor of OCD and studies have found the prevalence of OCPD in patients diagnosed with OCD as ranging only between 23 per cent and 34 per cent (Albert, Maina, Forner & Bogetto, 2004; Lochner, Serebro, der Merwe, Hemmings et al., 2011). However, regardless of whether OCPD is a risk factor for OCD, individuals diagnosed with comorbid OCPD and OCD do appear to exhibit more severe symptoms, are more functionally impaired, and are likely to develop other problems such as alcohol dependence and depression (Garyfallos, Katsigiannopoulos, Adamopoulou, Papazisis et al., 2010; Gordon, Salkovskis, Oldfield & Carter, 2013).

Chapter summary

This chapter has described a number of disorders that have important similarities with OCD. Four of those disorders are linked to OCD through their inclusion in the DSM-5 chapter on OCD, and these are Body Dysmorphic Disorder, Hoarding Disorder, Trichotillomania (Hair-Pulling Disorder), and Excoriation (Skin Picking) Disorder. Other related disorders exhibit OCD-like symptoms such as compulsions and ritualized behaviours, and this latter group includes Tourettes and tic-related problems, onychophagia (nail biting), mental contamination and Obsessive-Compulsive Personality Disorder (OCPD). While some evidence is available that all these related disorders are linked to OCD (e.g. because they have a higher prevalence in OCD sufferers than the general population), there is still considerable debate about what those links exactly are. Some of these disorders are claimed to be risk factors for subsequent OCD (e.g. OCPD, tic-related problems), while arguments can be made that some others are simply variants of OCD (e.g. Body Dysmorphic Disorder, Hoarding Disorder). Future research on OCD, its causes, and the mechanisms through which it is maintained should shed further light on the relationship between OCD and these related disorders.

Section One Summary

In this first section we have described and explored some of the main features of obsessive-compulsive disorder and its related mental health problems. Chapter 1 has dealt with a description of the main symptoms of OCD and how it is diagnosed using the most current diagnostic criteria outlined in DSM-5. As you will see when reading this section, OCD symptoms can manifest in a variety of ways including obsessional thoughts and a number of compulsive forms of behaviour. Although we have emphasized the diagnostic criteria for OCD in this section, it is important to be aware that OCD symptoms probably exist on a continuum from mild to severe and so a specific set of diagnostic criteria are not necessarily set in stone.

In Chapter 2 we dealt with the epidemiology of OCD and provided some information on its relative prevalence in the population. What is perhaps striking about the features of OCD we reviewed in this chapter is that it is a mental health problem that is highly comorbid with other problems – particularly anxiety and mood disorders. Although there are some cultural and ethnicity factors that can increase the risk of developing OCD symptoms (such as high levels of religiosity), cultural differences in symptoms are quite small. Finally, we reviewed the course of OCD throughout the lifespan, and found OCD symptoms to be an important way in which anxiety manifests itself in childhood.

Finally, the importance of OCD as a mental health problem has been recognized in DSM-5 with the disorder being given its own chapter. This chapter also recognizes that there are many other psychological disorders that have features resembling OCD, and we discussed these in detail in Chapter 3.

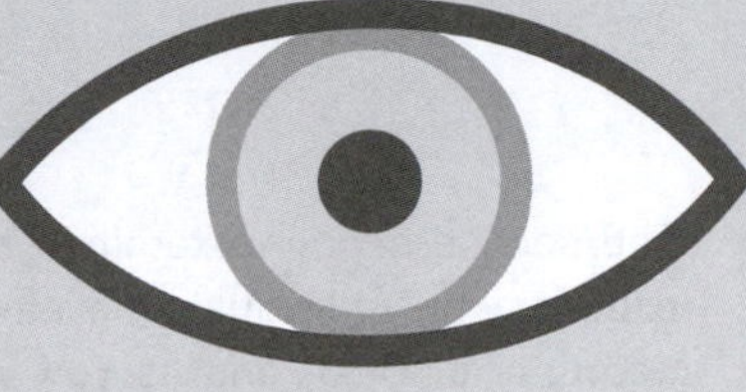

Section Two

What Causes OCD?

Preface

The second section examines theories that have been proposed to explain why individuals develop OCD. Chapter 4 covers cognitive accounts of OCD, and as you will see, many different theories fall under 'cognitive accounts'. Cognitive processes, such as biases in memory, attention and interpretation are covered in this chapter, as well as cognitive models including memory deficits, thought suppression, inflated responsibility, thought-action fusion, intolerance of uncertainty, metacognitive therapy and the mood-as-input theory. In Chapter 5, we review explanations of OCD that come from behavioural, psychodynamic and sociocultural theories. In the behavioural section, the importance of conditioning, safety behaviours, and avoidance in the development and maintenance of OCD is presented. In the psychodynamic section, Freud's psychoanalytic theory of psychopathology is covered, with particular focus on unconscious conflicts and defence mechanisms. Freud's theory is illustrated with 'The Rat Man' case history. The final section of Chapter 5 examines cultural factors related to OCD, including religion and disgust. In Chapter 6, the biological accounts of OCD are discussed. These include biochemical, genetic, neuroanatomical, immunological and evolutionary accounts. Section 2 ends with an overall evaluation of the accounts of OCD covered in Chapters 4–6.

Chapter 4

Cognitive Factors

Obsessive and intrusive thoughts occur both in the general population and in those with OCD (Rachman & de Silva, 1978). However, it is the way that the thoughts are interpreted and appraised that is thought to underlie the distress experienced by individuals with OCD. In this section we will consider cognitive factors that are known to lead to an anxious interpretation of unwanted intrusive thoughts. The first part of the section will consider cognitive biases and the second will examine cognitive models of OCD.

Cognitive biases in OCD

Cognitive biases are a tendency to selectively process information, leading to a skewed representation of events and can be considered to be maladaptive structures or **schemas** that affect the way information is processed. Cognitive biases are a feature of many psychological disorders relating to anxiety (e.g. OCD and GAD (Generalised Anxiety Disorder)) and depression. In OCD cognitive biases are thought to result in the individual giving increased information processing resources to threat-relevant information. Preferential processing of information has been observed in a number of cognitive processes in OCD. Some of the most commonly researched cognitive biases in OCD are **attentional biases, interpretation biases** and **memory biases**. Evidence for each type of bias in OCD will be discussed below.

Memory biases

One way in which anxiety is maintained in individuals with OCD is through experiencing heighted or improved memory for threatening stimuli as compared to non-threatening stimuli. For example, individuals with contamination fear, OCD may be more likely to recall information about potentially contaminating objects than about neutral objects. If that threat-relevant material is more easily available, this may influence the number of intrusions an individual has, which can make people feel more threatened, thus heightening the need to perform compulsions. An early example of memory biases in recall was demonstrated by Bower, Monterio & Gilligan (1978) who found that when participants learnt word lists while in a negative mood, they recalled more of those word lists when also in a negative mood than when in a positive mood. However, while there are many studies on memory biases across the anxiety disorders (many of which have conflicting results; see Coles & Heimberg, 2002 for a review), there are relatively few studies on memory biases in OCD. Wilhelm, McNally, Baer & Florin (1996) examined explicit memory biases in OCD by asking individuals with OCD or a non-anxious control group to either remember or forget (known as a directed forgetting paradigm) neutral, negative or positive words. The authors found that while they replicated the standard finding in this type of task where participants recalled more 'remember' words than 'forget' words, participants with OCD had greater difficulty forgetting negative forget words as compared to positive and neutral forget words, than the control group did. These findings suggest that individuals with OCD encode negative words more elaborately than positive or neutral words, regardless of the instructions they were given. This study was replicated and extended by Tolin, Hamlin & Foa (2002). In the replication they found support for the findings of the previous study where participants with OCD were less likely to forget negative words. Tolin et al. (2002) also extended the study to include OCD relevant words and they found that the relevance of the word to OCD was more important than its positive or negative valency. This means that individuals with OCD had more difficulty forgetting OCD relevant words, regardless of whether these words were negative or positive. One possible explanation for this is that positive OCD words may still be relevant to a general feeling of threat and individuals may be using more elaborate encoding for threat relevant words regardless of the valency of that word.

While studies such as those reported above support the existence of memory biases in OCD, other published studies have not found support for this. For example, Foa, Amir, Gershuny, Molnar & Kozak (1997) examined explicit and **implicit memory biases** in OCD and found an implicit memory bias for threat in individuals with and without OCD. To further clarify the role of memory biases in OCD, Radomsky & Rachman (1999) proposed to examine memory biases in individuals who were sensitive to specific threats, in this case contamination fear. They believed that examining individuals who had specific contamination threats would clarify the existence of memory biases in OCD as these specific contamination fears should be accompanied by specific associations and the increased strength of these specific associations could be the essential factor in producing the memory bias. Radomsky & Rachman (1999) examined memory biases for contamination relevant objects in individuals with OCD (who expressed fear of contamination) as compared to anxious individuals (who did not have OCD) and a non-anxious control group. When looking at behavioural responses to clean and dirty objects, they found that the OCD group and the two control groups were more anxious about touching dirty objects than clean ones, but the OCD group were more anxious about touching any objects (clean or dirty) than the anxious control group and the anxious control group was more anxious about touching objects than the non-anxious control group. However, interestingly, only individuals with OCD had a biased memory for objects perceived as dirty as compared to clean (as evidenced by their being able to recall more contamination relevant items from a list than clean items), while the other control groups did not. Importantly, overall recall ability was no different in the OCD group as compared to the two control groups, rather the OCD group had an *explicit* memory bias for preferential recall of dirt related objects. In fact, participants were able to remember dirty objects better than clean ones, without being able to remember which objects were clean or dirty. This led the authors to suggest that the threat observed by the participants was not the dirty object, but the dirt itself. As such, those who remembered which objects were dirty without remembering what the contaminated object was, were showing an *implicit* memory bias towards remembering threatening material. To further clarify the existence of memory biases in OCD, Radomsky & Rachman (2004) examined studies that either, showed or failed to show, memory biases in OCD. They concluded that in studies where **ecological validity** was low, they were unlikely to reliably detect a memory bias in OCD. Radomsky and Rachman suggested that experimental paradigms should have significance and relevance to individuals with OCD.

Attentional biases

An attentional bias involves showing preferential attention towards, or selectively attending to, threatening or anxiety provoking information, relative to neutral information. Attentional biases are important in both the development and maintenance of OCD. For example, being more attentive to threatening material may mean that intrusions are interpreted as being threatening and having a heightened attention to threat-relevant information may make one more likely to perform compulsions to seek anxiety reduction. According to Cisler & Koster (2010), attentional biases can be observed through three key characteristics: a) facilitated attention (e.g. detecting threat stimuli faster than non-threat stimuli), b) difficulty in disengagement (e.g. it is more difficult to disengage attention from threat stimuli compared to non-threat stimuli), and c) attentional avoidance (e.g. attention is allocated to locations opposite to the location of a threat) (Cisler & Koster, 2010). However, evidence for attentional biases in OCD is inconsistent and evidence both supporting and disconfirming the role of attentional biases in OCD will be discussed in this section.

In order to examine attentional biases in OCD, one strategy has been to examine attentional biases relevant to OCD specific threats such as biases towards contamination stimuli. One technique used by researchers (e.g. Foa & McNally, 1986) is the **dichotic listening task**. In this study a different stream of information was presented to each ear at the same time, but participants were instructed to concentrate only on one stream of information. Using this task, researchers found that individuals with OCD were better at detecting fear-relevant words that were presented in the information that they were *not* attending to than non-threat words presented in the non-attention ear. Furthermore, after the OCD group received a therapeutic intervention in the form of *exposure response prevention* treatment, this difference in ability to detect threat over non-threat words disappeared. This enabled the authors to conclude that threat relevant attention biases in OCD could be manipulated and could thus be diminished with treatment. Although attentional biases are well documented in anxiety disorders, OCD researchers have focused on *content specific* attentional biases (you will remember from the section above that this is also the case with memory biases), meaning that individuals with OCD and specific contamination fear showed a bias towards threatening material only when it was relevant to contamination, but not when it was relevant to other types of anxiety such as social anxiety (Tata, Leibowitz, Prunty, Cameron & Pickering, 1996). These findings indicate that biases in OCD are not a response to a general feeling of anxiety, but are specific to threats associated (in this case) with contamination fear specific OCD.

As noted above there are three core components of attentional biases (facilitated attention, difficulty in disengagement, attentional avoidance). One way to unpick the role of attentional biases in OCD is to examine which components can be observed in individuals with OCD. Cisler & Olatunji (2010) examined core components of attentional biases in contamination fear (CF). CF was chosen because it is a subtype of OCD that is associated with strong evidence for attentional biases. In CF they found that attentional biases were characterized by individuals having difficulty disengaging from threat and they suggested that this may be due to individuals with CF being unable to remove attention from sources of threat, or that they purposefully maintain attention onto threat because they perceive threat-relevant stimuli as harmful.

Although attentional biases in anxiety disorders are well documented, more recently researchers have reported inconsistencies in findings relating to attentional biases in OCD (e.g. Moritz et al., 2008; Moritz & von Muhlenen, 2008). Moritz and colleagues have pointed out that there are a number of published articles which did not find evidence for attentional biases in OCD and they present experimental data looking at attentional biases in a *Stroop task* (Moritz et al. 2008) and examining attention towards and ability to disengage from OCD relevant stimuli (Moritz & von Muhlenen, 2008). In both cases the authors concluded that there was no evidence to indicate that participants with OCD demonstrated attentional biases. However, Amir, Najmi & Morrison (2009) have suggested that the lack of evidence for attentional biases in OCD in these studies could be accounted for by taking into account the possibility that the attentional bias may actually diminish over the course of the experiment. When Amir et al. (2009) examined attentional biases in individuals with OCD over a number of time points, they observed that the bias diminished after the first block of trials, which they suggest may mean that individuals are *habituating* to the perceived threat over time. As many attentional bias experiments have used differing numbers of trials on experiments of differing lengths, this may explain the inconsistencies in research findings.

Interpretation biases in OCD

An ***interpretation bias*** occurs when an ambiguous event or situation is interpreted as a threat. Interpretation biases are a central cognitive processes in OCD and Rachman (1997) proposed that a key difference between a 'normal obsession' and a 'clinical obsession' is the interpretation of the significance of the obsession. A key characteristic of OCD is that individuals will make a catastrophic interpretation of an intrusive thought. In terms of OCD symptoms this anxiety-relevant interpretation may make an individual interpret an intrusion as being threatening, which in turn will increase anxiety and also increase the desire to perform compulsive behaviours. Studies of the interpretation biases that drive this catastrophic interpretation response have focused on various aspects of interpretation such as a perception of inflated responsibility for harm in ambiguous situations, or the tendency to view a thought as the same as an action (thought-action fusion). These different aspects of interpretation have been given a central role in cognitive models of OCD (Rachman, 1997; Salkovskis, 1985) and will be discussed in more detail in the cognitive models section below.

Summary

This section has examined common cognitive biases in OCD. We have discussed three cognitive biases relevant to OCD; these are memory biases, attentional biases and interpretation biases. Cognitive biases have a role in the onset and maintenance of OCD as these biases make individuals more likely to give preferential cognitive resources to threat-relevant information. This has important implications for OCD symptoms as having a bias for threat-relevant information will make one be more likely to perceive intrusive thoughts as being important. This in turn will trigger compulsive behaviours in a bid to reduce anxiety. Looking at the research for memory biases and attentional biases, we have seen that there have been mixed experimental findings for these biases in OCD. These mixed results can be accounted for by looking at the experimental methods used to study these biases. There are a number of different interpretation biases relevant to OCD that are prominent in cognitive models of OCD, which will be examined below.

Cognitive models of OCD

The cognitive account of OCD proposes that certain beliefs contribute to the development and maintenance of the disorder. The cognitive model (as opposed to a biological or social model) focuses on dysfunctional beliefs and maladaptive appraisals, such as an inflated sense of responsibility or intolerance of uncertainty to explain OCD symptoms. A number of different (yet often complimentary) cognitive models have been proposed to provide an explanation of the mechanisms that drive obsessive thinking in OCD and that serve to develop and maintain OCD symptoms. The cognitive model emphasizes that intrusive thoughts are actually a normal experience, yet it is the way in which these thoughts are appraised or evaluated that has implications for whether the thoughts are perceived to be distressing or not. For example, if one has an intrusion of harming one's family, one way of appraising it would be to think that it was simply a thought and not a true state of affairs. However, if you were experiencing feelings of excessive responsibility, another way of appraising the thought is as a potential threat that you must prevent from occurring. Cognitive models examine a number of different cognitive processes proposed to be important in explaining intrusive obsessive thinking and subsequent compulsions. The models discussed in this section will be memory deficits, thought suppression, thought-action fusion, inflated responsibility, perfectionism, intolerance of uncertainty and meta-cognitions. These are not necessarily competing models, these different cognitive models serve to explain different characteristics of the OCD process.

Memory deficits

Many people with OCD report feelings of doubt or uncertainty when they consider whether they have carried out an action correctly. This uncertainty is especially noticeable in compulsions where it may result in the need to repeatedly check that doors are locked or that hands have been washed properly. Commonly observed behaviours in OCD such as repeated checking have led researchers to examine what causes these feelings of doubt. Two broad hypotheses emerged, either individuals with OCD actually have a memory deficit, or that individuals with OCD have less confidence in their memory.

Do individuals with OCD have a general memory deficit?

Studies examining general memory deficits in OCD have tended to focus on deficits in *episodic memory* (as opposed to **semantic** or **procedural memory**) because episodic memory (recall of personal events in the past) is particularly relevant to OCD symptoms such as checking and is vulnerable to forgetting (Muller & Roberts, 2005). Early studies found that in a non-clinical sample, individuals who scored highly on a scale of checking behaviours had poorer memory functions than those who scored less highly on measures of checking behaviours (Sher, Mann & Frost, 1984). This study was also replicated with a clinical (although non-OCD) sample, where individuals who were high checkers were found to have deficits in memory, especially for recently completed actions (Sher, Frost, Kushner, Crews & Alexander, 1989). More recently the relationship between OCD checking and memory deficit has been examined with a clinical OCD sample (who had checking as a predominant symptom) by using neuropsychological tests of visual memory and memory for actions (Tallis, Pratt & Jamani, 1999). When using this clinical sample and more stringent tests of memory, Tallis et al. actually found no difference between the OCD group and a group of healthy controls on immediate memory for actions. This mixed pattern of results concerning memory deficits in OCD is represented in number of published studies (for a review see Muller & Roberts, 2005). It has been suggested that this lack of support for a global memory deficit in OCD should lead to research into other possible triggers of impaired performance, including cognitive biases such as inflated responsibility, or intolerance of uncertainty (e.g. Moritz, Ruhe, Jelinek & Naber, 2009).

Do individuals with OCD have less confidence in their memory?

An alternative explanation for the repeated checking carried out by individuals with OCD is that rather than having problems recalling what they did, they actually lack confidence in their recall of having completed a behaviour adequately. There is now evidence to suggest that confidence in recall, rather than recall ability itself, influences checking behaviours in OCD. A number of studies have examined confidence in memory recall in OCD. Tolin, Abramowitz, Bartholomew et al. (2001) examined memory confidence in individuals with OCD compared to an anxious and a non-anxious control group. In line with research discussed in the above section, no differences were found between groups for memory accuracy, but individuals with OCD showed a decrease (compared to the control groups) in their memory confidence over repeated trials. This suggests that the more OCD checkers checked, the less confident they became in their checking. This paradoxical effect has now been demonstrated in a number of studies. Marcel van den Hout and colleagues have examined memory distrust in OCD. In a number of experimental studies they have shown that when healthy individuals repeatedly check threat-relevant objects, the more they check, the less they trust their memory of the object. They propose that repeated checking causes familiarity with the object and this promotes **conceptual processing** and inhibits **perceptual processing**, which makes recollections of the object less vivid, which means that the memory of the object feels less trustworthy (van den Hout & Kindt, 2003). These findings suggest that individuals with OCD do not have impaired memory, but actually have less confidence and trust in their memory, which leads to repeated checking behaviours, which in turn reduces their confidence and certainty that they have adequately checked a threat-relevant object.

Thought suppression

As discussed in Chapter 1, we all experience unwanted and distressing thoughts. However, it is the way we deal with these thoughts that has implications for our psychological well-being. Cognitive models of OCD (e.g. Salkovskis, 1996; Rachman, 1998) view attempts to control unwanted thoughts as a key maintaining factor in the disorder. This section will examine a prominent thought control technique of **thought suppression.**

How many times have you tried to stop thinking about an unpleasant thought or event, only to find that the more you try to stop thinking about it, the more you think about it? This is a common effect in thought suppression, where trying to suppress, or dismiss the thought, paradoxically means that you think about it more. This effect was first documented by Wegner, Schneider, Carter, and White (1997). They asked non-clinical participants *not* to think about a white bear for 5 minutes, but to ring a bell if they did think about it. Interestingly, they found that participants were unable to suppress the thought of a white bear. They then asked participants to think about the white bear for 5 minutes and they found that those who had been asked to suppress the thought of a white bear had many more thoughts about the bear than another group who had been asked to think about the bear from the outset. This finding has particular relevance in OCD where individuals often attempt to control their intrusive thoughts by ignoring, neutralizing or suppressing them.

Salkovskis (1996) proposed that unwanted distressing thoughts develop into obsessions when attempts to suppress those thoughts actually result in the thoughts becoming more frequent. There is evidence to suggest that individuals with OCD and sub-clinical OCD report attempting to suppress intrusive thoughts (Freeston & Ladouceur, 1997) and that people with OCD report more thought suppression attempts than a non-clinical control group (Wegner & Zanakos, 1994). Wegner et al. (1987) termed an increase in the frequency of the suppressed thought during a period of suppression as the '**immediate enhancement effect**' and the increase in frequency of the thought after a period of suppression the '**rebound effect**'.

Despite the effects of though suppression on thought frequency being well documented in the literature, the experimental evidence for this effect is mixed. Salkovskis and colleagues have found that thought suppression increases the frequency of thought (Lavy & van den Hout, 1990; Salkovskis & Campbell, 1994; Trinder & Salkovskis, 1994). However, a number of studies have not found an increase in the frequency of a thought after suppression (Janeck & Calamari, 1999; Purdon, Rowa & Antony, 2005; Najmi, Riemann & Wegner, 2009), although in some cases there was an increase in reports of distress and negative mood after suppression, which will be discussed below. One possibility for these mixed experimental findings is methodological issues such as the type of instructions given to participants in the control conditions and the methods used to record thought occurrence. A detailed discussion of these methodological issues is beyond the scope of this book, however interested readers may wish to refer to articles by Abramowitz, Tolin & Street (2001) and Wenzlaff & Wegner (2000).

The effects of thought suppression on appraisals and mood

Another way that thought suppression has been thought to play a role in OCD is through the distress that results from trying to suppress unwanted thoughts and the negative appraisals associated with failing to suppress the unwanted thought. Purdon et al. (2005) did not find that thought suppression (in a clinical sample) was associated with an increased frequency of the unwanted thought. However, they did report that failure to suppress unwanted thoughts was appraised as being negative and resulted in an increase in negative mood. Purdon and colleagues proposed that it is not the appraisal of the intrusive thought itself that is distressing, it is the appraisal of failing to control or suppress the intrusive thought that is distressing. Similarly, Najmi, Riemann & Wegner (2009) propose that individuals with OCD try to suppress intrusive thoughts to reduce anxiety related to the thought. Once thought suppression techniques have failed and anxiety is not reduced there is a rebound in distress, which further increases anxiety and distress.

Inflated responsibility

Individuals with OCD tend to make a negative interpretation of unwanted cognitive intrusions and one reason why people with OCD appraise intrusions as being important is because they hold inflated beliefs of responsibility for causing harm to themselves and to others. **Inflated responsibility** (IR) can be defined in terms of the individual's belief in his or her power to cause negative outcomes (Rheaume, Ladouceur, Freeston & Letarte, 1994; Wilson & Chambless, 1999) and it can take a number of forms. For example, holding an inflated sense of responsibility can affect a person's behaviour; in an extreme case a person may feel so responsible for events that they may confess to a crime they have not committed as they feel excessive responsibility, not only for their own actions, but for the actions of others as well (Rachman, 1993). IR is understood to be a causal feature of OCD generally (Cougle, Lee & Salkovskis, 2007; Salkovskis, 1985; Salkovskis, Shafran, Rachman & Freeston, 1999; Salkovskis, Gledhill, Morrison et al., 2000; Rachman, 1993, 1997) and compulsive checking specifically (Bouchard, Rhéaume & Ladouceur, 1999; Foa, Sacks, Tolin, Prezworski & Amir, 2002; Rachman, 2002). IR is often measured by the Responsibility Attitudes Scale (RAS); Salkovskis, Wroe, Gledhill, et al., (2000), which is designed to measure responsibility beliefs as applied to OCD. Responsibility attitudes are measured on a 7-point scale ranging from 'totally agree' to 'totally disagree'. For an example of the RAS see Box 4.1.

Box 4.1 Responsibility Attitude Scale (RAS; Salkovskis, Wroe, Gledhill et al., 2000)

This questionnaire lists different attitudes or beliefs which people sometimes hold. Read each statement carefully and decide how much you agree or disagree with it. For each of the attitudes, show your answer by putting a circle round the words which BEST DESCRIBE HOW YOU THINK. Be sure to choose only one answer for each attitude. Because people are different, there is no right answer or wrong answer to these statements.

To decide whether a given attitude is typical of your way of looking at things, simply keep in mind what you are like MOST OF THE TIME.

1. I often feel responsible for things which go wrong.

TOTALLY AGREE	AGREE VERY MUCH	AGREE SLIGHTLY	NEUTRAL	DISAGREE SLIGHTLY	DISAGREE VERY MUCH	TOTALLY DISAGREE

2. If I don't act when I can foresee danger, then I am to blame for any consequences if it happens.

TOTALLY AGREE	AGREE VERY MUCH	AGREE SLIGHTLY	NEUTRAL	DISAGREE SLIGHTLY	DISAGREE VERY MUCH	TOTALLY DISAGREE

3. I am too sensitive to feeling responsible for things going wrong.

TOTALLY AGREE	AGREE VERY MUCH	AGREE SLIGHTLY	NEUTRAL	DISAGREE SLIGHTLY	DISAGREE VERY MUCH	TOTALLY DISAGREE

4. If I think bad things, this is as bad as doing bad things.

TOTALLY AGREE	AGREE VERY MUCH	AGREE SLIGHTLY	NEUTRAL	DISAGREE SLIGHTLY	DISAGREE VERY MUCH	TOTALLY DISAGREE

5. I worry a great deal about the effects of things which I do or don't do.

TOTALLY AGREE	AGREE VERY MUCH	AGREE SLIGHTLY	NEUTRAL	DISAGREE SLIGHTLY	DISAGREE VERY MUCH	TOTALLY DISAGREE

6. To me, not acting to prevent danger is as bad as making disaster happen.

TOTALLY AGREE	AGREE VERY MUCH	AGREE SLIGHTLY	NEUTRAL	DISAGREE SLIGHTLY	DISAGREE VERY MUCH	TOTALLY DISAGREE

7. If I know that harm is possible, I should always try to prevent it, however unlikely it seems.

TOTALLY AGREE AGREE VERY MUCH	AGREE SLIGHTLY	NEUTRAL	DISAGREE SLIGHTLY	DISAGREE VERY MUCH	TOTALLY DISAGREE

8. I must always think through the consequences of even the smallest actions.

TOTALLY AGREE AGREE VERY MUCH	AGREE SLIGHTLY	NEUTRAL	DISAGREE SLIGHTLY	DISAGREE VERY MUCH	TOTALLY DISAGREE

9. I often take responsibility for things which other people don't think are my fault.

TOTALLY AGREE AGREE VERY MUCH	AGREE SLIGHTLY	NEUTRAL	DISAGREE SLIGHTLY	DISAGREE VERY MUCH	TOTALLY DISAGREE

10. Everything I do can cause serious problems.

TOTALLY AGREE AGREE VERY MUCH	AGREE SLIGHTLY	NEUTRAL	DISAGREE SLIGHTLY	DISAGREE VERY MUCH	TOTALLY DISAGREE

11. I am often close to causing harm.

TOTALLY AGREE AGREE VERY MUCH	AGREE SLIGHTLY	NEUTRAL	DISAGREE SLIGHTLY	DISAGREE VERY MUCH	TOTALLY DISAGREE

12. I must protect others from harm.

TOTALLY AGREE AGREE VERY MUCH	AGREE SLIGHTLY	NEUTRAL	DISAGREE SLIGHTLY	DISAGREE VERY MUCH	TOTALLY DISAGREE

13. I should never cause even the slightest harm to others.

TOTALLY AGREE AGREE VERY MUCH	AGREE SLIGHTLY	NEUTRAL	DISAGREE SLIGHTLY	DISAGREE VERY MUCH	TOTALLY DISAGREE

14. I will be condemned for my actions.

TOTALLY AGREE AGREE VERY MUCH	AGREE SLIGHTLY	NEUTRAL	DISAGREE SLIGHTLY	DISAGREE VERY MUCH	TOTALLY DISAGREE

15. If I can have even a slight influence on things going wrong, then I must act to prevent it.

TOTALLY AGREE AGREE VERY MUCH	AGREE SLIGHTLY	NEUTRAL	DISAGREE SLIGHTLY	DISAGREE VERY MUCH	TOTALLY DISAGREE

16. To me, not acting where disaster is a slight possibility is as bad as making that disaster happen.

TOTALLY AGREE	AGREE	NEUTRAL	DISAGREE	DISAGREE	TOTALLY
AGREE VERY MUCH	SLIGHTLY		SLIGHTLY	VERY MUCH	DISAGREE

17. For me, even slight carelessness is inexcusable when it might affect other people.

TOTALLY AGREE	AGREE	NEUTRAL	DISAGREE	DISAGREE	TOTALLY
AGREE VERY MUCH	SLIGHTLY		SLIGHTLY	VERY MUCH	DISAGREE

18. In all kinds of daily situations, my inactivity can cause as much harm as deliberate bad intentions.

TOTALLY AGREE	AGREE	NEUTRAL	DISAGREE	DISAGREE	TOTALLY
AGREE VERY MUCH	SLIGHTLY		SLIGHTLY	VERY MUCH	DISAGREE

19. Even if harm is a very unlikely possibility, I should always try to prevent it at any cost.

TOTALLY AGREE	AGREE	NEUTRAL	DISAGREE	DISAGREE	TOTALLY
AGREE VERY MUCH	SLIGHTLY		SLIGHTLY	VERY MUCH	DISAGREE

20. Once I think it is possible that I have caused harm, I can't forgive myself.

TOTALLY AGREE	AGREE	NEUTRAL	DISAGREE	DISAGREE	TOTALLY
AGREE VERY MUCH	SLIGHTLY		SLIGHTLY	VERY MUCH	DISAGREE

21. Many of my past actions have been intended to prevent harm to others.

TOTALLY AGREE	AGREE	NEUTRAL	DISAGREE	DISAGREE	TOTALLY
AGREE VERY MUCH	SLIGHTLY		SLIGHTLY	VERY MUCH	DISAGREE

22. I have to make sure other people are protected from all of the consequences of things I do.

TOTALLY AGREE	AGREE	NEUTRAL	DISAGREE	DISAGREE	TOTALLY
AGREE VERY MUCH	SLIGHTLY		SLIGHTLY	VERY MUCH	DISAGREE

23. Other people should not rely on my judgement.

TOTALLY AGREE	AGREE	NEUTRAL	DISAGREE	DISAGREE	TOTALLY
AGREE VERY MUCH	SLIGHTLY		SLIGHTLY	VERY MUCH	DISAGREE

24. If I cannot be certain I am blameless, I feel that I am to blame.

TOTALLY AGREE	AGREE VERY MUCH	AGREE SLIGHTLY	NEUTRAL	DISAGREE SLIGHTLY	DISAGREE VERY MUCH	TOTALLY DISAGREE

25. If I take sufficient care then I can prevent harmful accidents.

TOTALLY AGREE	AGREE VERY MUCH	AGREE SLIGHTLY	NEUTRAL	DISAGREE SLIGHTLY	DISAGREE VERY MUCH	TOTALLY DISAGREE

26. I often think that bad things will happen if I am not careful enough.

TOTALLY AGREE	AGREE VERY MUCH	AGREE SLIGHTLY	NEUTRAL	DISAGREE SLIGHTLY	DISAGREE VERY MUCH	TOTALLY DISAGREE

The role of inflated responsibility in the development and maintenance of OCD

IR is also known to affect the way intrusive thoughts are interpreted and appraised. Specifically, individuals with obsessive compulsive tendencies often interpret their intrusions as indicating that they may be responsible for unacceptable and preventable harm to themselves and others. This negative interpretation of intrusive thoughts will result in **neutralizing behaviours** such as returning to the house to check the door is locked (overt neutralizing) or mentally repeating a phrase a specific number of times (covert neutralizing). Neutralizing usually results in reduced discomfort (at least in the short term) (Hodgson & Rachman, 1972; Roper, Rachman & Hodgson, 1973), which allows the development of obsessional behaviour as a strategy for coping with stress. IR is strongly associated with two types of compulsive behaviours, **checking compulsions** and **cleaning compulsions**. With both checking and cleaning compulsions it is rarely possible to achieve a sense of certainty that the future negative event has been avoided, thus compulsive behaviours have no obvious end-point and the actions intended to reduce anxiety actually results in a self-perpetuating cycle (Rachman, 2002, 2003; van den Hout & Kindt, 2003; Boschen & Vuksanovic, 2007).

Beliefs concerning responsibility for causing or preventing harm to others or oneself are known to be involved in both the development and maintenance of OCD. Refer to Figure 4.1 for a diagrammatic example of the onset and maintenance of the OCD cycle with responsibility as a key cognitive appraisal (from Salkovskis, Wroe, Gledhill, et al., 2000).

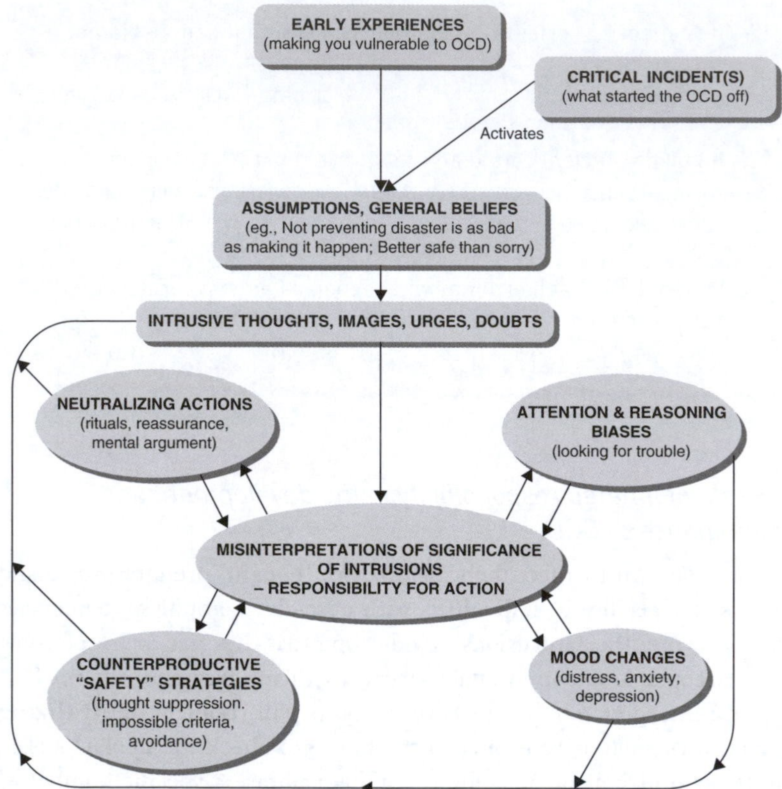

Figure 4.1 A cognitive model of obsessive-compulsive disorder showing the origins and maintenance of obsessive symptoms
Source: Salkovskis, Wroe, Gledhill et al., 2000

Salkovskis, Shafran, Rachman & Freeston (1999) propose that attitudes to responsibility typically develop early in life (although these attitudes may develop through a number of routes) and are often learned assumptions formed to cope with early experiences. When these beliefs develop, they are not necessarily maladaptive. However, if a critical incident (such as failing to prevent an accident they believed was preventable) occurs, this may activate assumptions concerning responsibility for harm. In turn this may result in the desire to suppress, avoid or neutralize, which may then trigger OCD maintenance cycles, which we will discuss below in more detail.

Beliefs concerning responsibility for others and the self also serve to maintain obsessional problems. Salkovskis, Wroe, Gledhill et al. (2000) provide a schematic representation of OCD which highlights the importance of early experiences as the origins of inflated responsibility assumptions and show how a later critical incident may activate these beliefs. Once beliefs about responsibility are activated intrusive thoughts will be misinterpreted as being important and inflated feelings of responsibility signal the need to act, which will result in the person doing things which they think may reduce the possibility of them causing harm to self or others. Responsibility appraisals will also trigger other reactions such as attentional biases, neutralizing behaviours, or safety behaviours, which will serve to maintain obsessional beliefs and fuel the re-occurrence of intrusions and then compulsions.

Responsibility and mood

Responsibility has also been found to have a causal effect on perseverative behaviours such as checking when experienced in combination with negative mood. The **mood-as-input model** is a hypothesis that suggests that people use their concurrent mood as information about whether they have successfully completed a task or not (Davey, 2006; Meeten & Davey, 2011). MacDonald & Davey (2005) examined the effects of inflated responsibility in conjunction with negative mood on a perseverative checking task. They found that inflated responsibility significantly facilitated checking perseveration only in the context of a negative mood, but that inflated responsibility in the absence of negative mood was not a sufficient condition for checking perseveration to occur. One explanation for these findings is that being in a negative mood signals dissatisfaction with performance, thus when holding inflated responsibility beliefs and also being in negative mood, one is less likely to feel that they have done enough to prevent a negative outcome occurring, thus they persevere with the checking task (MacDonald & Davey, 2005). These findings have implications for understanding the mechanisms that underlie excessive perseveration as these results indicate that responsibility beliefs alone are unlikely to cause excessive task perseveration, unless accompanied by negative mood.

Perfectionism

Perfectionism is another cognitive factor implicated in OCD and has been described as a tendency to keep high standards of performance and employing extremely self-critical evaluations (Frost, Marten, Lahart & Rosenblate, 1990). Shafran and colleagues have examined perfectionism in psychopathology through their work on 'clinical perfectionism'. This is defined as 'the overdependence of self-evaluation on the determined pursuit of personally demanding self-imposed standards in at least one highly salient domain, despite adverse consequences' (Shafran, Cooper & Fairburn, 2002, p. 778). Perfectionism has been linked with OCD symptoms as a control strategy. For example, individuals who experience dysfunctional perfectionism will seek to maintain control over threat by reducing the risk of harm and increasing safety (Mallinger, 1984), which in OCD would manifest through compulsive behaviour. Perfectionism has also been linked to distorted appraisals of negative intrusions in OCD (Rheaume, Freeston, Dugas, Letarte & Ladouceur, 1995). The evidence for perfectionism as a cognitive factor in OCD will be discussed below.

Perfectionism has long been associated with OCD (Rheaume et al., 1995; Frost & Steketee, 1997; OCCWG, 2005), but has received less attention in the literature than other prominent OCD cognitive factors such as inflated responsibility. Rheaume et al. (1995) sought to examine the contribution of perfectionism to OCD symptoms relative to that of responsibility. They used a non-clinical sample and found that both perfectionism and responsibility were significantly correlated with OCD symptoms. However, they also found that perfectionism was still a significant predictor of OCD symptoms once responsibility had been partialled out. This means that perfectionism was correlated with OCD symptoms independently of measures of responsibility. Bouchard, Rheaume & Ladouceur (1999) experimentally examined the relationship between perfectionism and responsibility in OCD. They concluded that perfectionism may predispose individuals to overestimate their perceived responsibility for negative events and this increase in responsibility is proposed to lead to increased checking as an attempt to prevent a negative event from occurring.

Perfectionism and 'Not just right experiences'

Perfectionism has also been implicated in OCD through the study of '**Not just right experiences**' (NJRE). NJRE is a term used to describe reports by individuals with OCD where they report feeling that things are not 'just right' and that they are driven to perform an action to reduce the uncomfortable sensation (Coles, Frost, Heimberg & Rheaume, 2003). This feeling has been described by Janet in 1903 as 'an inner state of imperfection' and Coles et al. (2003) sought to examine the relationship between NJRE and perfectionism in relation to OCD. Using a non-clinical sample, they found that NJRE were related to both OCD features and maladaptive perfectionism features such as concern over mistakes, and doubts about actions. In a second study NJRE were found to be strongly related to specific OCD symptom clusters such as checking and ordering and NJREs were significantly more strongly correlated with OCD symptoms than symptoms relevant to other psychopathologies. These findings indicate that like cognitive intrusions, NJRE occur in the general population, but their intensity and the importance assigned to them had the highest correlations with OCD symptoms. Thus it is not the presence of NJRE that have implications for psychopathology, but it is the interpretation of these experiences that have relevance for OCD. Furthermore it is possible that NJREs represent a specific form of perfectionism that has a unique relationship to OCD features (Coles et al., 2003).

Thought-action fusion

Another cognitive variable that is thought to influence the distress and anxiety caused by unwanted and intrusive thoughts and play a role in the development of OCD is **Thought-Action Fusion** (TAF). TAF refers to the belief that thoughts and actions are linked and that having an unacceptable thought can also influence the real world. Salkovskis (1985, p. 579) described TAF as 'Having a thought about the action is like doing the action'. In this way the responsibility associated with a negative thought is also transferred to an action (Shafran & Rachman, 2004). There are two types of TAF, Likelihood TAF and Moral TAF. Likelihood TAF refers to the belief that unacceptable thoughts can cause adverse events. There are two types of Likelihood TAF, 'Likelihood self', where thoughts cause an event to happen to oneself, and 'Likelihood other', where the event happens to others. Moral TAF refers to the belief that having an unacceptable thought is the moral equivalent of carrying that thought out (Shafran, Thordarson & Rachman, 1996). TAF is another example of how appraising unwanted and intrusive thoughts as meaningful, can cause distress. Having TAF beliefs not only increases distress and feelings of responsibility, but also increases the urge to neutralize the unwanted thought by using either cognitive or behavioural strategies (Rachman, 1998; Salkovskis, 1985).

In order to be able to examine the role of TAF in OCD, one needs to be able to measure it. Shafran, Thordarson & Rachman (1996) developed a measure of TAF which measures both Moral TAF and Likelihood TAF. An example of a question measuring Moral TAF is 'Having violent thoughts is almost as unacceptable to me as violent acts' and an example of a Likelihood TAF question is 'If I think of a friend falling ill this increases the risk that he will fall ill'. The TAF scale has been used to examine TAF in non-clinical and clinical samples. As one would expect, TAF was found to be higher in individuals with OCD than in a non-clinical sample (Rassin, Merckelbach, Muris & Schmidt, 2001). However, there was no difference between TAF scores by those with OCD and those with other anxiety disorders. This and other published findings suggests that TAF may not be a specific feature of OCD, but may also be a feature of other anxiety disorders (e.g. Rassin et al., 2001; Abramowitz, Whiteside, Lynam & Kalsy, 2003).

The role of TAF in the development and maintenance of OCD

One possibility is that TAF has a causal role in the development of OCD. Experimental work has examined whether inducing TAF appraisals has an effect on OCD symptoms. A technique commonly used to induce TAF is a sentence paradigm where individuals are asked to think of a friend or relative who they are close to and then complete a sentence such as 'I hope that (insert name) is in a car accident' and then to close their eyes and think of that situation (see Rachman, Shafran, Mitchell, Trant & Teachman, 1996 for further information on this technique). This induction technique has been found to induce anxiety, discomfort and the urge to neutralize, which is thought to represent the TAF construct (Shafran & Rachman, 2004). Other studies have experimentally induced TAF beliefs and found that increased TAF resulted in an increase in intrusions, more reported discomfort, and more resistance to intrusions. These findings suggest that TAF beliefs have a causal role in the development of OCD (Rassin, Merckelbach, Murris & Spann, 1999).

Intolerance of uncertainty

So far we have discussed a number of different maladaptive beliefs identified in the etiology and maintenance of OCD. Another important belief identified by the Obsessive Compulsive Cognitions Working Group (1997) is **Intolerance of Uncertainty** (IU). IU can be defined as 'a dispositional characteristic that results from a set of negative beliefs about uncertainty and its implications' (Dugas & Robichaud, 2007, p. 24). Individuals who appraise uncertainty as intolerable and distressing are thus likely to perceive ambiguous situations as threatening (Butler & Mathews, 1983, 1987) and report increased probabilities of negative events in uncertain situations (MacLeod, Williams & Bekerian, 1991), both of which ultimately result in increased anxiety and worry. Those with high IU are also likely to show hyper-vigilance for uncertainty and demonstrate attentional biases towards potential sources of uncertainty. Consequently, individuals who are intolerant of uncertainty may either avoid uncertain situations, or when faced with uncertainty may engage in compulsive rituals in an attempt to restore a feeling of certainty and reduce distress associated with uncertainty. Both checking and washing compulsions are associated with indecisiveness and doubt (Rachman, 2002) and compulsive checking actually increases doubt in both normal and clinical populations (e.g., van den Hout & Kindt, 2003; Radomsky, Gilchrist & Dussault, 2006; Boschen & Vuksanovic, 2007).

IU is a characteristic that is also implicated in the onset and maintenance of **Generalized Anxiety Disorder**. However, more recently IU has been considered to be a **transdiagnostic construct** underlying a number of different anxiety disorders, including OCD (e.g. Sexton & Dugas, 2009; McEvoy & Mahoney, 2011; Carleton, Mulvogue et al., 2012; Carleton, Weeks et al., 2012; Mahoney & McEvoy, 2012). IU is measured by The Intolerance of Uncertainty Scale short version (IUS-12; Carleton, Norton & Asmundson, 2007) and is used to measure IU. Example questions are:

> Uncertainty keeps me from living a full life
> When I am uncertain I can't function very well
> I must get away from all uncertain situations

Evidence for the role of intolerance of uncertainty in OCD

Rachman (2002) proposes doubt to be a key factor in compulsive checking and negative appraisals of doubt have long been implicated in OCD (e.g. Carr, 1974, Kozak, Foa & McCarthy, 1987; Rasmussen & Eisen, 1989). Doubt is a central feature of IU and more recently a literature has developed examining the role of IU in OCD. Tolin, Abramowitz, Brigidi & Foa (2003) examined IU in individuals with OCD where some individuals had checking compulsions and some did not and there was a non-anxious control group. Levels of IU were elevated in the OCD group who had checking compulsions as compared to both the OCD group without checking compulsions and the control group. Similarly, Holaway, Heimberg & Coles (2006) also found IU to be highly correlated with doubting and checking compulsions as compared to other compulsive behaviours such as washing or hoarding.

There is now a body of evidence supporting the role of IU in OCD, especially in relation to checking behaviours (Rachman, 2002; Tolin et al., 2003). More recently, the relationship between IU and other cognitive factors implicated in the maintenance of OCD has been explored. Lind & Boschen (2009) examined the relationship between IU, responsibility beliefs and compulsive checking. Using a sample with both clinical obsessive compulsive checkers and non-clinical participants they found that IU significantly mediated the relationship between responsibility and checking behaviours. In other words the relationship between responsibility and checking behaviours can be explained by taking into account IU ratings. Lind and Boschen suggested that beliefs about responsibility for harm promote checking by making uncertainty a more aversive and less tolerable experience and it is the unpleasant experience of doubt that is related to the checking behaviour. This type of study suggests that although cognitive factors in OCD (such as IR, IU, memory doubting and TAF) are well defined, the relationship between these factors and their relative contributions to OCD symptomology are still being explored.

Metacognitive theory

The **metacognitive model** of OCD (Wells & Mathews, 1994; Wells, 1997, 2000) emphasizes the importance of beliefs about the meaning and significance of intrusive thoughts. The term metacognition refers to knowledge or beliefs about thinking and strategies used to regulate and control thinking processes (Moses & Baird, 1999). The metacognitive model of OCD (Wells, 1997; 2000) proposes two subcategories of beliefs that are important in the maintenance of OCD. Fisher & Wells (2005) describe the first of these as:

Metacognitive beliefs about the meaning and consequences of intrusive thoughts, feelings and beliefs. There are three types of metacognitive beliefs about intrusions:

1. Thought-action fusion (TAF; Wells, 1997): TAF in the metacognitive model of OCD is the belief that a thought alone can cause one to act on that thought.
2. Thought-event fusion (TEF; Wells, 1997): TEF is the belief that a thought is evidence that an event has occurred.
3. Thought-object fusion (TOF; Wells, 2000): TOF is the belief that thoughts or memories can be passed onto other people or objects.

As we have seen in other cognitive models of OCD, in the metacognitive model these three beliefs are thought to be activated by normally occurring intrusions, but they lead individuals with OCD to appraise the intrusions as being important or threatening. The second subcategory is:

Beliefs about performing rituals. This has two components:

1. Positive beliefs about the need to perform rituals e.g. 'I need to perform rituals otherwise I will be unable to relax' (Myers, Fisher & Wells, 2009).
2. A programme for guiding behaviour and actions. This programme is used when performing rituals such as washing hands or repeatedly checking the stove is switched off because there is usually no objective signals about when to stop performing the task. In this case the individual will rely on a subjective stop criteria or stop signal such as a feeling of 'rightness' or time spent washing or a number of washes. However these criteria are maladaptive as they are flexible and may be hard to achieve so they act to exacerbate OCD symptoms (Myers, Fisher & Wells, 2009).

Evidence for the metacognitive model of OCD

The metacognitive account of OCD has received considerable attention over the last ten or so years and there is now a growing evidence base for the approach. Using a clinical sample, Fisher & Wells (2005) experimentally modified metacognitive beliefs about intrusions by first using exposure response prevention (see Chapter 7 for more on this), then providing participants with a rationale based on metacognitive theory to explain why their feared outcome did not occur. As predicted (when compared to participants in a control group who received traditional exposure response prevention with no metacognitive rationale) they found that reducing metacognitive beliefs resulted in a decrease in anxiety and distress, metacognitive beliefs and the urge to neutralize.

Myers, Fisher & Wells (2008) found further support for the metacognitive model. They asked 238 students to complete the Obsessive Beliefs Questionnaire (OBQ-44; Obsessive Compulsive Cognitions Working Group, 2005) and when they examined the underlying factors that contributed to scores on the OBQ-44, they found that metacognitions as measured by the importance/control of thoughts factor of the questionnaire reliably predicted unique variance in obsessive-compulsive symptoms beyond the contributions made by threat, worry, responsibility and perfectionism. Myers et al. (2008) proposed that these findings suggest a central role for metacognitive beliefs in explaining OCD symptoms. Myers, Fisher & Wells (2009) also provide evidence for three central features of the metacognitive model, namely fusion beliefs, beliefs about rituals and stop signals. In a series of hierarchical regression analyses they found that each of the beliefs was significantly positively associated with measures of obsessive compulsive symptoms and when each metacognitive belief was entered in the order specified by the model, it incrementally explained more variance in two different measures of obsessive compulsive symptoms. Myers et al. (2009) proposed these findings show that in the development of obsessive compulsive symptoms, beliefs about thought-fusions are initially activated, followed by beliefs about rituals, and this is followed by stop signals. These studies are examples of evidence for the role of metacognitive beliefs in the etiology and maintenance of OCD. Readers who would like further reading on the metacognitive account of OCD should visit the OCD research section of the Metacognitive Institute website: http://www.mct-institute.com/

Chapter summary

This chapter has examined cognitive factors relevant to OCD. The first part of the chapter examined cognitive biases in OCD, looking at memory biases, attentional biases and interpretation biases. The second part of the chapter examined cognitive models in OCD. Models examining memory deficits, thought suppression, inflated responsibility, perfectionism, thought-action fusion and intolerance of uncertainty all seek to better understand how an individual's appraisals and their response to appraisals contribute to the development and maintenance of OCD. The metacognitive model takes a slightly different approach in that it assumes that it is individuals' thoughts about their cognitive processes and the regulatory strategies they use to control their thoughts that have relevance for understanding OCD symptoms.

Chapter 5

Behavioural, Psychodynamic and Social Factors

Behavioural factors

The previous chapter examined some prominent cognitive theories of OCD. However, there are a number of different theoretical approaches that have sought to explain the onset and maintenance of OCD. This chapter will examine the Behavioural and Psychodynamic approaches to understanding OCD. Then we will look at the impact of social factors on OCD, exploring how cultural factors, religion and perceptions of disgust may influence our understanding of OCD.

Behavioural and learning accounts

As discussed in the previous chapter, it is now widely accepted that OCD can be understood from a cognitive behavioural perspective. However, some of the earlier formations of OCD that were important in helping to shape our understanding of the disorder today were based solely on behaviourist principles. **Behaviourism** became a popular method through which to study psychology as frustration grew with the psychoanalytic approach that had been popular prior to the 1970s. The behavioural movement sought to study observable behaviours with experimental methods, thus rejecting the study of thoughts or feelings because they were not observable, measurable events.

Until behaviourist theories were applied to OCD, it was considered to be largely untreatable and there was little understanding about how people developed obsessions and compulsions. However, behaviourism came to play a key role in helping researchers understand obsessive behaviours from work extrapolated from animal studies. Based on studies of learnt behaviour in animals (by scientists such as I. P. Pavlov, B. F. Skinner), Behaviourists explained the occurrence of obsessive compulsive symptoms by proposing that all behaviours are learned. This section will examine behavioural accounts of OCD and outline the role of classical conditioning and operant conditioning in a behavioural model of OCD.

At the heart of behavioural approaches to understanding OCD is **learning theory.** Mowrer (1939) proposed a two factor theory that can be applied to the development and maintenance of anxiety and avoidance behaviours in OCD. Central to this theory was the idea that anxiety was a learnt response. In the first stage of the theory, using **classical conditioning** to explain fear learning, Mowrer proposed that a neutral stimulus or event (conditioned stimulus; CS) can come to elicit fear or anxiety when paired with an aversive event (unconditioned stimulus; UCS), which produces anxiety (unconditioned response). In this way, obsessions are produced when a neutral object e.g. a hat, comes to be associated with fear (conditioned response) after you are robbed of your mobile phone by a person wearing a hat. This classical conditioning response is depicted in Table 5.1. However, the CS can be both a mental event, such as a thought, and/or a physical object. Once the relationship between fear and the neutral object has been formed though classical conditioning, then the once neutral object will elicit a fear response.

The second stage of Mowrer's two factor theory of anxiety provides a behavioural account of OCD whereby obsessions are reinforced by compulsive behaviours though **operant conditioning**. In operant conditioning a behaviour is repeatedly paired with either a rewarding or punishing outcome such that the behaviour becomes associated with its consequence. In OCD, once an individual experiences a distressing obsessive thought they will carry out a compulsion in order to reduce their feelings of anxiety. The reduction in anxiety serves to *negatively reinforce* the compulsion. However, a reduction in anxiety is only temporary until the next obsession occurs, in which case the compulsion will be

Neutral stimulus = Hat	**Conditioned stimulus = Hat**
Unconditioned stimulus = being robbed	
Unconditioned response = anxiety	Conditioned response = Anxiety

Table 5.1 Classical conditioning response

performed again to reduce the anxiety and thus the cycle of obsessions and compulsions is established.

Behavioural models provide a framework in which we can understand both the acquisition and perpetuation of fear. However, these models largely ignore the cognitive processes that also affect the development and maintenance of OCD such as the processes that affect how we appraise intrusive thoughts (see Chapter 4 for Cognitive factors in OCD). Today, scientists and clinicians often seek to understand OCD by taking both approaches into account from a cognitive behavioural perspective (e.g. Salkovskis, 1985). However the behavioural account of OCD paved the way for a now widely used therapeutic technique for OCD called *Exposure and Response Prevention (ERP)*. This technique is based on a basic principle of learning theory: if you can learn to associate a behaviour with a response (e.g. performing a ritual with the outcome of anxiety reduction), then you can also unlearn that association. ERP is discussed in detail in Chapter 7.

Safety seeking behaviours

Safety seeking behaviours are any actions in a feared situation that aim to prevent catastrophes and reduce harm (Salkovskis, 1985). A safety behaviour provides temporary relief of anxiety, but Rachman, Radomsky & Shafran (2008) suggest it is a major cause of persisting anxiety and avoidance. Examples of common types of safety behaviours employed in response to intrusive thoughts are compulsions, neutralizing and thought suppression. Compulsions are repetitive behaviours (overt compulsion such as checking the stove is turned off or washing ones hands a certain number of times) or mental acts (covert compulsion such as silent counting or monitoring for threats) that an individual feels driven to perform. There are many different types of compulsion, but the most common types of compulsion are checking and washing compulsions. A compulsion will be performed with the goal of preventing a negative outcome occurring and reducing feelings of anxiety. The term neutralizing is used fairly generally in the OCD literature to refer to acts that are performed with the aim of reducing distress. Freeston & Ladouceur (1997) define neutralizing as 'a voluntary, effortful cognitive or behavioural act that is directed at removing, preventing and attenuating the intrusive thought and the associated discomfort' (Freeston & Ladouceur, 1997, p. 344). Veale (2007) proposes that neutralizing is similar to a compulsion in that they both seek to reduce anxiety, but neutralizing has the specific aim of undoing the perceived harm, whereas compulsions are largely involuntary and repetitive. Thought suppression is another form of safety behaviour where an individual with OCD may try to reduce anxiety associated with an intrusion by attempting to suppress the thought.

Excessive reassurance seeking (ERS) is another behaviour associated with the maintenance of OCD symptoms. For example an individual with contamination fear OCD may wash their hands, then repeatedly ask others to check that their hands do actually look clean. Parrish & Radomsky (2010, p. 211) define ERS as 'the repeated solicitation of safety-related information from others about a threatening object, situation or interpersonal characteristic, despite having already received this information'. ESR is particularly common in those with checking compulsions, but also occurs across the full range of OCD presentations (Kobori, Salkovskis, Read, Lounes & Wong, 2012). For example, individuals with contamination fears may check with others that an object has not been contaminated. Individuals with OCD report that their reassurance seeking is motivated by a need for certainty relating to the possible occurrence of harm and their responsibility for it (Kobori et al., 2012). Seeking reassurance only serves to reinforce the belief that potential harm was avoided by acting on the situation, and this reinforces the avoidance behaviours.

Avoidance behaviours

Safety behaviours are performed to reduce the anxiety (albeit temporarily) associated with obsessions. Another behaviour that serves this function is avoidance. Avoidance behaviours are an attempt to avoid coming into any contact with stimuli that elicit anxiety. Avoidance is most commonly related to contamination obsessions (Starcevic, Berle, Brakoulias et al., 2011). Examples of avoidance behaviours in those with contamination obsessions are refusal to touch the toilet door handles or sit on a toilet seat, avoidance of shaking hands with others or touching the railings on the bus. Avoidance can also relate to other potential harmful outcomes, for example if one has had an intrusive thought about harming a loved one, they may then avoid that person. Avoidance can also occur mentally where one may try to avoid thinking about anxiety provoking triggers (Veale, 2007).

Like compulsions and other safety behaviours, avoidance behaviours play a key role in the maintenance of OCD symptoms. Typically, when using avoidance strategies the individual with OCD will find that their feared outcome has not occurred and this will reinforce the use of the avoidance behaviours as an anxiety reduction technique. Of course it may not be possible to always maintain avoidance behaviours. Veale (2007) suggests that in these cases where avoidance behaviours fail, other safety behaviours will be performed.

Summary

In this section we have examined behavioural accounts of OCD and looked at how safety behaviours maintain OCD beliefs. Based on studies of learning in animals, behaviourists proposed that anxiety is a learnt response, so for example we learn through our past experiences that a certain event or trigger is anxiety provoking. In order to deal with the anxiety we may perform safety behaviours such as compulsions, which are negatively reinforcing when they temporarily reduce anxiety. Safety behaviours and compulsions thus become a way of coping with the anxiety, but they only bring temporary relief from anxiety and the individual becomes stuck in cycle of needing to perform safety behaviours repeatedly, but never gains long-term anxiety reduction. Behaviourists also recognized that if we can learn a feared response to a trigger, we can also unlearn the response through exposure to the fear trigger in the absence of safety behaviours. This forms the basis of Exposure Response Prevention treatment for OCD, which will be discussed in Chapter 7.

The psychodynamic approach to understanding psychopathology

In this part of the chapter we will look at another psychological approach to understanding OCD: the **psychodynamic approach**. This approach was famously developed by Sigmund Freud, undoubtedly one of the most influential practitioners to have worked with individuals experiencing mental health problems. Psychodynamic approaches to OCD are based on the notion that our feelings and behaviours are influenced by unconscious desires and conflicts. This section will provide an introduction to the principles of Sigmund Freud's psychoanalysis, the first psychodynamic theory. The next section will then present the traditional Freudian view of OCD in terms of unconscious conflicts and defence mechanisms. Finally, we will look at one of Freud's most famous case studies, 'the Rat Man'.

From hypnosis to repression

Psychoanalytic theory originated from work conducted by Freud with Josef Breuer. They used hypnosis to try and understand patients who were experiencing psychological stress and symptoms that did not appear to have a biological cause, such as hysteria and spontaneous paralysis. Freud found that some of his patients would show improvements in their symptoms after undergoing sessions of **hypnosis**. During these sessions, patients recounted distressing emotions and childhood trauma. Consequently, he developed a theory that emphasized the importance of repressed emotions and traumatic experiences from childhood. Freud's theory of psychoanalysis approached the understanding of human functioning in terms of psychological mechanisms that operate with the aim of defending the individual against the experiences of anxiety and depression. Psychoanalytic theories hold that repressing memories and thoughts might be one way that the experiences of anxiety and depression can be avoided. This is because repressing such thoughts avoids the conflict and stress associated with the thoughts and memories.

Three forces that shape personality

Freud's theory of psychoanalysis focuses on three aspects of personality: the **id**, the **ego**, and the **superego**. According to psychoanalytic theory, the id represents our instinctual needs, especially those of a sexual nature, but also nutrition and defecation. The idea of the id evolved from Freud's observation that young children appear to gain pleasure from nursing, defecating and masturbating. He suggested that these 'sexually' related behaviours are driven by a need to fulfil the desires of the id. In contrast to the id's instinctual drives, the ego is related to rational thinking. Freud proposed that the ego develops when we learn that the environment itself cannot satisfy all our instinctual desires. The ego is said to control the impulses of the id through the use of defence mechanisms, which are deployed in an attempt to control unacceptable id impulses and reduce the anxiety that these impulses might evoke. The last part of the personality to develop, according to Freud, is the superego. This is said to evolve out of the id and ego, and attempts to integrate the 'values' that we learn from society and/or our parents. If we don't think our thoughts or behaviours meet the standards implicit in the values learnt from our parents or society, we judge ourselves negatively and feel guilty and stressed.

Freud theorized that the id, ego and superego are often in conflict, and that when this occurs, we may begin to show signs of psychopathology.

Stage of development	Normal age to reach stage	Description
Oral	0–18 months	Pleasure is obtained primarily from the mouth.
Anal	18 months–3 years	Pleasure is obtained through expelling and withholding faeces.
Phallic	3–5 years	Child focuses on their genitals and the opposite-gender parent (e.g., Oedipus conflict). Child resolves this stage by identifying with the same-gender parent.
Latency	5–12 years	Boys and girls do not engage in much interaction with one another.
Genital	12 years–adulthood	Pleasure is obtained primarily through the genitals and the individual strives to establish independence.

Table 5.2 Freud's psychosexual stages of development

He suggested that one way we attempt to control the conflict is through the use of **defence mechanisms**. The purpose of these mechanisms is to prevent further stress and anxiety. We will examine the defence mechanisms that may play a role in OCD at a later stage of this chapter.

Psychosexual stages of development

One additional aspect of psychoanalytic theory that is critical to Freud's explanations of psychological disorders is his model of the **psychosexual stages of development**. This model states that normal development includes a number of important stages, shown in Table 5.2, which individuals pass through from infancy to maturity. If an individual successfully navigates their way through each of these important stages then, according to Freud, they will experience psychological health and personal growth. If, however, an individual is unsuccessful in negotiating each of these stages, the individual will become fixated at the stage of development that they had difficulty with.

Traditional Freudian view of OCD

Unconscious conflicts

Freud viewed OCD as a result of fixation at the anal stage of development. He suggested that during the **anal stage of development**, the child is in conflict. There is conflict between the child's natural desire to be messy and aggressive, and their parents' desire that they are clean and tidy. According to psychoanalytic theory, children who do not manage to successfully resolve this conflict may become fixated at this stage, and continue to be preoccupied with cleanliness. There are themes of aggression and dirt in the obsessions of many individuals with OCD. This has led some psychoanalysts to suggest that such individuals experienced disruption during the anal stage of psychosexual development, and that this contributes to their development of OCD.

There is evidence to suggest that individuals with OCD do experience greater levels of latent aggression, defined as 'hostility/aggression towards (certain) other people that is not openly expressed but manifests in fantasies or in disguised form which is not always consciously available' (Moritz, Kempke, Luyten, Randjbar & Jelinek, 2011, p. 180). In their study, Moritz et al. (2011) gave 46 individuals with OCD and 23 individuals without OCD a questionnaire designed to measure latent aggression. The questionnaire is called the Responsibility and Interpersonal Behaviors and Attitudes Questionnaire, and it contains 60 items that can be grouped into three themes, or 'factors'. These three factors are (1) 'excessive worry and responsibility' (e.g., 'I am a very moral person and cannot forgive myself even small mistakes'), (2) 'latent aggression and calculating behaviour' (e.g., 'I am less moral than I pretend to be') and (3) 'suspiciousness/distrust' (e.g., 'I rather take the burden of responsibility on myself, because I cannot rely on my friends'). Moritz et al. (2011) found that the individuals with OCD scored significantly higher on the 'latent aggression and calculating behaviour' factor than individuals without OCD. However, given that psychodynamic theories hold that such aggression is 'not openly expressed' valid questions exist around how individuals are expected to endorse experiencing this on a questionnaire measure. Use of tasks that do not require the individual to provide a self-report of their latent aggression, such as the use of Implicit Attitude Tests (IAT) that have been successfully used in prejudice research (e.g., Greenwald, McGhee & Schwartz, 1998), might provide a more valid assessment of latent aggression. IAT tests are conducted on a computer. Participants are instructed to classify target words into one of two categories (e.g., the target 'scientist' must be paired with either 'male' or 'female'). Faster responses indicate a stronger implicit association held by the individual. A modified version of the IAT might give a more objective measure of latent aggression than self-report questionnaire measures.

Defence mechanisms

Defence mechanisms are probably the most widely accepted and adopted aspect of Freud's work by the clinicians and researchers working in the field of psychopathology. Reference to defence mechanisms is found in the Adaptive Functioning Scale of the Diagnostic and Statistical Manual of Mental Disorders (4th edn, APA, 2000) where they are described as 'automatic psychological processes that protect the individual against anxiety and from the awareness of internal or external dangers or stressors'. Anna Freud (1937), Freud's youngest daughter, placed the control of defence mechanisms firmly in the hand of the ego, claiming that they are the way in which the ego 'wards off unpleasure and anxiety, and exercises control over impulsive behaviour, affects and instinctive urges'.

Freud (1909) speculated that three defence mechanisms play a role in OCD: isolation (and displacement), **undoing** and reaction formation. *(1) Isolation and displacement*. Isolation occurs when the emotions associated with a thought, idea or image are separated from it and are pushed out of conscious awareness. In some cases, the separated emotion will be displaced onto another target. For example, we might shout at a loved one when we are angry at someone we can't shout at, such as our boss. *(2) Undoing*. Undoing occurs when an individual feels compelled to carry out a behaviour or thought (a compulsion) with the goal of preventing or undoing the anticipated consequences of an obsessional thought. An example of this might be someone feeling that they need to engage in compulsive praying to undo thoughts of a family member coming to harm. *(3) Reaction Formation*. Reaction formation occurs when an individual consciously adopts particular patterns of thoughts and/or behaviours that are in direct contrast with their impulses. An example of this might be being nice to a family member that you have impulses to harm. Or, considering the other end of the spectrum, perhaps the tendency for little boys to be mean to little girls at school – ah first love, nothing like a Chinese burn to show you care... [NB. we do not endorse Chinese burns].

Evidence seems to suggest that individuals with OCD are more likely to use 'immature' defence mechanisms compared to individuals without OCD. For example, Blaya et al. (2006) gave people the Defense Style Questionnaire-40, a questionnaire that assesses the amount that individuals use 'mature' (sublimation, humour, anticipation, rationalization and suppression), 'neurotic' (undoing, pseudo-altruism, idealization and reaction formation) or 'immature' (projection, passive-aggression, acting out, isolation, devaluation, 'autistic fantasy', denial, displacement, dissociation, splitting and somatization) defence mechanisms. The individuals in Blaya et al.'s study were either diagnosed as having major depressive disorder, social anxiety disorder, panic disorder or obsessive-compulsive disorder, or they were control participants (i.e., they didn't have a diagnosis of depression or anxiety). The diagnoses were established through a structured clinical interview. Individuals with anxiety or depression were significantly more likely to endorse 'immature' defence mechanisms than the control group. In particular, the OCD group were more likely to use 'acting out'. The use of 'immature' defence mechanisms by individuals with OCD has also been shown across cultures, for example, in an Iranian sample (Shabanpour, Zahiroddin, Janbozorgi & Ghaeli, 2012). However, self-report measures, such as the Defense Style Questionnaire-40, rely on the participants' awareness of how they think and act in situations.

Case study: psychoanalysis of the Rat Man

One of Freud's most famous case studies is that of a 29-year old man referred to by Freud as '**The Rat Man**' (for reasons that will become clear if you refer to Case History 5.1!). Although nowadays it would be deeply frowned upon as a breach of patient confidentiality, we actually know a surprising amount about the identity of 'Rat Man'. His real name was Dr Ernst Lanzer, and he was a lawyer from Austria (Mahony, 1986).

Our understanding of the Rat Man is aided by Freud's case notes (Freud, 1909), despite Freud's assertion that it would 'probably be intelligible to no one outside our immediate circle' (McGuire, 1974, p. 238). The details that are shown in Case History 5.1 are based on the 1990 English translation Case Histories II, edited by Angela Richards. Long case histories were used by Freud to communicate ideas about his psychological models of mental disease. Before this point, theories of mental illness had been predominantly physical in origin, and the methods used in the physical sciences did not necessarily lend themselves to describing the models that Freud was developing. A medical doctor by trade, it is suggested that Freud borrowed heavily from the medical case history format when he began to write about his patients using long case histories. While Freud's case studies have the advantage of being rich in detail, Freud did not make notes during his sessions (Freud, 1990), and

Case History 5.1

The Rat Man first visited Freud in 1907 and reported that he had a lifetime experience of obsessional thoughts but that these obsessions had got progressively worse during the past four years. During an early therapy session, he recounted a tale to Freud of an incident that occurred when he was serving in the military. The Rat Man lost his pince-nez and became embroiled in an unnecessarily complicated ritual regarding paying back the individual who had paid for his new pince-nez. He claimed that this ritual was precipitated by an officer telling him about a method of torture that involved having a bucket attached to one's anus. The bucket contained rats, and the Rat Man learned that during this torture method, the rats would burrow into the torture victim's anus. You begin to see where the name came from ... Horrified, the Rat Man began to experience obsessions that this method of torture might befall two people he cared deeply for, his father (who strangely enough was actually dead at the time) and a lady that he was romantically attached to.

consequently the reliability of what he recorded later is questionable. What is more, Freud himself plays a large role in what is reported – he is a character in the case studies (Sealey, 2011). While this has the advantage of acknowledging the importance of interpersonal factors, it does somewhat complicate the neutrality of what is reported.

In his case notes, Freud describes the Rat Man's difficulties as arising from an unconscious conflict regarding harbouring hateful feelings towards his loved ones:

> In the case of someone who was closer to him, of his wife for instance, he would wish his feelings to be unmixed, and consequently, as was only human, he would overlook her faults, since they might make him dislike her – he would ignore them as though he were blind to them. So it was precisely the intensity of his love that would not allow his hatred – though to give it such a name was to caricature the feeling – to remain conscious. (Freud, 1909, p. 61)

Freud suggested that the Rat Man experienced symptoms that prevented him from having to make difficult decisions, and the anxiety that such decisions might have provoked. He also emphasized the importance of the Rat Man's early sexual experiences, as well as his relationship with his father, who the Rat Man had secretly wished would die so that he could inherit his money and marry a wealthy lady. Within this case history, Freud began to develop his ideas on defence mechanisms that might play a role in the symptoms we now know as OCD. He suggested that individuals may use rationalization, undoing and displacement, which we read about earlier. He also highlighted the importance of doubt in OCD, and suggested that compulsions were a way of dealing with the discomfort that doubt induced. Freud reported that his psychoanalysis with the Rat Man was successful, but sadly, the Rat Man was killed in combat during the First World War, so no long term follow-up of the case was possible.

Psychodynamic summary

We have seen in this section that psychodynamic accounts of OCD are grounded in ideas of repression of anger, conflict at the anal stage of development, and the use of defence mechanisms to minimize anxiety, particularly undoing, isolation, displacement and reaction formation. In comparison to other accounts of OCD (see Chapters 4 and 6 for details on cognitive and biological accounts), the psychodynamic account of OCD is not widely used in current day **formulation**, research or treatment. The major challenge in determining the role that psychodynamic processes have in OCD is the difficulty in establishing unconscious thought processes. Consequently, psychodynamic accounts have largely fallen out of favour in our increasingly evidence-based healthcare system.

Socio-cultural factors

Cross cultural factors

Up to this point in the book we have considered the cognitive and behavioural factors that influence the development and maintenance of OCD. However, we have considered these factors as though they are universal characteristics; what we have not yet examined is how cultural factors may influence the clinical manifestation of OCD (see Chapter 2 for cultural differences in OCD prevalence). Broadly speaking, the term culture refers to the 'behaviour patterns and value system shared by a group of people' (Sica, Novara, Sanavio, Dorz & Coradeschi, 2002) and it is likely that people who share a culture will also share common concerns and anxieties.

Given that one of the primary triggers for anxiety in OCD is an intrusive thought, it is likely that the content of the intrusive thought would have culture-specific references and that the presentation of OCD may differ from culture to culture. de Silva (2006) proposed four possible pathways of cultural influence on OCD. These were:

1 The content of obsessions and compulsions may reflect common concerns within a culture.
2 Obsessions and compulsions may be linked to religious beliefs or practices.
3 Those with strict religious beliefs may be more prone to developing clinical obsessions as a result of attaching high significance to unwanted and intrusive thoughts.
4 Superstition in a culture may be reflected in the OCD symptoms in members of that culture.

We will return to the theme of religion in more detail later in this chapter. More broadly, what these factors suggest is that culture is likely to play a role in the type of unwanted intrusions reported in OCD and the type of compulsions performed as a response to these intrusions. However, this is only part of the picture. What about the core cognitive factors (such as inflated responsibility, thought-action fusion, intolerance of uncertainty) that are implicated in the development of OCD, are they influenced by culture? Evidence looking at the influence of culture in the presentation of OCD will be examined below.

A study using non-clinical participants examined OCD relevant factors of inflated responsibility, perfectionism, guilt, anxiety and depression in an Australian and Italian sample (Kyrios, Sanavio, Bhar & Liguori, 2001). They found no significant gender differences between the two cohorts on outcome measures and few differences between the two cohorts in typically reported OCD phenomena and measures of affect (emotion) and OCD relevant beliefs. However, they did find that the Australian sample reported a stronger relationship between OCD phenomena and self-orientated perfectionism and a measure of behavioural urges/worries associated with OCD. The authors suggested that the Australian sample may be more concerned about issues of self control than the Italian sample and that these differences could be explained by cultural factors. Another study examined OCD symptoms and magical thinking in a sample of Australian students and Icelandic students (Helgadottir, Menzies & Einstein, 2012). They found that the Icelandic sample exhibited higher levels of magical thinking, superstitious thinking and OCD symptoms, but there were no differences between the two cohorts in levels of superstitious behaviour and TAF beliefs. The authors suggested these differences could be attributed to cultural differences, especially when taking into account the fact that the Icelandic culture is known to have elevated beliefs in telepathy and the paranormal. A study examining cross-cultural factors in OCD vulnerability factors and symptoms between a sample of Canadian and Turkish students (Yorulmaz, Gençöz & Woody, 2010) also found some interesting cultural differences. Yorulmaz et al. (2010) reported that there were differences in the type of thought control used by the two samples; the Turkish students were more likely to use worry and thought suppression and the Canadian students were more likely to use punishment thought control strategies. However, the authors did report that there were a number of commonalities between the two samples. Examples of commonalities in correlations between vulnerability factors and OCD symptoms were in endorsements of neuroticism, appraisals of responsibility, threat estimation, perfectionism, need for certainty and TAF. The authors concluded that the support for common factors indicated the cross-cultural validity of some factors, but that cultural features may be operative in some cognitive processes relevant to OCD symptoms.

In summary, the evidence reviewed above suggests that there are a number of common cognitive and behavioural factors that will influence the onset and maintenance of OCD, culture-specific factors do influence OCD symptoms. Due to space constraints only a small sample of the literature examining cross-cultural factors in OCD could be examined and interested readers may like to refer to the de Silva (2006) for other interesting references. One reason why it is important to examine culture-specific influences in OCD is the bearing that this may have on treatment. In order to provide treatment for OCD, one must first have a good understanding of the beliefs that are driving the OCD symptoms and this will necessarily involve taking into account the individual's cultural experiences.

Religion and disgust

Other typical socio-cultural factors that are known to influence the nature of OCD are religion and disgust propensity and sensitivity. Religion is a particularly relevant factor in OCD when considering that a person's beliefs about the significance of unwanted thoughts may influence appraisals of responsibility of harm and perfectionism and superstition. Disgust beliefs are also known to be important in OCD, especially when considering contamination fears. Evidence concerning the role of religion and disgust in OCD symptoms will be examined below.

Religion

The cognitive-behavioural model of OCD recognizes that strict religious beliefs and moral codes can influence the intensity and content of obsessions (see also Chapter 2 for a discussion of OCD prevalence and religion). The original meaning of obsession is 'actuation by the devil or an evil spirit from without' (Greenberg & Witztum, 1991, p. 173), highlighting the traditional association between religious and obsessive thinking. The term **scrupulosity** is often used to refer to obsessions and compulsions with religious themes, strict moral codes and concern about sin (Greenberg & Witzum, 2001; Abramowitz, Huppert, Cohen, Tolin & Cahill, 2002). One reason why scrupulosity may be implicated in OCD is that strict adherence to moral codes may contribute to the evaluation of and importance given to intrusive thoughts. Intrusions with a moral content are likely to be over-evaluated and distressing for someone holding strict religious beliefs (Rachman, 1997, 2006). Scrupulosity is thus a potential risk factor for OCD and religion was identified as being in the top five most common themes of obsessions (Foa et al., 1995). Evidence concerning the relationship between scrupulosity and OCD will be examined below.

The positive relationship between religious beliefs and OCD is now well documented (e.g. Steketee, Quay, & White, 1991; Shafran, Thordarson, & Rachman, 1996; Shafran, Watkins, & Charman, 1996; Abramowitz, Huppert, Cohen, Tolin, & Cahill, 2002; see Chapter 2, section 2.1 for some specific Case Histories). When considering how religion is related to the beliefs and the cognitive appraisals implicated in the development of OCD, research suggests that a number of cognitive factors may be important in this relationship. For example, Nelson, Abramowitz, Whiteside & Deacon (2006) found that scrupulosity was correlated with a number of cognitive factors implicated in OCD such as beliefs about the importance of thought and the need to control thought and an inflated sense of responsibility and moral thought-action fusion. Nelson et al. suggest that the reason for the relationship between strict religious belief and OCD related cognitive factors is that holding a strict moral code may be more likely to make one more sensitive to intrusions of a sexual or sacrilegious nature. As such, these types of intrusions would be considered particularly important to control and may be particularly distressing.

More recently research has also begun to examine OCD cognitions and symptoms in different religious contexts. Yorulmaz, Gençöz & Woody (2009) examined the relationship between religiosity and OCD cognitions in a sample of student Muslims and Christians from Turkey and Canada respectively. They reported some differences between religious categories, in that Muslim participants scored higher on measures of OCD and reported more concerns on their thoughts and about controlling their thoughts and reported using worry to manage their unwanted thoughts more than the Christian participants. Degree of religiosity was found to make a difference in endorsement of moral thought-action fusions beliefs, especially in the Christian participants. However, they also found a number of similarities in both religion categories. Regardless of religion category, participants who reported holding strict religious beliefs also reported more obsession thoughts and checking. These findings support the view that there is a relationship between religiosity and OCD when examined in two religious categories, but that the characteristics of OCD may differ across religions. Inozu, Clark & Karanci (2012) also looked at the mechanisms underlying the relationship between religiosity and OCD in both Muslim and Christian non-clinical participants in Turkey and Canada respectively. They reported that highly religious Muslim participants scored higher on compulsive symptoms measures than highly religious Christian participants. However, in both religious categories the relationship between religiosity and obsessionality was mediated by importance/control of thoughts, responsibility/threat beliefs and guilt. The authors suggest that in both these religious categories a heightened sense of personal guilt and beliefs that they are responsible for controlling unwanted intrusive thoughts explains the high incidence of obsessionality. Furthermore the higher incidence of compulsions in the Muslim participants is likely due to differences in the characteristics of the two religions in that the Muslim faith is a ritualistic religion that primarily focuses on following strict rules and the Christian faith is characterized by a belief in Jesus, with relatively few behavioural rituals (Inouz et al., 2012).

Disgust

OCD has traditionally been considered an anxiety disorder, but there is also evidence to suggest that **disgust** plays an important role in the development and maintenance of **contamination-related OCD**. The term disgust relates originally to a food-rejection emotion whose purpose is to prevent the transmission of illness and disease through the oral incorporation of contaminated items. However, the term disgust is now also applied to thoughts, such as moral disgust. Rachman (2004) defines contamination as the intense, subjective experience of directly or indirectly contacting a stimulus (e.g., a person, object, thought) appraised as contaminated, impure or spoiled. In contamination-related OCD, recurrent thoughts of contagion lead to excessive washing and cleaning. These neutralizing behaviours reduce distress associated with contamination obsessions, but only temporarily. Consequently the safety behaviour negatively reinforces the belief that certain stimuli must be avoided due to risk of contamination (Rachman, 1994). The next section will examine the role of disgust in contamination-related OCD.

Individuals with contamination-relevant OCD have reported that they are not fearful of objects perceived as contaminated, but they are disgusted by them (Tallis, 1996). Furthermore, after performing safety behaviours such as washing, an individual with contamination-relevant OCD will report a reduction in feelings of disgust rather than anxiety (Sieg & Scholz, 2001). These findings suggest that in contamination-related OCD, **disgust sensitivity** may play an important role in the development and maintenance of contamination-related OCD. Tolin, Woods & Abramowitz (2006) examined the relationship between disgust sensitivity and OCD symptoms in a large non-clinical sample. The results indicated that washing-related OCD symptoms had the strongest relationship with disgust sensitivity to hygiene related stimuli. However, disgust sensitivity was also found to relate to other domains of OCD such as checking and ordering, although the authors suggest that these relationships may actually be a product of participants' washing concerns. Importantly this data indicated a role for disgust sensitivity in washing-related OCD and suggests that disgust reduction may be a useful therapeutic approach when dealing with contamination fears in OCD.

To further examine the role of disgust in contamination-relevant OCD, research has also looked at **disgust propensity** (the intensity with which disgust is experienced; Olatunji, 2010) as well as disgust sensitivity. One example is a study by Olatunji, Tart, Ciesielski, McGrath & Smits (2011) where they examined whether disgust was specifically related to OCD or whether it was also related to other anxiety disorders such as Generalized Anxiety Disorder (GAD). When an OCD group, a GAD group and a non-clinical control group completed measures of disgust propensity and disgust sensitivity, they found that individuals with OCD more strongly endorsed disgust propensity as compared to the other two experimental groups. However, individuals with OCD were no different in their endorsement of disgust sensitivity than individuals with GAD, although both groups endorsed this measure more highly than the non anxious control group. This finding sheds further light on the relationship between disgust and OCD by indicating that disgust propensity may have a more robust relationship with OCD than disgust sensitivity. This type of finding may be especially useful when thinking about how to maximize therapeutic gain in that therapeutic approaches may target disgust propensity to maximize symptom reduction.

Chapter summary

This chapter has examined the behavioural, psychodynamic and social factors implicated in OCD. Early behavioural experiments on animals were pivotal in helping to form the learning theory account of fear acquisition. Learning theory explains how fear responses are learned though classical conditioning and how the negative reinforcement of behavioural rituals serves to maintain the use of safety behaviours. Behaviourist studies of learning also discovered that compulsive behaviours in the response to fear can be reduced due to **habituation** and this forms the basis of ERP therapy for OCD. The Psychodynamic approach proposes that unconscious conflicts are responsible for OCD symptoms. However, it is very difficult to formulate and test hypothesis based on Psychodynamic theory and it is not considered to be part of an as evidenced-based approach to understanding OCD. In the second part of this chapter we examined socio-cultural factors that can influence the manifestation of OCD. OCD is recognized in many different cultures and there are many similarities in its presentation across cultures. However, some studies have highlighted interesting cultural differences in OCD presentation and these are often reflected in cultural norms relating to superstition and religion. Religious themes are common in intrusive thoughts and it stands to reason that different religious view-points will differentially influence the content of intrusions. Research shows that characteristics of OCD can differ across different religions and these can often be understood by looking at behavioural norms within different religions. Lastly we examined the role of disgust in OCD. The emotion of disgust is thought to be particularly relevant to contamination-related OCD where repeated intrusive thoughts concerning contamination lead to the development of safety behaviours, which serve to prevent the disconfirmation of the need for these behaviours. Interventions in contamination-related OCD may usefully target disgust reactions as a means to reducing reliance on safety behaviours.

Chapter 6

Biological Models of OCD

Common biological approaches to explain psychopathology include **biochemistry, genetics** and *neuroanatomy*. Each of these approaches has been applied in the quest to understand OCD. We will begin by reviewing neurotransmitter models, and then consider what is known about the genetics of OCD, before turning to look at neuroanatomical accounts. Finally, we will consider immunological and evolutionary accounts of OCD. We will revisit some of these accounts in Chapter 8 when we look at biological treatments of OCD.

Biochemical factors

The **neurons** in our brain communicate with one another through chemicals called **neurotransmitters**. Some theories of OCD suggest that there are problems with the neurotransmitter systems in individuals with OCD, and that these problems give rise to obsessions and compulsions. Figure 6.1 shows the important structures involved in communication between brain cells. When a neuron has a chemical message to communicate, neurotransmitters stored in **vesicles** are released by a neuron (the **presynaptic neuron**) and travel across the gap between this neuron and the neighbouring neuron. This gap is called the **synaptic cleft**. The neurotransmitter molecules bind to **receptors** on the neuron (the **postsynaptic neuron**) on the other side of the synaptic cleft. Once enough neurotransmitter molecules have docked on the receptors on the postsynaptic neuron, an electrochemical message will travel along the neuron. Problems can occur if there are abnormalities in (1) the amount

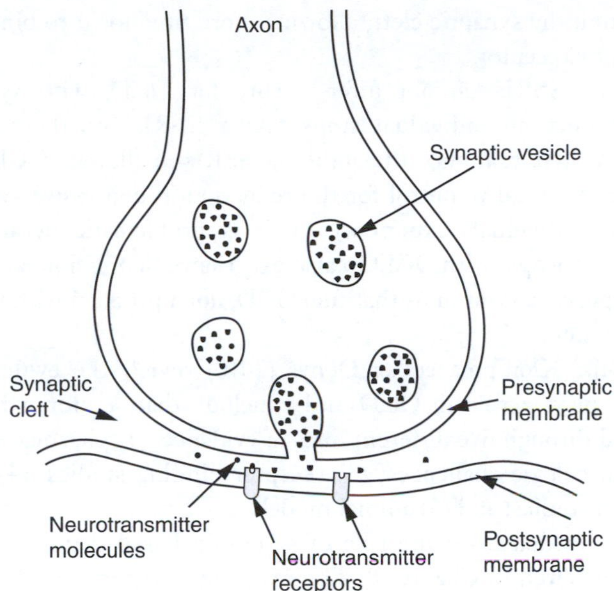

Figure 6.1 A schematic diagram of neurotransmitter communication across a synaptic cleft

of neurotransmitter that is released by the presynaptic neuron; (2) the rate that the neurotransmitter is cleared from the synaptic cleft; and (3) the number of postsynaptic receptors. As we shall go on to see, evidence suggests that these kinds of abnormalities may exist in the neurotransmitter systems of individuals with OCD.

The serotonin theory of OCD

One neurotransmitter system that has received lots of interest in OCD research is the ***serotonin*** system. Serotonin has many functions, and in fact, 90 per cent of the serotonin in our body resides in our gut! However, the 10 per cent that is in our brain is involved in important processes including regulating mood, appetite and sleep. Given that some people with OCD experience a reduction in their symptoms when they take a form of antidepressants called *selective serotonin-reuptake inhibitors* (SSRIs; for information on SSRIs, see Chapter 8) it has been argued that individuals with OCD may have a dysfunctional serotonergic system. This is because SSRIs work by reducing the rate at which serotonin is cleared from the synaptic cleft, allowing more time for it to bind with a postsynaptic receptor.

However, SSRIs do not offer a cure for OCD, with symptoms returning once an individual stops taking SSRIs. Furthermore, the studies that have examined the ability of SSRIs to alleviate OCD symptoms do not typically control for the reduction in depressive symptoms that these individuals experience. This is problematic because it is common for people with OCD to also experience depression, and it may be the depressive symptoms that fuel OCD, not a problem with the serotonergic system.

Van Dijk, Klompmakers & Denys (2010) review the evidence that serotonin plays a role in OCD and conclude that serotonin has been implicated through five different lines of evidence: (1) pharmacotherapy; (2) pharmacologic challenges; (3) receptor binding studies; (4) genetic association studies; and (5) animal models.

(1) The evidence for the role of serotonin-based drugs in treating OCD is reviewed in Chapter 8. The main support for the role of serotonin based on pharmacotherapy comes from the finding that only antidepressants that block the serotonin transporter have been shown to be effective as stand-alone drug treatments for OCD. However, while this highlights that blocking the re-uptake of serotonin can offer a means for treating OCD it does not necessarily mean that serotonin plays a role in the cause of OCD. After all, not all people with OCD respond to SSRIs.

(2) *Pharmacological challenges* involve exposing individuals with OCD to a biological substance that acts as a serotonin receptor **agonist**. Zohar, Mueller, Insel, Zohar-Kadouch & Murphy (1987) found that when individuals with OCD were given an agonist called meta-chlorophenylpiperazine (mCPP) that affects serotonin receptors (particularly 5-HT_{2C}), the participants' OCD symptoms worsened. However, Zohar et al. (1987) also included healthy controls in their study who were exposed to mCPP. These healthy control participants did not show the same exacerbation of OC symptoms that were observed in the participants with OCD. Consequently, increased activity at the serotonin receptor sites is not a sufficient cause of OCD on its own. Westenberg, Fineberg & Denys (2007) reviewed the evidence from pharmacological challenge studies. They concluded that the findings are inconsistent, with some studies supporting the finding obtained by

Zohar et al. (1987) and other studies failing to replicate this effect (e.g., Lesch et al., 1991). Westenberg et al. (2007) suggest that such inconsistencies are probably due to small sample sizes, participants having different OCD subtypes, and biological challenge agents that are nonselective in their action (i.e., they act on a number of receptors and the exact receptors that they act on varies across studies). Van Dijk et al. (2010) conclude that pharmacological challenge studies implicate a role for some serotonin receptors (particularly 5-HT_{2A} and/or 5-HT_{2c}, and possibly $5\text{-HT}_{1B/1D}$) in OCD.

(3) It is possible to examine the density of serotonin receptors by examining the amount that **radiotracers** bind to receptors. Using **single-photon emission computer tomography** (SPECT), Pogarell et al. (2003) found a 25 per cent higher availability of the *serotonin transporter receptor* (5-HTT) in the midbrain of individuals with OCD compared to healthy controls without OCD. When the participants were stratified by the age that their OCD symptoms had begun, it was found that the higher midbrain 5-HTT availability was only present in individuals who had an early age of onset. Conversely, a number of studies have found reductions in the 5-HTT availability in the midbrain, thalamus and upper brain stem (e.g., Stengler-Wenzke et al., 2004; Hesse et al., 2005). Although Hasselbalch et al. (2007) did report finding reduced midbrain 5-HTT availability in individuals with OCD, they did not find that the receptor availability correlated with OCD symptoms as measured by the Yale-Brown Obsessive-Compulsive Scale (YBOCS), raising questions about the role that serotonin transporter density plays in OCD. **Positron-emission tomography** (PET) studies have also supported a decrease in 5-HTT availability in the midbrain and thalamus (e.g., Reimold et al., 2007) but this has not always been found by other research teams using PET (e.g., Simpson et al., 2003).

(4) We will explore genetic studies in more detail below. The evidence for the notion that genes that play a role in the serotonin system also affect who develops OCD is inconsistent, and most studies have been negative (i.e., the evidence does not support individuals with OCD having particular alleles) (Van Dijk et al., 2010).

(5) Animal models have also been used to examine whether the serotonin system plays a role in OCD. In their review, van Dijk et al. (2010) report that three kinds of animal models have been developed

in OCD research: pharmacological, behavioural and genetic. The pharmacological animal models have mainly involved giving serotonin agonists to rodents and examining the effect that this has on marble-burying behaviour, which is used as a proxy for compulsive behaviour. 5-HT_{1A} agonists have been reported to lead to the inhibition of marble-burying, while the results for 5-HT_{2A} are less consistent. Genetic models use specially bred mice without particular genes, known as **knockout mice**. 5-HT_{2C} receptor knockout mice (i.e., mice without the gene that codes for the 5-HT_{2C} receptor, and consequently without the 5-HT_{2C} receptor) show more compulsive behaviours, such as increased non-nutritious clay chewing. Animal models have also implicated the 5-HT_7 receptor. However, it is difficult to tell how much compulsive behaviours observed in rodents truly mimic compulsions carried out by human beings. What is more, it is not possible to examine obsessions in animal models.

The role of dopamine and glutamate

Dopamine is another neurotransmitter that has been implicated in OCD. Dopamine levels increase in our brains when we experience a reward. What is more, dopamine plays a role in motor control. Evidence for the role of dopamine in OCD comes from the same lines of research that has suggested a role for serotonin in OCD. Firstly, **antipsychotics**, which influence the dopamine system, can be used successfully alongside **antidepressants** to reduce OCD symptoms (we will read more about the use of antipsychotic medications in Chapter 8). Pharmacological challenge studies using indirect agonists such as cocaine and amphetamine show mixed results. On the one hand, chronic cocaine use is associated with stereotypic behaviours including examining, searching and sorting (e.g., Satel & McDougle, 1991) but on the other hand, some studies have demonstrated that OCD symptoms improve after the administration of amphetamine (e.g., Insel et al., 1983). The mixed findings may arise because individuals who have low levels of dopamine are more likely to become chronic users of cocaine in the first place in an attempt to raise their dopamine levels. Receptor binding studies suggest that there is a higher density of the ***dopamine transporter (DAT)*** in the basal ganglia (e.g., Van der Wee et al., 2001; Kim et al., 2003) but this has not been replicated by all research groups (Pogarell et al., 2003). Zohar et al. (2012) suggest that there are higher dopamine concentrations in the synaptic clefts of individuals with OCD.

Glutamate abnormalities are also associated with OCD. Glutamate is the major mediator of excitatory signals in the mammalian central nervous system. Consequently, glutamate plays a role in many important brain processes, including cognition, learning and memory. Chakrabarty, Bhattacharyya, Christopher & Khanna (2005) examined the **cerebrospinal fluid** (CSF) levels of glutamate in 21 drug-naive individuals with OCD and 18 individuals without OCD. Chakrabarty et al. (2005) found that the CSF glutamate levels were significantly higher in the individuals with OCD than those without OCD. However, glutamate levels did not correlate with OCD symptoms as measured by the YBOCS making it unclear exactly what role glutamate might play in OCD. There are also reports of reduced glutamate levels in drug-naive children and adolescents with OCD in their anterior cingulate (Rosenberg et al., 2004), a region which we will see below has been implicated in abnormal OCD neurocircuitry. In addition, Arnold and colleagues have demonstrated an association between OCD and the glutamate transporter gene (SLC1A1) and the glutamate (NMDA) subunit receptor (GRIN2B) (Arnold et al., 2004, 2006).

Neurotransmitter summary

A greater understanding of the abnormalities in serotonin and dopamine systems in individuals with OCD has helped in finding ways of managing OCD symptoms in the form of antidepressants and antipsychotics, respectively (as we will see in Chapter 8). However, these treatments do not help everyone. What is more, many of these studies were conducted when people already had OCD, so it is not possible to determine whether the changes in the neurotransmitter systems are the cause of OCD, or a consequence of having OCD. **Longitudinal studies** will help us to discover more about the cause and/or effect of neurotransmitter abnormalities. The study of glutamate is in its infancy, and it is hoped that new medicinal treatments might be derived from research into the role of glutamate in OCD. The neurotransmitters that we have examined in this section do not operate in isolation. The future of research into the biochemical factors of OCD will need to examine the way that these different neurotransmitter systems – serotonin, dopamine and glutamate – interact with one another.

Genetic factors

OCD seems to run in families. One possible explanation for the familial nature of OCD and other anxiety disorders is that there are genes, passed from parents to offspring, which increase the risk of developing OCD. Our understanding of the role that genes play in OCD has been aided by a number of different kinds of studies. The main methods used are **family studies, twin studies, candidate gene analysis** and **genome-wide linkage studies** (GWLS). The first two methods, family and twin studies, have provided support for the idea that OCD is heritable, while the second two methods, candidate gene analysis and genome-wide linkage studies, have provided clues to specific genes and chromosome regions that may be involved in OCD.

Family studies

Family studies are conducted by identifying individuals with OCD, and then examining how many members of their family also have OCD. This is based on the premise that if there is a genetic basis to the disorder, individuals with OCD share their genes with their family members, and consequently it is probable family members will also have OCD. Given that OCD is a complex disorder that can be characterized by a continuum of symptoms, it is plausible that family members may not have clinically significant OCD, but may show high scores on dimensional measures of OCD. Similarly, it might be the case that family members have conditions related to OCD, rather than OCD itself, perhaps reflecting shared underlying genetics of OCD and related conditions, e.g., tic-related disorders.

Earlier family studies looked for signs of obsessional neurosis or obsessional symptomatology in the **proband** and their relatives. Generally, such studies suggested that first-degree relatives had an increased risk of experiencing obsessional symptoms (for a review, see Pauls, 2008). More recently, family studies have been based on operationalized criteria for establishing OCD, such as the DSM criteria that we read about in Chapter 1. In a review, Shih, Belmonte & Zandi (2004) report that studies based on family history, rather than clinical interview, lead to estimates of 0–8 per cent OCD symptomatology in first-degree relatives. This is compared to a prevalence rate in the general population of around 2.1 per cent (see Chapter 2 for more about the prevalence of OCD). This suggests that OCD is more common in relatives of people with OCD, but clearly environmental factors also play a role as the prevalence rate shows that most individuals who have a relative with OCD do not develop OCD. However, the difficulty with family studies based on family history is that it is difficult to be sure that there have not been errors in recall of the individual with OCD. More satisfactory are studies that involve direct interviews with the family members. Shih et al. (2004), in their review of studies that have interviewed family members, report that such studies produce estimates of 2.5–23.3 per cent of first-degree relatives showing OCD symptoms. However, the greater risk observed in first-degree relatives may be because they are more likely to share a more similar environment than second-degree relatives. This is a problem with all family studies – families do not only share their genetics, they also are more likely to live in similar environments, and be exposed to the same environmental risk factors.

Twin studies

One way of determining whether a disorder has a genetic component is to compare the ***prevalence*** of OCD in *monozygotic (MZ) twins* and *dizygotic (DZ) twins*. MZ twins are what we refer to when we say 'identical twins' and they share 100 per cent of their genes, whereas DZ twins share approximately half of their genes. Therefore, if a disorder was caused entirely by genes, we would expect 100 per cent ***concordance*** between MZ twins because they have the same genes: if one MZ twin had this disorder, we would expect their other twin to have the disorder as well. We would expect lower concordance rates in the DZ twins because they only share half of their genes: if one DZ twin had this disorder, the other twin may have it if they share that particular gene, but may not if they have another version of the gene.

Studies of the prevalence of OCD in twins have produced varying results. Some studies have shown quite high concordance while others have shown no concordance at all. For example, Carey & Gottesman (1981) conducted a study with 30 twin pairs, 15 MZ and 15 DZ. They found that concordance rates were higher in the MZ twins (13/15) compared to the DZ twins (7/15). In contrast, Andrews, Stewart, Allen & Henderson (1990) found absolutely no concordance in 48 twin pairs (0/18 MZ and 0/30 DZ). Both of these studies used DSM-III criteria to establish a diagnosis of OCD, so the way that OCD is measured is unlikely to have influenced these wildly different results. The results shown by twin studies that have examined both MZ and DZ twins using DSM criteria to establish the presence of OCD are shown in Table 6.1. In a review of twin studies in OCD, Nestadt et al. (2010) report that 54 of 80 (68%) MZ twins were concordant for OCD, whereas only 9 of 29 (31%) DZ twin pairs were concordant. Consequently, there is support for the idea that genes play a role in OCD, because the concordance rate for MZ twins is more than double the rate for DZ twins. However, clearly genes are not the whole picture in determining who develops OCD, because the MZ twins, who share identical genes, do not have 100 per cent OCD concordance. Evidently other factors play an important role as well, and one of the most useful aspects of twin studies may in fact be their ability to tell us about the contributions made by shared and non-shared environmental factors.

Despite twin studies providing an insight into the role of genes in OCD there are some difficulties with comparing MZ and DZ twin concordance rates. Firstly, it is likely that identical (MZ) twins are treated more similarly than DZ twins. MZ twins will also always be of the same gender, whereas DZ twins are not always. Consequently the environments of MZ twins are also likely to be more similar than the environments of DZ twins. If there are risk factors for OCD in the environment of one MZ twin, it is likely that the other MZ twin will also be exposed to these environmental risks. Secondly, our genes can be 'switched on and off' by modifications to the genetic material that do not change the underlying DNA sequence. Modifications in gene expression can be caused by environmental factors (this is explored within the field of **epigenetics**). Just because MZ twins have the same genes, it does not mean that the exact same genes are currently functional. Thirdly, the twin studies that have been carried out to date in OCD are largely either single case reports or studies with very small

Study	MZ concordance	DZ concordance
Inyoue (1965)	80%	50%
Carey & Gottesman (1981)	87%	47%
Torgersen (1983)	0%	0%
Andrews et al. (1990)	0%	0%

Table 6.1 The concordance rates of OCD in monozygotic and dizygotic twin studies that used DSM criteria to assess the presence of OCD

numbers of twins. The different studies have used different diagnostic criteria for OCD, making it hard to compare the findings across twin studies (Pauls, 2008). Lastly, as we saw in Chapter 1, OCD is really better characterized by a dimensional approach than a categorical one. A possible reason for the lack of concordance seen in some of the MZ–DZ twin studies reported above is that the twins may have showed higher rates of OC symptoms than individuals who did not have a twin with OCD, but did not reach the DSM criteria for OCD. In this vein, some researchers have examined dimensional measures of OC symptoms in twins using dimensional symptom checklists. Van Grootheest, Cath, Beekman & Boomsma (2005) reviewed these dimensional studies and reported that the evidence supported that OC symptoms are heritable, with genetic influence rates in children of 45–65 per cent and in adults of 27–47 per cent.

Adoption studies

As indicated above, it can be difficult to disentangle the influence of genes and the influence of the environment when trying to work out why OCD might run in families. In genetic research, adoption studies offer a way to assess the contribution of genes independently of the biological family environment. Unfortunately, adoption studies are challenging to conduct, and there are currently no documented adoption studies examining the heritability of OCD (van Grootheest et al., 2005). If these studies were to be conducted, people who were adopted who have a biological parent with OCD would be compared to adopted people who do not have a biological parent with OCD. In all cases, the adoptive parents would not have OCD. If adopted people who have a biological parent with OCD develop OCD away from the environment of a biological parent who has OCD at a greater rate than adopted people without a biological parent with OCD, a claim can be made that genetics are playing a role in the aetiology of OCD.

Candidate gene analyses

The research from twin and family studies we have just examined suggests that OCD is **heritable**. What this means is that a proportion of the individual differences in who experiences OCD within a population can be attributed to variability in **genes**. **Genetic polymorphisms** occur when two or more versions of a gene exist in a population. These different versions are known as **alleles**. These polymorphisms could be common (high frequency, with lots of individuals in the population having the allele associated with OCD) or rare (low frequency, with very few individuals in the population having the allele associated with OCD). Heritability in OCD could occur in different ways. It could be the result of single genes with high **penetrance**, which, in medical genetics, is when a large number of people with that gene show the disorder in question. Complete penetrance occurs when everybody with a particular gene develops the disorder. For example, achondroplasia (a form of dwarfism) has complete penetrance: 100% of people with a deficit in the gene for achondroplasia (Fibroblast growth factor receptor 3, FGFR3 gene) develop the condition (Rousseau et al., 1994). However, it is more likely (as you will see below) that OCD is the result of **non-Mendelian inheritance** and is a multifactorial trait determined by a combination of lots of low-frequency genetic polymorphisms. From the geneticist's point of view, this last option is the most challenging – spotting which combination of low-frequency genes is associated with variation in OCD symptomatology is like spotting a needle in a haystack!

It is possible to examine whether specific genes play a role in OCD. This is known as ***candidate gene analysis***. This form of genetic testing involves assessing whether genetic polymorphisms are associated with having OCD. Given the complexity of OCD, it is unlikely that a single, or even a few, specific genes can explain the heritability rates observed in family and twin studies.

Candidate gene studies have been guided by our current knowledge of the pathophysiology of OCD. Consequently, most candidate gene studies have examined genes that play a role in the serotonin and dopamine system, which, as we saw above, are neurotransmitter systems that have been implicated in OCD. Zohar, Greenberg & Denys (2012) report specific genes that are possibly involved in OCD: serotonin system genes (5-HT_{1B}, 5-HT_{2A}, 5-HTT/SLC6A4), genes affecting dopamine (DRD4, COMT), monoamine oxidase (MOA-O) and myelin oligodendrocyte glycoprotein (MOG-4).

OCD is a complex, multifaceted disorder, and different presentations may have different genetic influences. As we saw in Chapter 1, it may be possible to create meaningful OCD subtypes, and one valid distinction may between early- and late-onset OCD. It has been argued that these two subtypes may be underpinned by different genetic factors. Hemmings et al. (2004) report that the A7 allele of the dopamine receptor type 4 (DRD4) gene is significantly less common in individuals with early-onset OCD compared to late-onset OCD.

However, in two reviews of the genetics of OCD, the authors conclude that candidate gene studies have failed to find consistently **replicable** results about specific genes that might play a role in OCD (Pauls, 2008; Nestadt et al., 2010). Consequently, Nestadt et al. (2010) conclude 'the limited state of knowledge about pathophysiological pathways and networks of interacting genes in OCD, and conflicting results from association studies, makes it premature to restrict our focus to associations of OCD with specific candidate genes' (p. 4).

Genome-wide linkage studies

Genome-wide linkage studies (GWLS) allow researchers to examine common **single-nucleotide polymorphisms** (SNPs) to see whether these SNPs occur in affected versus unaffected family members. These SNPs act as genetic markers, which help localize the region on the chromosome where the genes that play a role in OCD are located. This is in contrast to candidate gene studies, where researchers look at specific genes. To date, there have been five genome-wide linkage studies in people with OCD (Hanna et al., 2002; Willour et al., 2004; Shugart et al., 2006; Ross et al., 2011; Mathews et al., 2012). These studies have led to the identification of 12 regions. However, only two of these regions, 15q14 and 9p have been identified in more than one study. While GWLS with a case-control design (i.e. one that has a group of affected individuals compared to a group of unaffected individuals) can identify a disease-causing genetic variant with a high penetrance, this methodology may not be sensitive enough to detect variants with low penetrance (Ohashi & Tokunaga, 2002). This is likely to be a problem in identifying genes that play a role in OCD, because the lack of identified replicable regions suggests that the genetic influence in OCD may be due to the combination of many different genes with low penetrance.

An exciting new avenue for genetic research is **genome-wide complex trait analysis** (GCTA – which also happen to be the letters designated to the nucleotides that make up DNA!). GCTA is a computer software package that allows researchers to examine how much variance in complex traits (e.g., differences in obsessive-compulsive symptoms between individuals) is accounted for, not by one SNP as we see in GWLS, but by all the SNPs either on a chromosome or even in the entire genome (Yang, Lee, Goddard & Visscher, 2011). This research method is in its infancy, and as of yet, the GCTA technique has not been used to assess genetic contributions to the variation in OCD symptoms – but watch this space!

Genetics summary

Studies into the role of genes in OCD began with family and twin studies. These have produced variable results but generally when the findings are interpreted together they indicate that OCD runs in families. One possible reason for the higher rates of OCD in family members is that parents pass on genes to their offspring that increase the risk of developing OCD. Candidate gene studies, which examine whether specific genes increase the risk of developing OCD, have also shown variable results, but promising findings include genes that play a role in the neurotransmitter systems we read about earlier in this chapter. Consequently genes may play a role in OCD through their influence on the serotonin, dopamine and glutamate systems. The other reason why OCD may run in families is that having an individual with OCD in the family may change the family environment (or even be caused by the environment that the family lives in), and OCD may be 'transmitted' via environmental influences, including the behavioural and social factors that we read about in Chapter 5. Technology for assessing the contribution of genes to OCD is rapidly developing. New advances, such as genome-wide complex trait analysis, will enable us to learn more about the precise way that different genes may interact to produce complex symptoms.

Neurocircuitry

Obsessions and compulsions may arise from dysfunctional **neurocircuitry**. There are, broadly speaking, two ways that we can think of the neurocircuitry as being dysfunctional in OCD. On the one hand, we can look for **structural abnormalities**, and on the other hand we can examine whether there are **functional abnormalities**.

Functional abnormalities

One area of the brain that has received lots of attention in OCD research is the **basal ganglia**. The basal ganglia are a series of structures located deep in the brain. The structures making up the basal ganglia are the striatum (which includes the caudate nucleus and putamen), the globus pallidus, the substantia nigra, the nucleus accumbens and the subthalamic nucleus. You can see some of the basal ganglia structures in Figure 6.2, as well as important cortical regions that are implicated in OCD, namely the orbitofrontal cortex and the cingulate cortex, which will come to in a moment. When the basal ganglia are functioning normally, they are believed to contribute to voluntary motor planning and action, and habit formation. Attention to the basal ganglia in OCD research arose initially because individuals with known problems with their basal ganglia (e.g. people who have Huntington's chorea or Parkinson's disease) develop OCD-like symptoms. Furthermore, **lesions** (i.e., injury or any other kind of pathological change) to a part of the basal ganglia called the striatum results in behaviour similar to symptoms seen in patients with OCD, as do lesions to the pallidum, a region of the basal ganglia that the neurons in the striatum project to (Laplane et al., 1989). However, it is not only the basal ganglia that are implicated.

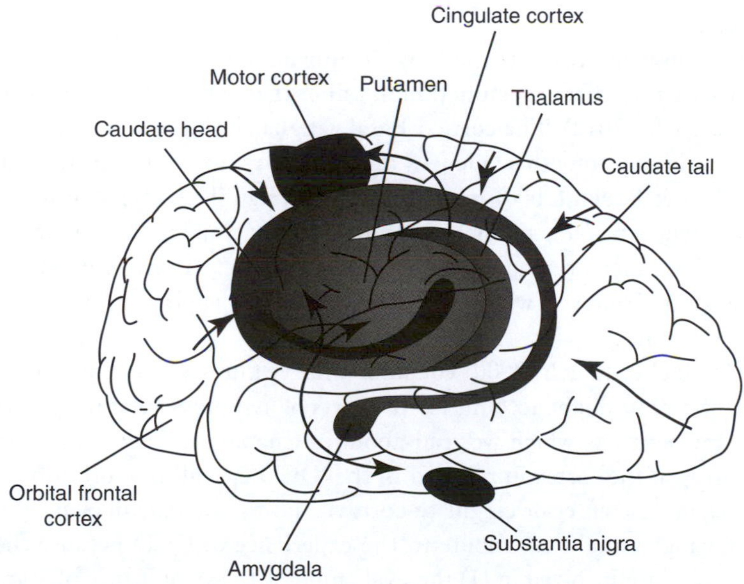

Figure 6.2 A schematic diagram of the brain showing brain regions implicated in OCD

Neuroimaging methods, including **functional magnetic resonance imaging** (fMRI), *positron emission tomography* (PET), and *single-photon emission computed tomography* (SPECT) have supported the notion that the basal ganglia show abnormal activity in individuals with OCD, and have also provided evidence that suggests that people with OCD also have abnormalities in the **orbitofrontal cortex** and the **anterior cingulate cortex**. You can see where these regions are in the brain in Figure 6.2. These cortical regions are both involved in decision-making processes.

There are three main strands of evidence from functional imaging studies that implicate the *cortico-basal ganglia circuit* in OCD. Firstly, activity in this circuit is increased at rest (i.e., when the participant is lying in the scanner, not doing anything in particular) compared to controls. Secondly, activity in this circuit is increased further when individuals with OCD are exposed to a situation that provokes their symptoms (e.g., a contaminated glove). Thirdly, activity in this circuit is reduced following successful treatment of OCD. Consequently, it is proposed that individuals with OCD have dysfunction in a cortico-basal ganglia circuit (Rauch & Jenike, 1993; Baxter et al., 1996; Hoehn-Saric & Greenberg, 1997; Graybiel & Rauch, 2000; Saxena et al., 2001).

It is possible that it is the flow of information between parts of the neurocircuitry that is dysfunctional, rather than a localized abnormality (Zohar et al., 2012). The cortico-basal ganglia circuit may be important for developing smooth sequences of behaviours, which is a process that Graybiel & Rauch (2000) refer to as 'chunking'. They hypothesize that this system, when functioning in an adaptive way, could reduce the amount of working memory capacity that is required to perform sequences of behaviours. However, when it is dysfunctional, it appears to give rise to OC symptoms.

Graybiel & Rauch (2000) consider what features of the cortico-basal ganglia circuit might account for the sorts of symptoms that people with OCD experience, which we read about in Chapter 1. They suggest that the areas of the cortex implicated in the 'OCD circuit' (the orbitofrontal cortex and the anterior cingulate cortex), and the caudate nucleus in the basal ganglia might contribute to the experience of OCD because these structures are involved in (1) the evaluation of the significance of stimuli as positive or negative; (2) aspects of **executive function**; and (3) habit learning and the performance of habits. Abnormalities in the basal ganglia may result in inappropriate habits (or compulsions) as stimuli in the external world are appraised as disproportionately negative. Evidence for this comes from single unit electrophysiological cell recordings (measurement of the activity of a single brain neuron), lesion studies and animal studies.

A number of questions remain, and indeed are raised, by neuroimaging research into OCD. Leckman & Bloch (2008) highlight that more needs to be done to examine whether findings of abnormalities in different brain regions, e.g., in the medial frontal region and right inferior parietal region (Menzies et al., 2008), represent a single abnormal circuit or multiple abnormal circuits. One possibility suggested by Leckman & Bloch (2008) is that different circuits may underpin different OCD symptom presentations.

Structural abnormalities

Studies that have examined the structure of the brain support the notion that individuals with OCD have abnormalities in the cortico-basal ganglia regions. Zohar et al. (2012) report that studies using fMRI have demonstrated that individuals with OCD have different volumes of particular brain regions, and these abnormalities have been found in areas of the basal ganglia including the caudate nucleus, the putamen and the globus pallidus, as well as the thalamus.

Structural abnormalities have been observed outside of the cortical regions typically incorporated into the cortico-basal ganglia OCD circuit. For example, **white matter** changes in the **parietal cortex** have also been observed. White matter is brain tissue consisting of **glial cells** and **myelinated axons**, which form part of the central nervous system. *Diffusion tensor imaging* (DTI), a variant of magnetic resonance imaging, maps the diffusion of molecules (typically water molecules) in the brain. Molecules interact with obstacles in tissue, such as membranes and macromolecules. Consequently, the pattern of diffusion can provide information about the tissue architecture. Menzies et al. (2008) conducted a DTI study with individuals with OCD and their first-degree relatives. They found that both the people with OCD and their relatives showed changes compared to healthy controls in their white matter. Menzies et al. (2008) found that there was increased **fractional anisotropy** (meaning that water molecules were more restricted in their movement) in right medial areas and decreased fractional anisotropy in the right inferior parietal region. White matter is important as it coordinates communication between different brain regions. When fractional anisotropy is decreased, such as was found in the parietal cortex, this can indicate that communication is disrupted between brain areas (Menzies et al., 2008). More research is needed to determine exactly how white matter abnormalities might give rise to the symptoms of OCD. Given that the unaffected first-degree relatives also showed these changes, they are unlikely to be as a result of OCD (or a sufficient cause on their own), but they may be a useful marker of risk of developing OCD (Leckman & Bloch, 2008).

In addition to white matter changes, it appears that some children with OCD who are drug-naive also show differences in the **gray matter** density in bilateral (both sides of the brain) orbitofrontal cortex and the putamen (Szesko et al., 2008). Because the children who participated in this research had not taken any medication for their OCD, we can be confident that the increase in gray matter observed by Szesko et al. (2008) is not due to the effect of taking medication.

Neurocircuitry summary

In this section we have reviewed the evidence for dysfunction in the neurocircuitry of individuals with OCD. Evidence from functional and structural imaging studies converge on a dysfunctional cortico-basal ganglia circuit. It also appears that there are other regions of the brain involved, such as the parietal cortex, and this is hypothesized to be due to these brain regions supporting compensatory processes (Zohar et al., 2012). A successful future for neurocircuitry imaging as a means for helping us to understand more about the causes of OCD is likely to hinge on researchers examining individuals with specific kinds of OCD. This is because research supports the idea that the symptom subtypes of OCD may be underpinned by different neurocircuitry abnormalities. However, we must bear in mind that the changes in brain neurocircuitry that are observed in individuals with OCD could be a consequence of experiencing the symptoms, such as repetitive actions. There is a great need for ***longitudinal studies*** that begin before symptom onset, so that cause and effect of neurocircuitry abnormalities can be satisfactorily explored. After all, as noted by Zohar et al. (2012) 'a primary pathological process underlying core OCD symptoms has yet to be identified' (p. 381).

Auto-immune accounts of child-onset OCD

The *immune system* has been implicated in a specific kind of OCD. It is suggested that some children develop OCD symptoms very rapidly after experiencing an infection caused by streptococcal bacteria (group-A β-hemolytic streptococci, GABHS). This subgroup of OCD comes under the name **Paediatric Autoimmune Neuropsychiatric Disorders Associated with Streptococcal infections** (PANDAS). The term 'PANDAS' was introduced by Swedo et al. (1998) in a paper in which they document 50 cases where children exposed to a GABHS infection rapidly developed OCD and/or tic disorder. Based on the observation of 144 episodes of GABHS-related infection, Swedo et al. (1998) proposed the following diagnostic criteria: (1) presence of OCD/tic disorder; (2) symptom onset between age 3 and puberty; (3) abrupt onset of symptoms and episodic symptom profile with recurrent exacerbation and remissions; (4) temporal association with GABHS infection; (5) association with neurological abnormalities during a symptom exacerbation.

However, the existence of PANDAS as a genuine post-streptococcal autoimmune disorder is not accepted by everyone. For example, de Oliveira and Pelajo (2010) report that many controversies remain. They state that the diagnostic criteria require validation and that there is inconclusive evidence of autoimmunity. Furthermore, de Oliveira & Pelajo (2010) raise concerns about whether GABHS infection is a true precursor, or simply exacerbates the symptoms in some cases, and they note that GABHS infections are common in childhood. de Oliveira & Pelajo (2010) suggest that PANDAS may represent a subgroup of children with child-onset OCD who experience worsening symptoms when they are exposed to GABHS infections, but that this is not the sole, or even the greatest, exacerbating factor.

Evolutionary accounts of OCD

Evolutionary accounts of psychopathology grounded in Darwinism explain psychopathology in terms of it evolving through ***natural selection*** because it has an evolutionary benefit in terms of ***inclusive fitness*** (Hamilton, 1964). In some cases, it has been argued that the symptoms of psychological illness were evolutionarily useful at a previous time in the history of human kind. For example, it has been suggested that the hyperactivity observed in patients with Anorexia Nervosa evolved in times when famine was more common. It has been suggested that this hyperactivity provided foragers with the ability to travel distances to search out food sources away from the depleted environment (Guisinger, 2003). However, most evolutionary theorists would not argue that the psychological disorders themselves are evolutionarily advantageous, but rather milder forms of some of the symptoms can be advantageous. When these advantageous systems become dysregulated, psychopathology can emerge.

Evolutionary accounts of OCD typically follow the approach of conceiving of symptoms of OCD as dysregulated versions of adaptive, useful behaviours. For example, Leckman & Bloch (2008) highlight that developing ritualistic behaviours is a normal part of typical child development. They cite work by Gesell, who suggested that young children develop rituals not to deal with emotional needs, but to enable them to master skills that are relevant to that particular stage of development. After all, rituals in childhood are very common, and 80 per cent of parents report that their three-year old child has a bed time ritual (Evans et al., 1997):

> Going to bed is also complicated for the 2 year old ... bedtime demands have often grown into an elaborated and rigid structure. There is a coming upstairs ritual, brushing the teeth ritual, getting into bed, pulling down the shades, kissing, and even a specially worded 'good night' ritual. (Gesell & Ilg, 1943, cited in Leckman & Bloch, 2008, p. 182)

What is more, children develop a variety of rituals that resemble behaviours and thoughts experienced by those with OCD. Leckman & Bloch (2008) report that following the establishment of a bedtime ritual, children develop a preoccupation with arranging things 'just right' and symmetrically, which is followed by concern about dirt and germs, and finally is followed by hoarding type behaviours such as collecting and storing objects. These behaviours peak at 3 years, except the hoarding-type behaviours which peak in typically developing children at age 6.

It has also been noted that phenomena associated with OCD symptoms can be experienced at specific time points across the lifespan. For example, hormonal changes observed when an individual falls in love are similar to those seen in OCD. Given the similarities between an 'over-valued idea' seen in the early stages of falling in love and an obsession, Marazziti, Akiskal, Rossi & Cassano (1999) examined whether the two conditions shared altered serotonin (5-HT) transporter protein levels. Marazziti et al. (1999) compared the 5-HT transporter levels in 20 people who reported falling in love in the past six months, 20 people who had OCD and were unmedicated and 20 healthy controls. Marazziti et al. (1999) found that there was a significantly lower density of the platelet 5-HT transporter in the groups of people who had recently fallen in love or who had OCD than in the healthy controls. Falling in love is an important part of human pair bonding, and consequently, the decreased 5-HT transporter density observed in people with OCD might have been evolutionarily conserved because of its function in assisting with the mating process. In August 2013, a poem about love and its relationship to OCD went viral on the internet. Neil Hilborn, who himself has OCD and Tics, recounted his experience of falling in love. In his poem, Hilborn describes the way that the object of his affection absorbed his attention in a way that, prior to falling in love, only obsessional thoughts and compulsions were able to. The love takes on an obsessional quality. You can view Hilborn reading his poem aloud on YouTube.

Another life event that is associated with similar states to those observed in OCD is when an individual has their first child. In a study conducted by Leckman et al. (1999), early parental preoccupations and behaviours (often centring on fear of harming the infant) were found to resemble the symptoms of OCD. Given that significant life events are associated with OCD-like phenomena, it seems likely that these cognitions and behaviours may serve some useful function, or at least, do not harm inclusive fitness.

We saw in Chapter 2 that there is a gender difference in terms of age of onset of OCD. Typically, males develop OCD at a younger age, and are more likely to have early-onset OCD, while females are more likely to develop OCD in young adulthood. Evolutionary accounts offer an explanation for this gender difference in terms of the more traditional gender roles occupied by our ancestors, and roles that are still typically of more relevance to one sex, e.g., females still are the predominant caregivers for young infants (Saad, 2006). It is plausible that it was more important for males to develop skills for hunting and so we see a higher incidence of repetitive, ritualistic behaviours in young males to ensure that they master skills. Conversely, females are more likely to develop OCD at around child-bearing age, when it may serve a function in terms of monitoring offspring and ensuring no harm befalls them. This heightened attention to the needs of her infant was documented by Winnicott (1958) in his writings on the 'primary maternal preoccupation'. In this sense, OCD may represent an over-activation of adaptive warning systems (Saad, 2006).

Chapter summary

In this chapter we have seen that some individuals with OCD have abnormalities in brain biochemistry and neurocircuitry. Individuals with OCD are more likely to have decreased levels of serotonin, and raised levels of dopamine and glutamate. There is also tentative evidence that some individuals with OCD may have particular alleles of genes related to these neurotransmitter systems. We also saw that individuals with OCD show abnormalities in their neurocircuitry, with increased activity in the cortico-basal ganglia circuit. In some cases of child-onset OCD, it appears that the onset is preceded by a bacterial streptococcal infection. However, it remains unclear whether this is a sufficient cause for a group of individuals, or whether it represents one of many precipitating factors. We discovered that there are evolutionary accounts that suggest that OCD symptoms arise from the dysregulation of evolutionarily adaptive systems, such as threat monitoring. To date, none of the biological abnormalities reviewed in this chapter have been observed in all participants with OCD, which likely reflects that OCD is a multifaceted and complex condition, which has a number of different causes. Future research into the biological aspects of OCD will be probably be advanced by paying more consideration to different OCD subtypes as it seems likely that these are underpinned by different genes and neurocircuitry abnormalities.

Section Two Summary

In Section Two, we have covered different theoretical accounts of what causes OCD. In Chapter 4, we reviewed cognitive accounts, in Chapter 5 we saw that behavioural, psychodynamic and social accounts have been proposed, and in Chapter 6 we discussed biological accounts. As you have seen in Chapters 4–6, each of these theories has strengths and weaknesses, and no single account that we have examined can explain every case of OCD.

When evaluating theories of what causes OCD it is vitally important that we do not view these as **mutually exclusive** explanations. What this means is that these theories need not be considered competing theories. Rather, they account for the symptoms of OCD at a different theoretical level of analysis. For example, in Chapter 6, we read about genetic theories, which implicated genes that play a role in neurotransmitter systems (another theory), which affect the communication between different brain regions (yet another theory) that play a role in many of the cognitive processes (more theoretical accounts!) that we covered in Chapter 4, such as doubting, attentional biases and interpretation biases.

Despite acknowledging that we can offer explanations of OCD at different levels, it may be that some levels of explanation are more useful, especially in terms of deriving treatments for OCD. For example, if an alien landed on planet Earth, and feeling peckish, nipped into a restaurant, they might see someone using a pen to put a squiggle at the bottom of a piece of paper. There are many different levels of explanation for this action. The alien could explain it in terms of the thought processes that determined the form that the squiggle should take, or the brain processes that coordinated the arm muscle movements, or the biochemical processes occurring in the arm muscles, or even the properties of physics that are at play in the energy and forces moving the arm. But in this instance, the most sensible and useful level of explanation is a social explanation: the squiggle observed is a signature, a means of confirming one's identity in the social world. The theories that are held in favour at the present time are predominantly cognitive and biological in nature. This is likely because, as we see in Section Three, these theoretical approaches have been translated into treatments for OCD.

It is plausible that the most appropriate level of explanation may differ depending on the subtypes of OCD that we are trying to understand. Early-onset OCD, for example, may be caused by different factors to adult-onset OCD. Future research into explanations of OCD will probably prove more fruitful if different OCD subtypes are taken into account. What is more, future work should aim to integrate some of the accounts at different levels of explanation so that a more complete understanding of what causes OCD can be established.

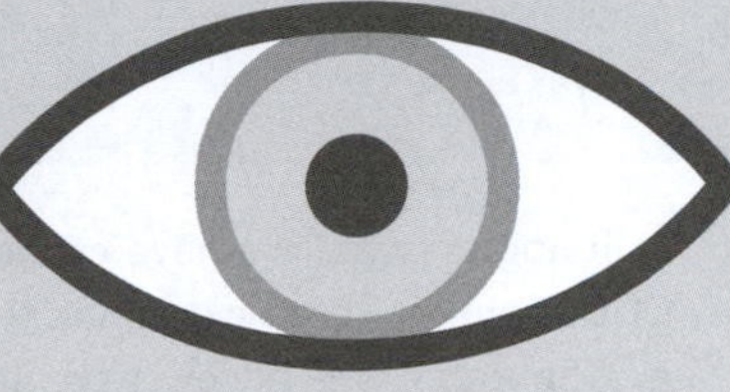

Section Three

How Do We Treat OCD?

Preface

Building on what we have covered in Section Two about what causes OCD, Section Three examines treatment options for people with OCD. In Chapter 7, we review psychological treatments for OCD including exposure and response prevention, cognitive behavioural therapy, metacognitive therapy, E-therapy and psychodynamic therapy. In Chapter 8, we turn to biological and pharmacological treatment for OCD such as antidepressant drugs, augmentation with antipsychotic drugs, neurosurgery, electroconvulsive therapy, deep brain stimulation and transcranial magnetic stimulation. In Chapters 7 and 8 we discuss the evidence that these different treatment methods help reduce symptoms of OCD and look at when they are recommended for use.

In the United Kingdom, the decisions that healthcare professionals make about the treatments to use with individuals who have OCD are guided by recommendations made by the **National Institute for Health and Care Excellence (NICE)**. NICE is a body, accountable to the Department of Health but operationally independent from the UK government. Groups of academic clinicians review the available evidence for treatments and make recommendations about the treatments that are most effective (both in terms of improving health and in terms of **cost-effectiveness**). The OCD guidelines (CG31) were published in 2005 and can be viewed online on the NICE website: http://www.nice.org.uk/. At a review in 2011, it was decided that the guidelines should not be updated at that time.

NICE uses a **stepped-care model**, which emphasizes that the treatment that is chosen for an individual with OCD should be tailored to the individual's severity of symptoms. A stepped-care approach involves starting with the least invasive treatment thought to confer a benefit for the current severity of the individual's symptoms. There are six steps in the OCD stepped-care model. Step 1 is the stage suitable for those with the mildest OCD symptoms and Step 6 is the stage for those with the most severe OCD symptoms. Generally, psychoeducation and self-help are recommended for the mildest symptoms. Then psychological treatments are proposed, in conjunction with medication for more severe cases. In the most severe cases, inpatient admissions to specialist units for people with OCD may be appropriate. Critical to the stepped care model is the idea of continual assessment of the individuals' symptoms and progress or remission so that they can be moved up and down the stepped-care model as necessary.

Chapter 7

Psychological Treatments

So far this book has examined current knowledge on what OCD is and what causes and maintains the disorder. You will have seen that there are a number of different approaches to explaining the development and maintenance of OCD. As we come to examine how OCD is treated from a psychological perspective, you will see that there are a number of different approaches to psychological treatment which have their roots in the different approaches to understanding OCD.

Exposure and Response Prevention (ERP)

The **Exposure and Response Prevention** (ERP) approach to OCD treatment has its roots in learning theory accounts of behaviour change. Central to the ERP approach is the view that engaging in safety behaviours prevents a reduction of fear (although OCD sufferers may report a decrease in anxiety after employing the safety behaviour, this is usually only temporary) and prevents the disconfirmation of maladaptive beliefs. The use of a compulsion is thus negatively reinforced as a coping mechanism. The roots of ERP can be traced back to a paper published by Victor Meyer in 1966. Meyer based his work on studies of learnt behaviour in cats and dogs which showed that experimentally induced fear could be reduced by exposing them to their fear stimuli, while not allowing them to avoid their fear in the normal way (e.g. they were not allowed to jump into another chamber, which would be a safety behaviour). After repeated exposure to the fear stimulus without being able to use any kind of avoidance or safety behaviours, the animals' fears reduced. This process is called **habituation**. Meyer (1966) then performed a similar experiment with individuals with OCD whereby they were exposed to their feared situation and were not allowed to perform any compulsive rituals. Meyer reported that 10 of the 15 participants improved due to their fear reducing after habituation to the feared stimuli.

Since the work of Meyer, ERP (sometimes also referred to as exposure ritual prevention; EX/RP) has been widely used in the treatment of OCD and is often combined with cognitive therapy to produce a cognitive behaviour therapy (CBT) treatment approach. The use of ERP has been refined since the 60s and there are a number of mechanisms though which ERP is proposed to work. Through engaging in ERP the individual will learn that their anxiety relating to their feared situation will reduce, even in the absence of ritualized safety behaviours. Furthermore, by repeatedly confronting their distressing situation, the maladaptive belief is disconfirmed as one learns that the feared outcome does not occur. For session by session guides to ERP refer to the following references (Kozak & Foa, 1997; Franklin & Foa, 1998; Abramowitz, 2006).

Abramowitz (2006) outlines a number of steps that will occur in a typical ERP treatment (See Case History 7.1 for an example of ERP treatment of OCD):

1 Socialization to the psychological model of OCD: Before actual treatment commences, the therapist familiarizes the client to a psychological model of OCD. The client is also given a clear rationale for how ERP is expected to help reduce OCD. This psychoeducational component is important because it helps to motivate the client to tolerate the distress that often accompanies exposure practice.
2 Planning of exposure exercise: The client and therapist will work together to plan the specific exposure exercises that will be pursued. This plan will include the construction of a **fear hierarchy** which will work from moderately distressing situations to very distressing situations. See Table 7.1 for an example of a fear hierarchy.
3 Familiarization to response prevention procedures: The educational stage of ERP will also acquaint clients with response prevention procedures. Here the therapist must convince the client to resist urges to perform rituals on their own.
4 Exposure exercises with mild stimuli: The exposure exercises usually begin with moderately distressing situations and will build up to the most distressing situations. Beginning with exposure

Case History 7.1

Jane's symptoms involve fears that she will harm or even kill others. When Jane experiences obsessional thoughts she performs compulsive rituals in order to stop harm occurring to friends and family. Her compulsive rituals include: (a) holding her hands closed to stop contamination of others, (b) praying for protection of others, (c) repeating certain phrases to protect those close to her, (d) avoidance of wishing people goodbye in case this will cause them harm, (e) performing washing rituals to prevent contamination of others. If she visits someone who is ill, she will involve her husband in washing rituals by insisting that he wash his hands and clothes in order to avoid him also becoming ill. Below is an outline of ERP treatment conducted with Jane:

Psychoeducation

Psychoeducation is used to help Jane understand her OCD and provide a working model of OCD. This model will help Jane map the relationship between obsessions and rituals. Psychoeducation is also used to reduce Jane's self-blame and help Jane objectify her OCD so she can work with the therapist to learn new ways to manage her OCD.

Providing a Rationale for EX/RP

The primary goal of EX/RP is to help Jane understand how her rituals are currently maintained, rather than looking for the roots cause of the ritual. This helps to provide the basis for EX/RP by providing a rationale for response prevention. For example, Jane learns that rituals (i.e., avoidance) actually fuel the obsessions, which consequently increase anxiety.

Identifying triggers

Once Jane is comfortable with the rationale for ERP, she works with the therapist to identify anxiety 'triggers', which helps her to recognize rituals. Jane uses self-monitoring forms to recognize and record examples of rituals. Once identified, the triggers can be used to build a fear hierarchy.

After a couple of sessions Jane develops a fear hierarchy in conjunction with the therapist. Exposures begin with fairly easy items (typically rated of 30 or less on a scale of 0–100) and work their way up to items rated as being more difficult. Exposure tasks are initially developed and carried out with the therapist, but then Jane does much of the exposure work as homework between therapy sessions and brings any difficulties she encounters to discuss in the next therapy session. Jane completes the more difficult items on her hierarchy before treatment ends.

Finishing treatment

By the end of treatment Jane has learned to identify and monitor her symptoms and she can continue her exposure work by using knowledge gained in the therapy session to plan and execute exposure sessions. During the final sessions, Jane works with the therapist to identify possible future challenges and prepare strategies to help her deal with them.

Adapted from Himle & Franklin (2009)

	Hierarchy items	Predicted anxiety
Easiest	Switch off the cooker without going back to check it is on.	
	Use hair straighteners and only go back once to check they are off.	
	Use hair straighteners and do not go back to check they are off.	
	Leave the house and only check once that appliances are turned off.	
Hardest	Leave the house and do not check that appliances are turned off.	

Table 7.1 Example fear hierarchy

tasks that evoke less anxiety makes it more likely that clients will learn to manage their distress and complete the exposure exercise successfully. At the end of each treatment session, the therapist instructs the client to continue exposure for several hours alone and in different environmental context.

5 Exposure exercises to high anxiety evoking stimuli. Exposure to stimuli high on the fear hierarchy is usually dealt with mid-way though the treatment. This allows time to repeat the most difficult exposure exercises in different contexts.

This treatment approach may seem fairly simplistic from a mechanistic view point, yet there are a number of factors that need to be taken into account if the treatment is to be delivered effectively. Gillihan, Williams, Malcoun, Yadin & Foa (2012) outline some of the key points for consideration in the effective use or ERP for OCD. Two examples of these points for consideration will be briefly examined to highlight some of the complexities of successful ERP treatment (for a full account of these issues readers should refer to the Gillihan et al.'s article).

1 Not going far enough in exposure: Gillihan and colleagues point out that ERP must fully address the avoidance and rituals that the individual falsely believes are preventing feared outcomes from occurring. Thus for example, when using a fear hierarchy, the top-most fear may be behaviour more excessive than is experienced in normal daily life e.g. eating food from a toilet

seat. Gillihan et al. point out that the most extreme fears must be addressed in order to prevent the individual attributing the lack of harm to the avoidance of their most feared obsession content.

2 Providing reassurance: In Chapter 5 we discussed the role of excessive reassurance seeking in the maintenance of OCD. Gillihan et al. suggest that an ERP therapist should try to determine whether providing reassurance is suitable in an ERP session or whether the individual seeking help actually uses reassurance seeking as a compulsion? If the latter is the case then the therapist will need to explain to the client why they are unable to provide any reassurance.

The points outlined above serve as examples of some of the complexities associated with effectively delivering ERP. The next section will look at the efficacy of ERP for the treatment of OCD.

ERP: what's the evidence?

ERP is recommended by the National Institute of Health and Clinical Excellence (NICE, 2006; see Section Three Preface for further information on NICE guidelines) as being a treatment of choice for OCD. In an analysis of treatment effectiveness for OCD, Fisher & Wells (2005) reported that ERP produces statistically reliable improvement in 75 per cent of clients and had a recovery rate of above 60 per cent. There is a large body of research examining how effective the approach is compared to other types of therapies, including both psychological and pharmacological treatments. Whittal, Thordarson & McLean (2005) compared the efficacy of ERP to the efficacy of CBT for OCD. In this study the CBT arm had both cognitive and behavioural aspects in their intervention, but the behavioural aspects included collecting evidence to support the notion of faulty beliefs and appraisal, rather than exposure work. When the two approaches were compared Whittal et al. (2005) found that they were comparable in outcome. Neither of the approaches had significantly better outcomes than the other. In a **meta-analysis** of treatments for psychological disorders, Butler, Chapman, Forman & Beck (2006) also reported that CBT and behaviour therapy had comparable outcomes for OCD. In a **randomized control trial** study (RCT) Foa et al. (2005) compared ERP to a pharmacological treatment. They found that ERP was superior to having medication without any other treatment and that adding medication to ERP showed no added treatment benefit. Evidence indicates that ERP is an effective treatment for

OCD, although one barrier to delivering this treatment effectively is the lack of therapists trained in its use (Abramowitz, Whiteside & Deacon, 2005).

New approaches to ERP

Despite evidence supporting the efficacy of ERP for OCD, there has recently been some evidence to suggest that safety behaviours could actually be usefully employed in behaviour therapy. This proposal has gained empirical support recently and one of the driving forces behind this alternative approach to ERP is that traditional ERP can be extremely demanding and distressing and refusal or drop out is often high (e.g. Cottraux, Bouvard & Milliery, 2005; Foa, Liebowitz, Kozak, et al., 2005; Whittal et al., 2005). In ERP therapy, the use of safety behaviours is considered to undermine treatment as the safety behaviour does not enable the individual to disconfirm their maladaptive beliefs. For example, if an individual believes they will contaminate others if they do not spend 15 minutes washing their hands before leaving the house, if they always wash their hands they will never see what would happen (i.e. that no harm would occur) if they did not perform their hand-wash ritual. The safety behaviour is thus assumed to be a maintaining factor in the obsessive compulsive cycle. Rachman, Radomsky & Shafran (2008) propose that although this view is central to cognitive theories, there is actually little empirical evidence to support the notion that safety behaviours must be completely removed for therapeutic gains to be made in ERP. Rachman et al. (2008) suggest that for those individuals who cannot tolerate traditional ERP or who do not respond to treatment, then the careful use of safety behaviours early on in treatment may actually facilitate therapeutic gains. As well as reducing ERP drop-out rates and increasing client co-operation, the use of safety behaviours early on in therapy can provide the client with a sense of increased control over the process, the duration of exposure can be extended, and an increased sense of safety can allow the client to better absorb corrective information concerning thinking biases (Rachman et al., 2008).

There is an emerging evidence base to support the use of safety behaviours in ERP. Rachman, Shafran, Radomsky & Zysk (2011) compared traditional ERP (where no safety behaviours were used) with Exposure + safety behaviours (E+SB) as an intervention for contamination fears in an undergraduate non-clinical sample. They found that both the ERP and E+SB conditions produced large, significant and stable reductions in contamination fear. This led the authors to conclude that if these results were replicated and extended to clinical population, then E+SB may improve the acceptability of cognitive behavioural treatments and may boost treatment effectiveness. These findings were supported in a replication study (van den Hout, Engelhard, Toffolo & van Uijen, 2011), which also included a no-treatment control group. van den Hout et al. reported that both the ERP and E+SB groups showed a reduction in contamination that was significantly greater than that in the control group. These findings further support the use of safety behaviours in exposure treatments using a non-clinical sample. The next stage of this research will be to examine the use of safety behaviours in ERP with a clinical sample.

Cognitive Behaviour Therapy (CBT)

The term **Cognitive Behaviour Therapy** (CBT) is a broad term that is often used to describe therapeutic approaches that may include both cognitive and behavioural aspects, or just Cognitive Therapy (an approach that emphasizes the identification and change of maladaptive cognitions; CT). The NICE (2006) guidelines for OCD indicate that CBT which also includes ERP should be a first line treatment for OCD. In the section above we examined ERP as a treatment for OCD. This section will examine contemporary cognitive therapy for OCD which emphasizes the importance of challenging cognitive biases and maladaptive beliefs, but this will not include ERP. That is not to say that CBT without ERP is a purely cognitive approach as CBT that focuses on challenging maladaptive cognitions will usually also include behavioural experiments.

The CBT model of OCD has its roots in seminal cognitive analyses of OCD (e.g. Salkovskis, 1985; Rachman, 1997). These theoretical approaches to the understanding of CBT placed maladaptive cognitive processes at the centre of processes thought to underlie OCD. Behavioural approaches to understanding and treating psychopathology had gained popularity in the 1960s and 70s and up to this point cognitions had been largely ignored. As such, the CBT approach represented a new way of conceptualizing psychopathology in that it sought to target the intrusive cognitions viewed as potential maintaining factors in OCD, and CBT provided a less anxiety provoking treatment alternative to ERP.

At the basis of the cognitive theory of OCD is the idea that intrusive thoughts are interpreted as being important and meaningful and that clients interpret these thoughts as an indication that they may be responsible for harm to themselves or others unless they take steps to prevent the harm (Salkovskis, 1985). Safety behaviours in the form of compulsions may produce temporary reduction of anxiety, but only serve to make the intrusive cognitions seem more meaningful and occur more frequently. A key part of CBT for OCD is thus helping clients to identify their obsessions and change their interpretations of these thoughts. Changing the negative and catastrophic response to intrusive thoughts will reduce subsequent anxiety and distress and in turn will decrease the urge to perform compulsions.

The exact content of CBT will vary depending on the presentation of OCD in each individual's case. However, there are a number of distinctive characteristics involved in modern CBT. CBT is a collaborative process between the therapist and client, it is structured, time limited and brief, and empirical and problem orientated (Westbrook, Kennerley & Kirk, 2010). CBT will typically involve homework between sessions; these may be thought or mood diaries or behavioural experiments. During the course of the therapy, clients learn to identify and re-evaluate beliefs about the potential consequences of engaging in or refraining from compulsive behaviours and subsequently begin to eliminate compulsions (Foa, 2010). The client and therapist will review progress together at pre-specified points in the course of the therapy. Common components of a CBT approach to OCD are outlined below:

- **Assessment and goal setting:** In the assessment stage the therapist will work with the client to identify how and when obsessions and compulsions occur. In the initial stages of CBT clients are encouraged to view their worries and fears as obsessions and to view their rituals as compulsions. By the end of the assessment stage the therapist and client will have formulated a shared understanding of the problem and will have agreed on goals of the therapy. Often the client will complete a measure of symptoms (using for example a psychometric scale such as the Yale Brown Obsessive Compulsive scale; Y-BOCS; Goodman, Price & Rasmussen et al., 1989) or a briefer measure of behavioural responses and moods after behavioural experiments. The purpose of using measurement in CBT is to inform the client and the therapist to evaluate the impact of interventions.

- **Homework:** A diary or thought record is used to help clients identify their obsessions and how they interpret them and indentify when and under what circumstances the obsessions occur. It is also important to note the response to the obsession and identify whether a compulsion was performed.
- **Identifying cognitive biases:** The therapist will use the thought record with the client to identify how the client interpreted their obsession. The therapist can then use Socratic questioning to challenge the interpretation of the intrusive thought, which helps the client identify the cognitive distortion.
- **Developing new perspectives:** Once the therapist and client have worked together to identify the cognitions that drive obsessive thinking, the therapist will help the client develop new perspectives. Techniques may include generating evidence for and against the belief related to the obsession, cost benefit analyses of maintaining obsessive beliefs and appraisals, and the generation and evaluation of alternative belief consequences. Once maladaptive beliefs relating to the obsessions have been examined and alternative ways interpreting obsessions have been analysed, the client may also be invited to perform some behavioural experiments.
- **Behavioural experiments:** Once the client and the therapist have developed a cognitive formulation of the beliefs that drive the obsessive thinking, the client may be invited to take part in behavioural experiments which will be designed to either test the validity of the beliefs they hold (e.g. if the belief is 'if I don't check all the sockets in the house 5 times before going to bed the house will set on fire and my family will die' the client may start to test the validity of this by not checking for two nights a row), or construct and test new alternative and more adaptive beliefs that were developed in collaboration with the therapist.
- **Ending therapy:** In CBT the course of the therapy will be decided at the outset and regular reviews will take place in therapy to check on the progress of agree therapeutic goals. Towards the end of the therapy course the therapist will work with the client to develop a blueprint well and dealing with problems that may arise after therapy has ended. Examples of this may include identifying what has been learned in therapy, identifying strategies that have been helpful, thinking about where problems may arise and how they may be dealt with.

CBT: what's the evidence?

A number of studies have assessed the effectiveness of CBT (here CT with behavioural experiments) as compared to ERP. In a randomized control trial study by Cottraux, Note, Yao et al. (2001) that compared CBT to ERP over a 16 week period, the two interventions had similar outcomes as measured by the Y-BOCS measure of OCD. However at a 1 year follow-up those who had ERP had improved further from their post-treatment Y-BOCS scores than those who had CBT. Fisher & Wells (2005) examined the efficacy of CBT and ERP by looking at recovery rates from five controlled trial studies rather than just comparing change on symptom scales between the two approaches. They concluded that ERP was the most effective treatment with 75 per cent of patients improving and 60 per cent reaching the cut-off score for being considered to be recovered. This compared to an improvement rate of 61 per cent for CBT and a 53 per cent recovery rate. In a meta-analysis of 19 studies, Rosa-Alcazar, Sanchez-meca, Gomez-Conesa and Marin-Martinez (2008) examined the effectiveness of ERP as compared to CBT and of the combination of ERP and CBT. Results indicated that all three treatment options were effective and that this may not be surprising when one considers that CBT usually involves some behavioural elements such as behavioural experiments and ERP involves some processes that can help clients to question their unrealistic beliefs and appraisals.

CBT: future directions

CBT that includes ERP is a recommended treatment for OCD (NICE, 2005). However, as discussed in the ERP section of this chapter, ERP can be anxiety provoking and distressing, which means that drop-out rates can be high. Consequently, researchers are beginning to examine other cognitively based approaches. One example of this is to develop CBT procedures for different manifestations of OCD. Radomsky, Shafran, Coughtrey & Rachman (2010) developed a cognitively based approach for their treatment of compulsive checking and suggest that targeting treatment procedures for specific OCD subtypes would enable delivery of more refined treatment approaches. Similarly Tolin, Frost & Steketee (2007) developed CBT specifically for compulsive hoarding. Using this intervention they saw significant improvements in measures of compulsive hoarding and proposed that by using a specialized CBT intervention it is possible to see treatment gains in a condition traditionally thought to be treatment resistant (See

Case History 7.2

Example of CBT for hoarding adapted from Tolin, Frost & Steketee (2007). Treatment was based on a cognitive-behavioural therapy manual for compulsive hoarding (Steketee & Frost, 2007).

Treatment outline

Participants took part in 26 sessions over a 7–12 month period. Sessions based in the therapist's office often lasted 1–1.5 h, and sessions in the participant's home often lasted 2 h. The initial 3–5 sessions always took place in the therapist's office. These sessions involved evaluation and treatment planning and formulation of a cognitive behavioural model of each patient's presentation. The assessment would take place both in the clinic and in patients' homes.

Therapists used interventions to target three key factors in hoarding: disorganization, difficulty discarding and compulsive acquisition. Treatment techniques consisted of (1) helping participants to target problems with organization, decision-making and problem solving though skills training (2) using imagined and direct exposure to tackle avoided situations, and (3) targeting hoarding-related beliefs though cognitive restructuring. In cognitive restructuring, methods are used to challenge the biases that a patient might hold about threats and negative outcomes (in this case relating to discarding objects) and to generate thoughts that are more accurate. Approximately 25 per cent of sessions were held in patients' homes or at sites where the individual would often acquire many objects (e.g., jumble sales, discount shops) and 75 per cent of sessions were conducted at the therapist's office. Of the 26 patients, 2 patients completed 'marathon' sessions at their home where the therapist helped with sorting, organizing and discarding. Patients also completed homework tasks between sessions and the therapist rated the homework compliance at each session. The final 2 sessions involved relapse prevention methods which would help patients to identify techniques with which to manage current and future stressors without reverting to hoarding behaviours.

Case History 7.2 for details of the treatment). Based on these examples, it is likely that refining treatment approaches to optimize best outcomes for specific OCD subtypes will provide an alternative treatment approach to ERP that is also evidence-based and effective.

Metacognitive therapy

Metacognitive therapy (MCT) for OCD is based on Wells' metacognitive model of OCD (Wells & Mathews, 1994; Wells, 1997, 2000; see Chapter 4 for details of the model). MCT for OCD is a more recent development in cognitive therapies for OCD; it has less exposure than ERP and focuses on the beliefs a client has about the importance and meaning of obsessional thoughts and symptoms. Fisher & Wells (2008) highlight some key similarities and differences between the metacognitive account of OCD and other cognitive accounts. From a therapeutic view point, the metacognitive account of OCD proposes that beliefs about thoughts and thought processes such as intrusions are of central importance and can account for the negative appraisal of intrusive thoughts – in a similar view to other cognitive models of OCD. However, rather than changing the content of the anxious beliefs associated with intrusions (such as feeling of responsibility for harm), the metacognitive intervention proposes that the metacognitive beliefs concerning the importance of intrusive thoughts should be modified.

Fisher & Wells (2008) describe the key stages in the metacognitive treatment of OCD, which will be summarized below (for further reading on MCT see Wells, 1997, 2000):

- **Stage 1:** Thoughts are thoughts – not facts: This stage increases awareness of the role that metacognition plays in symptom maintenance. The goal is to enable clients to change from treating their thoughts about their obsessions and compulsions as facts to being able to objectively evaluate their obsessions as merely mental events, which do not require further processing.
- **Stage 2:** Case formulation: A case formulation based on the metacognitive model of OCD is developed with each client followed. The client is familiarized to strategies that emphasize that beliefs about intrusions and rituals will be the main focus of treatment. For example, clients are helped to realize that if they no

longer hold metacognitive beliefs about obsessions e.g. 'thinking that I may poison someone means that I will', then they will be able to treat their intrusions as benign mental events.

- **Stage 3:** Targeting of Thought fusion beliefs (TFB): TFB are targeted using verbal reattribution. Behavioural experiments are also performed where clients are taught to respond to their intrusive thoughts with 'detached mindfulness' (Wells & Mathews, 1994; Wells, 2000). When using 'detached mindfulness' clients are asked not to engage with their obsessional thoughts in any way. Thus rather than use safety behaviours such as thought suppression, avoidance, reassurance seeking, or overt and covert neutralizing in response to their intrusive thoughts, they are asked to simply notice their obsessions and choose to let the thought naturally decay. In this way no importance or meaning is given to the thought. This strategy is used to increase awareness of the maintaining role of metacognitive beliefs in OCD, whilst also modifying both metacognitive beliefs about obsessions, as well as positive and negative beliefs about compulsions. Clients are then asked to implement the technique consistently between therapy sessions.
- **Stage 4:** Continuation sessions: Further treatment sessions involve further 'detached mindfulness' practice and the modification of beliefs about the necessity of performing compulsions in response to obsessions. Both positive metacognitive beliefs about rituals (e.g. 'my rituals prevent me from becoming a murderer') and negative beliefs about rituals (e.g. 'my compulsions are uncontrollable and will make me go mad') are addressed in therapy.
- **Stage 5:** Modification of goals used to guide compulsions: Once the previous stages have been mastered, the next stage is to modify the maladaptive internal criteria that OCD clients use to guide their overt and covert rituals. Clients will continue to perform their rituals until an internal goal state is achieved. This goal state is usually subjective and a number of different maladaptive strategies are used to assess the goal state. Strategies include being hypervigilant for internal and external threat cues or monitoring of mental events for absence/presence of intrusive thoughts. Clients will work with the therapist to analyse the advantages and disadvantages of these behaviours. Clients are then asked to ban

their maladaptive strategies and are reminded to use feelings of anxiety or inappropriate thought monitoring as a cue to implement detached mindfulness.

- **Stage 6:** Relapse prevention strategies: The final treatment sessions work on relapse prevention. Clients will leave therapy with a therapy blueprint which will include a formulation of the clients' OCD and an account of the main therapeutic strategies used during treatment. Clients will discuss situations and possible triggers for relapse and will be encouraged to implement these learnt strategies to prevent relapse and stay well.

Metacognitive therapy: what's the evidence?

Metacognitive therapy is a relatively new treatment for OCD and there is an emerging evidence base supporting its efficacy as an intervention. In an initial examination of metacognitive therapy for OCD, Fisher & Wells (2008) performed a case study with four clients with differing presentations of OCD. Each of the four individuals had their baseline symptoms measured (using the Yale Brown Obsessive Compulsive scale (Y-BOCS; Goodman, Price & Rasmussen et al., 1989) and other measures of mood and anxiety) for between 3–4 weeks to establish stable baseline symptoms measures. Clients then underwent the metacognitive therapy process described above and symptoms measures were repeated at the end of therapy and at 3 and 6 months follow-up. Results showed that post intervention all clients' Y-BOCS scores had substantially decreased at 3 months follow-up all 4 individuals showed clinically significant change on their Y-BOCS scores. At six months follow-up only 3 individuals' data was available and 2 of the 3 maintain recovery while the other individual continued to show significant improvement as compared to baseline scores. This initial examination of metacognitive therapy for OCD shows encouraging results. In a trial of group MCT for OCD, Rees & van Koesveld (2008) delivered group MCT to 8 adults who had a variety of OCD presentations. They reported that 7 of the 8 participants achieved recovery as measured by the Y-BOCS at a 3 month follow-up. These results support the potential efficacy of MCT for OCD, but further evidence is needed. According to the US clinical trials site, a randomized control trial comparing MCT with ERP is currently underway with an estimated completion date of 2014. For further details readers can visit the clinical trials page (http://clinicaltrials.gov/show/NCT01483339).

E-Therapy

There are a number of psychological interventions for OCD (e.g. ERP, CBT, CBT + ERP) that have acceptable treatment outcomes. However, not everyone is able to access these evidence-based interventions. In 2000 the Psychiatric Morbidity Survey reported that per 1000 people aged 16–74, 38 people had OCD. Stobie, Taylor, Qiuigley, Ewing & Salkovskis (2007) found that individuals received their diagnosis, an average of 8.5 years after symptoms starting impacting on daily life and clinical experience suggests that it can take people up to 15–20 years to seek professional help. There are a number of possible reasons why people delay in seeking help. They may initially be sent to the wrong service, or may experience feelings of stigma or shame, especially if they consider their intrusions to be shameful. Another barrier to accessing services may be a lack of trained specialists, or difficulty getting to services. An alternative route to accessing evidence-based therapy that may overcome some of the traditional barriers to accessing therapy is computerized cognitive behavioural therapy (CCBT).

The term CCBT refers to a number of methods of delivering CBT via an interactive computer interface. It can be delivered on a personal computer, over the Internet or via the telephone using interactive voice response (IVR) systems. As with CBT, pre-therapy assessment is recommended to ensure that people are suitable for therapy (NICE, 2006). A key question concerning CCBT for OCD is whether individuals who are seeking help perceive CCBT to be an acceptable choice. Wootton, Titov, Dear, Spence & Kemp (2011) examined acceptability of CCBT for OCD using an internet study with individuals who had OCD and found that 93 per cent of the sample would consider using CCBT. One potential advantage to CCBT is that it may offer a cost effective intervention for some individuals and may be a useful add on or follow-up to face-to-face therapy for others. Of course, for CCBT to be advantageous, one must first have evidenced-based programs that are effective.

There are a number of online CCBT programs for anxiety and depression and programs such as Beating the Blues (Ultrasis plc; www.beatingtheblues.co.uk) and FearFighter (ST Solutions Ltd; www.fearfighter.com) are recommended by NICE (2006) as part of a **stepped care** treatment for depression and panic/phobia respectively. By comparison there are relatively few CCBT interventions designed for OCD. There have been some small trials of CBT self-help manuals delivered via a computer (e.g. Clark, Kirkby, Daniels & Marks, 1998; Andersson, Ljótsson, Hedman et al., 2011). One program that is currently assessed (though not recommended) by NICE is called OC Fighter (previously known as BTSteps). OC Fighter is an online program that uses CBT and ERP techniques presented in a paced therapy package with email or phone support from a mental health professional. The earlier BTSteps version used a treatment manual and a computer-driven IVR system, which the client phoned to receive tailored self-help for OCD. The program content in the two systems is the same, but the more recent version is delivered online rather than using the IVR system. The package includes 9 steps where steps 1–3 concern education and self-assessment. Steps 4–9 guide daily self-exposure to triggers of rituals and obsessions, followed by self-imposed ritual prevention for at least one hour until discomfort and the urge to perform rituals decrease: These steps include planning self-exposure homework, carrying out and reporting of that homework, and preventing relapse.

CCBT: what's the evidence?

Compared to other common mental health problems such as anxiety and depression there is relatively little research on the efficacy of CCBT for OCD. Clark et al. (1998) examined an interactive computer program to deliver vicarious exposure (e.g. exposure via the computer) and ritual prevention for obsessive-compulsive disorder (OCD). They found that after 3 forty-five minute sessions, participants' Y-BOCS scores fell, but not significantly. It was suggested that this computer based treatment may be useful when employed alongside therapy. The majority of CCBT research for OCD has been performed on the BTSteps program (Marks, Baer, Greist et al., 1998; Nakagawa, Marks, Park et al., 2000; Greist, Marks, Baer et al., 2002; Kenwright, Marks, Graham, Franses, & Mataiz-Cols, 2005) where individuals used a self-help manual and reported progress to a computer operated IVR before the online version of this program became OCFighter.

In a small pilot study Nakagawa et al. (2000) reported that patients with OCD improved nearly as much with home self-treatment guided by a manual plus computer (BTSteps), as with treatment guided by a behaviour therapist. In a larger control trial study Greist et al. (2002) compared CBT for OCD as delivered by BTSteps, to therapist delivered CBT, or a control group who received systematic relaxation guided by a manual. They found that after 10 weeks change scores on the Y-BOCS were significantly greater in the therapist led CBT than the computer CBT (BTSteps) and Y-BOCS change scores were significantly greater in both CBT groups as compared to the relaxation group. They concluded that CCBT for OCD was a useful first treatment step when therapist guided CBT was unavailable. Kenwright et al. (2005) examined the BTSteps program, but with added phone support from a therapist. There is evidence to suggest that phone or email support to CCBT decreases dropout (Christensen, Griffiths, Mackinnon & Brittliffe, 2006) and Kenwright and colleagues found that scheduled phone support from a therapist when using CCBT for OCD as compared to participant requested phone calls reduced dropout and improved adherence to the treatment and outcomes. Andersson et al. (2011) completed a trial of a 15 week internet-based CBT intervention with therapist support. They examined Y-BOCS scores pre and post trial and concluded that participants made significant improvements and that internet-based CBT with therapist support may be a useful treatment for OCD, but that larger, randomized trials were necessary. From this literature we can conclude that the CCBT for OCD may a useful intervention for those who do not wish to or cannot engage in face-to-face therapy. More research is needed to confirm the efficacy of program such as OCFighter as the majority of research to date examines an earlier version of this package. A randomized control trial study (the Obsessive Compulsive Treatment Efficacy Trial; OCTET) examining the efficacy of OCFighter as compared to a self-help book and a **waitlist control** group is underway and results are expected in 2015.

Psychodynamic therapy

Until the 1960s psychoanalysis was widely viewed as the treatment of choice for OCD, although this was not due to its clinical effectiveness (as will be discussed below), but due to there being few other therapeutic options. Psychoanalysis is defined as 'a treatment that aims at a comprehensive exploration and understanding of unconscious conflicts, character, and personality development' (Horowitz, 1998, p. 261).The psychoanalytic approach to OCD has its roots in Freud's theories of neuroses (see Chapter 5 for psychodynamic explanations of OCD), although more recently others have also proposed psychoanalytic formulations of OCD (e.g. Wells, 1990; Esman, 2001). This section will give an overview of psychodynamic approaches to the treatment of OCD and will then consider the evidence for the effectiveness of this approach.

Traditional psychoanalysis differs from CBT-based therapies in that it is not necessarily brief, or time-structured. The client may see the therapist a number of times a week and therapy can last for months or years (NICE, 2006). Treatment emphasizes the relationship between the therapist and patient and will often involve **transference** and **countertransference,** which are proposed to allow the therapist to better understand the patient's unconscious feelings. Lane, Quintar & Goeltz (1998) propose that psychoanalysis is based on a number of key assumptions: (1) that there is an unconscious mind that influences our behaviour and experiences, (2) the specific life experience, history and psychic needs of an individual will powerfully influence that person's perceptions and behaviours, (3) pathology exists on a continuum and mental illness is a matter of degree, (4) the adult's dysfunction is determined by the individuals developmental history, (5) all individuals are unique. From these we can see a number of core themes that define psychoanalysis. For example, the importance of the unconscious and past experiences in shaping behaviour and the view that it is an individual's past experience that define that person's view and understanding of the world. From a psychodynamic perspective, psychopathology is assumed to arise from internal conflict and the inner conflict is represented by symptoms (Lane et al., 1998). Feelings of anxiety were proposed to trigger the defence system and Salzman (1983) proposed that a key part of psychoanalysis for OCD is to alter the **defence mechanisms** that maintain the feelings of anxiety and distress.

Psychodynamic therapy for OCD: what's the evidence?

As mentioned above, OCD was traditionally treated with psychoanalysis, but this was because there were few other treatment options. The NICE (2006) treatment guidelines highlight the fact that psychoanalytic therapy for OCD has become far less frequent, mainly due to there now being treatments for OCD that have an evidence base. Foa (2010) highlights the fact that while there are a number of psychoanalytic formulations of OCD, these formulations did not lead to treatments that demonstrated a reduction in OCD symptoms. A barrier to assessing the efficacy of psychoanalytic interventions for OCD is the lack of randomized or controlled studies on the topic.

There is little literature examining the efficacy of psychoanalytic therapy for OCD, but there is consensus that reports of therapeutic gains using psychoanalysis are virtually non-existent (e.g. Perse, 1988; Malan, 1979; Jenike, Baer & Minichiello et al., 1997). NICE guidance (2006) proposes that, given the lack of evidence as to the efficacy of psychodynamic therapy for OCD, there is doubt as to whether there is a place for the approach in mental health services for OCD.

Chapter summary

This chapter has examined psychological treatments for OCD. A brief summary will be provided for each approach. The chapter started off by looking at Exposure Response Prevention (ERP). This approach has its roots in learning theory. ERP seeks to expose clients to their feared situations whilst not allowing them to use their safety behaviours. The result is that the client learns that their feared outcome does not occur and that their safety behaviours are actually maintaining their anxiety. ERP has acceptable effectiveness rates, but there is high drop-out and treatment refusal due to the anxiety provoking nature of the treatment. Cognitive Behavioural Therapy (CBT) seeks to challenge the maladaptive response to unwanted intrusions and to develop new perspectives concerning the beliefs about their intrusions. Behavioural experiments are used to test out competing theories and demonstrate that their maladaptive beliefs are not valid. To increase the efficacy of CBT, scientists and clinicians have begun to formulate CBT-based therapy approaches that target specific subtypes of OCD such as washing compulsions or checking compulsions.

Metacognitive therapy (MCT) for OCD takes a different approach to CBT. Rather than trying to change the content of cognitions, MCT focuses on the beliefs a client has about the importance and meaning of obsessional thoughts and symptoms. The MCT approach examines beliefs about the importance of intrusions and teaches clients to relate differently to these beliefs by using a technique termed 'detached mindfulness'. Two belief types that are targeted are positive beliefs about the need to perform compulsions (e.g. I need to perform this compulsion to prevent harm occurring to my loved ones) and negative beliefs about the need to perform compulsions (e.g. my compulsions are uncontrollable and will send me mad). There is an emerging evidence base that supports the use of MCT for OCD.

As we have seen from the evidence presented above there are a number of acceptable cognitive and behavioural approaches for treating OCD. However, many people who have OCD either do not get diagnosed for many years, or for a number of different reasons are unable to access services. E-therapy and specifically computerized cognitive behavioural therapy (CCBT) has been examined to test whether therapeutic gains can be made when therapy is accessed via a computer. There is evidence to suggest that CCBT for OCD may provide useful therapeutic gains when employed alongside face to face therapy or when supported by phone calls or emails from a therapist. Further research trials are underway to assess whether the package OCFighter is a useful therapeutic tool for OCD when examined in a randomized control trial.

Finally this chapter reviewed the psychodynamic approach to the treatment of OCD. Psychopathology from a psychodynamic perspective is assumed to arise from internal conflict and the inner conflict is represented by the OCD symptoms. A key part of psychoanalysis for OCD is to alter the defence mechanisms that maintain the feelings of anxiety and distress. Psychoanalysis is not time structured or brief like many other therapeutic approaches and the treatment can last for months or years. In psychoanalysis emphasis is placed on the relationship between therapist and client and the therapist will encourage the client to use techniques such as transference to explore past relationships and emotions that are thought to affect the current psychological state of the client. There is however little evidence to support psychoanalysis as an effective treatment for OCD and this treatment approach is not recommended by NICE guidance.

Chapter 8

Biological and Pharmacological Treatments

As we saw in Chapter 6, there is evidence that some individuals with OCD have abnormalities in aspects of their biology, such as their levels of neurotransmitters and the ways that different parts of the brain communicate with one another. This raises the possibility that we might be able to reduce the symptoms of OCD by targeting these biological abnormalities. In this chapter, we will find out about the most common form of biological treatment for OCD, antidepressant medications, and the guidance on how, when and for whom these should be prescribed. We will then turn to some of the more drastic measures that have been undertaken to try to correct biological abnormalities, including neurosurgery, electroconvulsive therapy, transcranial magnetic stimulation and deep brain stimulation. We will find out a bit more about what each of these treatments involves and what evidence there is that they can help. But first, we shall begin by thinking about how we know if a treatment for OCD is effective.

How do we determine whether a treatment for OCD 'works'?

In order to determine whether a treatment for OCD, be it psychological, pharmacological or surgical, is effective, we need to be able to see improvements in OCD symptoms, as measured by symptom checklists. A treatment is usually deemed effective if there is a 25 per cent or more reduction in OCD symptoms as measured by the Yale-Brown

Obsessive-Compulsive Scale (YBOCS; Goodman et al., 1989; Decloedt & Stein, 2010).

However, it is not very reliable to work out if a treatment works by simply looking at whether symptoms of OCD are reduced by 25 per cent following an intervention of some kind. This is because psychological conditions can get better even if we don't treat them, a process known as **spontaneous remission**. It might be that a group of patients show a reduction in their symptoms after taking a medicine, but that they were always going to get better anyway. Another important reason why we can't just give patients a medicine and see if they get better is that the effect that a medicine has on how we feel isn't solely based on pharmacology; our mind also plays a role. During the past sixty years, this has been well-documented in the form of the *placebo effect*. A placebo effect occurs when an individual experiences improvement that is not attributable to a medication, or a procedure that has been conducted, and can occur because an individual expects that the medicine will help them. Consequently, it is important that when we are assessing whether a medicine or another kind of treatment works, we include a condition where patients do not receive the treatment that we are interested in but instead they receive a placebo. In drug trials this is quite straightforward to carry out – the participants in the control condition can be given a drug that looks identical to the active drug, but doesn't contain the active ingredients. If participants in the group who receive the active treatment show greater reductions in their symptoms than participants who receive the placebo (sometimes called a 'dummy pill'), then we can be more confident that the improvements are not simply due to the placebo effect (people believing that they will get better by taking the medicine) or spontaneous remission (people getting better naturally without intervention). However, one criticism of placebo-controlled trials is that sometimes the **side effect profile** of the active drug and the placebo are different. Consequently, if a participant experiences side effects known to be associated with the active product, they may work out that they are taking the active drug and have increased hope and belief that the treatment will be effective (Kirsch, Scoboria & Moore, 2002). In surgical trials, it is possible to conduct '*sham surgery*' where an incision is made but the surgical procedure is not conducted. There are ethical issues associated with this because undergoing an anaesthetic to have surgery carries a small but significant risk. It is much harder to find a suitable control in trials of psychotherapy, although *befriending* has been used in some cases (e.g., Sensky et al., 2000), and it is possible to measure participants' expectations about whether the sessions will help them and statistically control for this.

The 'gold standard' method for examining whether a treatment is successful or not is the *double-blind*, **placebo-controlled**, *randomized controlled trial* (RCT) (Sibbald & Roland, 1998). In these studies, individuals who agree to take part in research (known as 'participants') are randomly assigned (usually by a third party in really top quality RCTs) to conditions in the experiment. At a minimum, placebo-controlled RCTs include the treatment that the researchers are testing (often referred to as the active condition) and a control condition. Sometimes other conditions, such as treatments that are already known to be effective at reducing symptoms will also be included. The double-blind part means that neither the participant, nor the clinician/researcher who is measuring the symptoms after the intervention, know which condition the participant was randomly assigned to receive/experience.

Antidepressants

As we saw in Chapter 6, the ***serotonin*** system is thought to be important in OCD because some patients who take **antidepressant drugs** go on to experience fewer obsessions and carry out fewer compulsions. There are different kinds of antidepressants, but those used to treat OCD include **tricyclic antidepressants** (TCAs) and *selective serotonin-reuptake inhibitors* (SSRIs). TCAs and SSRIs both have very similar mechanisms of action: they increase the level of serotonin in the brain. As we saw in Chapter 6, serotonin is important because it is a neurotransmitter that carries messages from one neuron to another. It does this by binding to receptors on the post-synaptic neuron. Problems with chemical messaging (passing on the message from one neuron to the next) can occur if there are not enough of the neurotransmitters in the synaptic cleft. Generally, neurons recycle the neurotransmitters that signal messages by taking them back into the cell. If the neurotransmitters are taken up by the cell to be recycled too quickly, then there may not be an adequate quantity of serotonin molecules docked on the postsynaptic nerve cell receptors to result in the message being registered by the nerve cell, and consequently it also won't be passed on to other nerve cells.

TCAs and SSRIs are able to increase the amount of serotonin because they block the reabsorption of serotonin molecules, meaning that there are more molecules in the synaptic cleft that can assist nerve cells with communication. SSRIs are selective (the first S!) because they seem to only inhibit the reuptake of serotonin. In contrast, TCAs inhibit the reuptake of **noradrenaline** (as well as serotonin).

The very first study that showed that antidepressants help individuals with OCD to experience fewer symptoms was conducted over 45 years ago, by Fernandez and Lopez-Ibor (1967), and involved the TCA clomipramine. Since this first study, more studies have been conducted to examine the effectiveness of different antidepressants in treating OCD. One way to make sense of the findings from many different studies is to conduct a systematic review of the findings from separate studies looking to answer the same question. In 2008, a *Cochrane Review* was published, which systematically reviewed the evidence for the efficacy of SSRIs in treating OCD based on data from 17 studies conducted on a total of 3,097 participants (Soomro, Altman, Rajagopal & Oakley Browne, 2008). These 17 studies included different SSRIs: five studies of sertraline versus placebo, five studies of fluvoxamine versus placebo, three studies of fluoxetine versus placebo, three studies of paroxetine versus placebo, and one study comparing citalopram to placebo. The studies varied in length, between 6–13 weeks, making this a systematic review of short-term outcomes. SSRIs were found to be superior to placebo. In 13 of the studies, data was provided on the number of participants who met specified criteria for being classed as a 'responder', which was typically a 25 per cent reduction on the YBOCS. This data was used to calculate the relative risk of recovery in the two groups (SSRI versus placebo). Soomro et al. (2008) report that the relative risk was 1.84, which means that people who received a SSRI were almost twice as likely to show clinical improvement compared with people who received a placebo. The authors also conducted a meta-analysis for each of the different SSRI types. They found that there was no significant difference between the effectiveness of the SSRIs compared to placebo – all were equally effective. Despite this, the side effect profiles of the different SSRIs varied, and Soomro et al. (2008) concluded that more research is required using head to head drug trials (where one SSRI is compared to another SSRI) to find the most suitable SSRIs for OCD based on efficacy and on side effects profiles. A systematic review of TCAs and SSRIs in children and adolescents also found that these drugs (particularly clomipramine, a TCA, and sertraline, a SSRI) should be considered as first-line treatment options in young people who develop OCD (Gentile, 2011).

So which is the best drug to prescribe in the first instance for patients with OCD – a TCA or a SSRI? In their review of the pharmacotherapy of OCD, Fineberg & Gale (2005) report that all the ***meta-analyses*** that have looked at the question of whether clomipramine (TCA) or SSRIs are better at reducing symptoms of OCD have shown in their primary analysis that clomipramine is superior to SSRIs. There is a lot of heterogeneity in the separate studies that are included in meta-analyses, and it is possible to control for things such as the year of publication, length of trial, and severity of OCD. Ackerman & Greenland (2002) did just that, and found that while clomipramine remained superior to placebo when controlling for these factors (and a few others), it was no longer superior to SSRIs. Therefore, it appears that clomipramine's superiority to SSRIs might actually just be a result of the studies with clomipramine being conducted early, in drug-naive participants, when the placebo effect was weaker, which resulted in larger effects for clomipramine against placebo, compared to SSRIs against placebo. Despite comparable efficacy, the side effects of clomipramine are worse than those of SSRIs, making it a less appealing first drug of choice. The side effects of clomipramine are probably worse because TCAs, of which clomipramine is an example, don't just affect the neurotransmitter levels of serotonin, but also of noradrenaline. However, Fineberg & Gale (2005) report that the drop-out rate (i.e., people who stop participating in a drug trial) is comparable for both groups of antidepressants, suggesting that the side effects of TCAs are not so bad that participants can't tolerate taking the medication.

So how effective are antidepressants at helping to reduce OCD symptoms? Pallanti & Quercioli (2006) report that 40-60% of people who receive SSRIs for OCD will meet criteria for a clinical response (a 25-35% reduction in their YBOCS score). In comparison to CBT with ERP, which you read about in Chapter 7, a recent review suggested that pharmacotherapy was significantly less effective (Cuijpers et al., 2013) but it still provides a valid option for individuals (1) who cannot engage in CBT, (2) who do not wish to engage in CBT, (3) for whom CBT has not been effective, or (4) who are currently on a waiting list to receive CBT.

Deciding whether to take medication for mental health problems can be a challenge for some people. In Case History 8.1, based on an extract from an anonymous online blog, one lady explains how her OCD symptoms made this even more of a challenge. Eventually, this lady decided to

Case History 8.1

A woman, let's call her Lucy, had been experiencing OCD for a number of years and was encouraged by medical staff to think about using medication to help manage her OCD symptoms. Lucy was very anxious about taking medication. Lucy believes that aspects of her OCD made it harder for her to decide whether to use medication or not (you can read about some of the cognitive aspects of OCD in Chapter 4). For example, Lucy found uncertainty very difficult to deal with; the uncertainty of whether medication may or may not help Lucy's symptoms made her feel very anxious. Lucy also strives for perfection, and this resulted in Lucy wanting the correct drug at the correct dose straight away. Broader issues contributed to Lucy's difficulties in deciding whether to take medication. As you read in Chapter 3, comorbidity is common in OCD. Lucy also experiences health anxiety and was particularly concerned about the side effects that the medication might have. What is more, Lucy found some social situations, such as making phone calls to psychiatrists to discuss her options, very nerve-racking, and believes that this led to her adopting rituals around phone call making.

After a year of obsessive and ritualized decision making, Lucy decided to give medication a go. In Lucy's case, the medication proved to be helpful, and Lucy attributes taking medication to helping her reach a point where she was able to engage in psychological therapy.

If you are interested in reading the blog that this case study is based on visit http://exposingocd.blogspot.co.uk/

give antidepressant medication a try, to see if it would help her manage her OCD symptoms. She reflects on the benefit she found from her medication in helping her to engage in psychological therapies, which you read about in Chapter 7.

Augmenting antipsychotics

Given that many individuals who are prescribed an antidepressant for OCD do not show clinical improvements, researchers and clinicians have examined what happens when these patients are also given *antipsychotic drugs*, alongside their antidepressant. This is known as **augmentation**. Antipsychotics have been investigated because, as we saw in Chapter 6, there is evidence of a potential role for dopamine in OCD, and antipsychotics target the dopamine system (Decloedt & Stein, 2010). In a recent meta-analysis, Dold, Aigner, Lanzenberger & Kasper (2013) identified all of the studies that were double-blind, placebo-controlled randomised controlled trials investigating whether adding an antipsychotic to an antidepressant significantly reduced symptoms of OCD. Dold et al. (2013) identified 12 studies investigating five different antipsychotics between them: quetiapine (5 studies), risperidone (3 studies), olanzapine (2 studies), aripiprazole (1 study), and haloperidol (1 study). A total of 394 patients took part in these 12 studies. Dold et al. (2013) found that significantly more patients responded (as measured by a 35% reduction on the YBOCS) when they were given an antidepressant augmented with an antipsychotic than when they were given an antidepressant with a placebo. Interestingly, the efficacy depended on which antipsychotic was added. Dold et al. (2013) reported that risperidone resulted in significantly more patients responding to the treatment, but that quetiapine and olanzapine did not. More research needs to be conducted regarding aripiprazole and haloperidol as there was only one study that was identified for each of these antipsychotics.

However, while the results from the Dold et al. (2013) meta-analysis suggest that it might be useful to add risperidone to antidepressants for patients who have not responded to antidepressants alone, this potential gain should be weighed up against the side effects that some patients experience when taking risperidone. For example, in a study conducted by Matsunaga et al. (2009), patients who were given atypical antipsychotics had significant increases in body mass index and fasting blood glucose compared to patients who were not, suggesting that the antipsychotics may be putting their physical health at an increased risk.

The Matsunaga et al. (2009) study also highlights the illness severity in patients with treatment-resistant OCD. In their study, the 44 patients who were given an antipsychotic with a SSRI had significantly higher YBOCS scores than the patients who were responsive to a SSRI within a 12-week trial. So it seems that patients who are not responsive to SSRIs are experiencing a more severe form of OCD. What is more, Matsunaga et al. (2009) found that the scores of patients who received antipsychotic augmentation still had higher YBOCS scores after one year of treatment than patients who had responded to a SSRI, indicating that even with antipsychotic augmentation, it is difficult to obtain a good clinical outcome in SSRI treatment-resistant OCD patients.

NICE guidance on prescribing medication for adults with OCD

In the Preface to Section Three, we discussed that treatment for OCD in the UK is guided by the *National Institute for Health and Clinical Excellence* (NICE). Medication for OCD is generally prescribed by a **psychiatrist** or in special cases by **GPs with a Special Interest in Mental Health**. In the section below, the recommendations that NICE made regarding the use of medication in the treatment of OCD are summarized. You will notice when you read the recommendations that NICE makes that they differentiate between recommendations made for adults and recommendation made for children.

Adults

Antidepressants: NICE recommends that patients should be advised verbally and in writing of the following: (1) craving and tolerance do not occur when taking antidepressants; (2) discontinuation/withdrawal effects may occur when the patient stops taking the drug, misses a dose or reduces the dose; (3) there are a range of possible side effects associated with taking antidepressants (including worsening anxiety, suicidal thoughts and self-harm), and that these need to be carefully monitored during the first few weeks of taking the medication; (4) the onset of a therapeutic benefit can be delayed by 12 weeks (although symptoms of depression can improve earlier than this); (5) taking medication should not be viewed as a sign of weakness.

Selective Serotonin Reuptake Inhibitors (SSRIs): NICE recommends that individuals with OCD with a mild functional impairment who have not responded to a low intensity treatment (e.g., brief (10 hours) individual CBT including exposure and response prevention (ERP) using self-help materials or over the phone, or group CBT including ERP) should be offered the choice between a course of a SSRI or more intensive CBT including ERP. This choice should be offered in the first instance to individuals who are unable to engage in CBT or who have a moderate level of functional impairment arising from their OCD.

NICE recommends that prescribing clinicians consider other medications that the patient is taking as there is a risk of drug interactions. Furthermore, patients should be monitored for suicidal thoughts and/or self-harm on a regular, appropriate basis. If patients have a significant risk of suicide, a limited amount of SSRIs should be prescribed, and, if appropriate, further support should be arranged, such as regular direct contact with primary care staff or telephone calls. Suicide risk should also be monitored if the dose of SSRIs is altered. NICE recommends that SSRI use should be reviewed if the patient exhibits marked or prolonged restlessness or agitation.

If a patient is unresponsive to a SSRI NICE recommends that, after checking that the prescribed dose has been taken, and that there is no interference from alcohol or substance misuse, a gradual increase in the dose of the SSRI should be considered in line with the **Summary of Product Characteristics**. When increasing the dose of a SSRI, clinicians should be mindful of the therapeutic response, adverse effects and the patient's preference. If a patient shows clinically significant benefit from a SSRI, NICE recommends that the SSRI should be continued for at least 12 months to avoid relapse and to allow for any further benefit. If a decision is made to continue the SSRI after this 12 months, regular review should be implemented. When a decision is made to stop a SSRI (either because there is no longer a clinical need (and 12 months of continued treatment post-remission has been administered) or because the patient/doctor wishes to stop the treatment because of adverse effects) the dose should be gradually reduced over several weeks according to the patient's needs. Things to take into account include the starting dose, the drug half-life and the particular profile of adverse effects. NICE recommends that doctors advise patients to seek advice if they experience significant withdrawal/discontinuation symptoms.

Tricyclics: NICE recommends that the tricyclic Clomipramine should be considered if any of the following apply: (1) an adequate trial of at least one SSRI proved ineffective; (2) the SSRI was poorly tolerated (i.e. it was accompanied by adverse side effects); (3) the patient has a preference for clomipramine; (4) the patient showed a previous good effect when taking clomipramine. There is an increased risk of cardiovascular problems associated with clomipramine, and consequently, NICE recommends that if a patient is at risk of cardiovascular disease an **electrocardiogram** and blood pressure measurement should be obtained before deciding whether to prescribe clomipramine. It is also important, as with SSRIs, to assess suicide risk. If the patient is at a significant risk of suicide, the prescribed dose should be small because of the toxicity of clompiramine in overdose.

If the patient does not show improvement after an adequate trial of clomipramine, NICE recommends that the clinician considers increasing the dose in line with the Summary of Product Characteristics. Conversely, NICE recommends that if a patient has shown therapeutic benefit from clomipramine it should be continued for at least 12 months to allow for further improvement. NICE recommends that clomipramine treatment is reduced slowly to minimize potential discontinuation/withdrawal symptoms.

Prescribing medication for children and adolescents with OCD

Selective Serotonin Reuptake Inhibitors (SSRIs): For children and young people (under 18) who have moderate to severe OCD and have not shown improvements in their OCD symptoms following a full trial of CBT (including ERP, lasting for 12 weeks, and including their caregiver where appropriate) (see Chapter 7), NICE recommends that following a *multi-disciplinary review*, a selective serotonin reuptake inhibitor (SSRI) should be offered. Currently, the only two SSRIs licensed for use in the UK in children are fluvoxamine and sertraline. If a child has *comorbid* depression, then fluoxetine (Prozac) should be prescribed, and the NICE guidelines for managing childhood depression should also be followed. Antidepressants should be prescribed alongside CBT with ERP.

There is some evidence indicating that children may be at an increased risk of feeling suicidal and engaging in self-harm behaviours when they are taking antidepressants. Consequently, NICE recommends that (1) all children taking antidepressants are carefully monitored by their psychiatrist; (2) parents and young people are informed about the possibility that the child may feel suicidal, engage in self-harm or self-neglect; (3) parents and young people are advised on what to if such behaviours or thoughts do occur (the child's medical practitioner should be contacted urgently, or they should go straight to A&E in an emergency); (4) maximum recommended doses for children should not be exceeded.

Tricyclics: Clomipramine is recommended by NICE for consideration when a child has failed to show improvements in the OCD symptoms after taking SSRIs (bearing in mind that this needs to be long enough to allow for a delay of 6–12 weeks in symptoms improvement after beginning the SSRI treatment). Despite this, NICE guidance suggests that there is not very good quality evidence that clomipramine gives much benefit to young people with OCD, and it is not currently licensed for use in children. However, sometimes the clinical need is so great – the child may be showing severe symptoms, high levels of distress, and no improvement with CBT or SSRIs – that psychiatrists will prescribe clomipramine.

Other forms of medication: NICE does not recommend the use of antipsychotics as routine treatment for OCD in children and young people. However, NICE suggests that antipsychotics can be considered as part of augmentation therapy (i.e., prescribed alongside a SSRI).

Non-drug physical interventions

While pharmacological and psychological treatments can help to reduce the majority of individuals' OCD symptoms, a smaller group of patients do not show improvements. For individuals with chronic, severe OCD, life can become unbearable. Case History 8.2 details one anonymous individual's experience of living with treatment-resistant OCD. In such cases, more invasive procedures may be considered. NICE does not recommend **neurosurgery** for individuals with OCD, but in rare cases, neurosurgery in the form of **anterior cingulotomy** is performed in an attempt to manage OCD that has not responded to first line treatments.

Case History 8.2

A 25 year-old male university student, who developed OCD during his childhood, had been experiencing very severe OCD for approximately four years. He found himself in a cycle of self-harming when his OCD became unbearable and subsequent psychiatric hospital admissions. Lots of different therapeutic approaches were tried in the hope of relieving the OCD symptoms – outpatient and inpatient OCD psychological therapy, sessions alone, with his family, and in a group, medication and combinations of medication. The young man's OCD, and the attempted treatments, significantly interfered with his studies and took over his social life.

Other techniques have also been used in cases of severe, treatment-resistant OCD including **electroconvulsive therapy** (ECT), **deep brain stimulation** (DBS) and *transcranial magnetic stimulation* (TMS). The evidence for these alternative treatment methods being effective is not sufficient enough for NICE to recommend them. What is more, in some cases, not enough is known about the potential side effects. In this section, we will explore the options for those individuals with OCD who cannot be helped by drugs or psychotherapy.

Neurosurgery

Neurosurgery has a murky past – on the one hand, a Nobel Prize was awarded to Egas Moniz, the neurologist who pioneered frontal leucotomy (lobotomy), on the other hand, hundreds of patients died during or after such surgery, due to imprecise methods, infection and complications.

Nowadays, neurosurgery for OCD is a final resort, and is only recommended when significant effort has been put into treatment using more conventional pharmacological and psychological therapies. Outcomes for patients have drastically improved, with very few patients who undergo these procedures dying. What is more, surgical techniques have improved, as have brain imaging techniques, which allow neurosurgeons to be more precise. Importantly, great progress has been made in the implementation of informed consent – patients must understand the possible benefits and risks of a procedure, and then decide whether they want to undergo the procedure, or not. Neurosurgery isn't commonly carried out in the treatment of OCD in the UK, and is only conducted at two sites: Dundee and Cardiff. You can read more about the service provided by the Ninewells Hospital & Medical School in Dundee on their website: http://www.advancedinterventions.org.uk/.

Anterior cingulotomy

There are different neurosurgical procedures that can be conducted, but the most commonly used in Europe is anterior cingulotomy, and so we will focus on that here. Cingulotomy is a surgical procedure that involves creating a lesion in the anterior cingulate gyrus. The technique was initially developed to help individuals with intractable pain, but it was observed that the patients who also suffered from anxiety or depression had the best outcomes, and consequently its efficacy for psychiatric problems was explored (Greenberg, Rauch & Haber, 2010). The cingulotomy procedure is performed by creating **burr holes** in the side of the skull using drills, and then inserting thin electrodes. The procedure is carried out under general anaesthetic. The electrodes are guided **stereotactically**, or, more recently by **magnetic resonance imaging** (MRI). The tips of the electrodes are then heated to around 80–85°C, which destroys the surrounding brain cells in a process known as thermocoagulation. Surgeons begin by creating a small lesion, but if this proves unsuccessful in treating the patient's OCD, more surgery may be undertaken to enlarge the lesion.

Greenberg et al. (2010) report that since 1962, over 1000 cingulotomies have been performed at Massachusetts Hospital in the United States. Dougherty et al. (2002) investigated the efficacy of cingulotomy for OCD by following up 44 patients who had undergone the procedure. The patients had severe, treatment-refractory OCD prior to the cingulotomy. In order to be deemed eligible for the surgery, each patient had undergone pharmacotherapy (at least 10 weeks of at least 3 SSRIs, plus for one of the SSRIs, at least one month of augmentation with two of the following: lithium, clonazepam, buspirone or a neuroleptic) and psychotherapy (a trial of CBT that included at least 20 hours of exposure and response prevention). Dougherty et al. (2002) reported that 32 per cent (14/44) of patients were treatment responders to the cingulotomy, and 14 per cent (6/14) were partial responders. Side effects were observed in 20 per cent (9/44) of patients, and included memory deficits and seizures.

Electroconvulsive Therapy (ECT)

One of the most well-known kinds of non-drug physical interventions used in the treatment of mental illness is ECT. 'No publicity is bad publicity', or so the saying goes. Unfortunately, when it comes to ECT and public opinion, this does not seem to have been the case. ECT received a grim portrayal in 'One Flew Over the Cuckoo's Nest', featuring Jack Nicholson. It was a portrayal that was described by Dr Susan Benbow, spokesperson for The Royal College of Psychiatrists, as 'doing for shock therapy what "Jaws" did for sharks'. As a result, this treatment has never quite recovered from the publicity. Despite the general public's perception of ECT, in reality, thousands of people with treatment-resistant depression undergo ECT each year in the UK (Bickerton, Worrall & Chaplain, 2009).

ECT involves electrically inducing seizures while the patient is under anaesthetic and has been given a muscle-relaxant. The anaesthesia and muscle-relaxant, which have been used since the 1950s, mean that the horrific shuddering and convulsing portrayed by Jack Nicholson simply does not happen when patients undergo ECT these days. However, it is not without risk, and some patients who undergo ECT experience side effects including memory deficits. In a large, prospective, longitudinal study of individuals with Major Depressive Disorder, Sackeim et al. (2007) found that individuals who received ECT were significantly more likely to have deficits in both short-term and long-term memory six months after receiving ECT compared to individuals who had not received ECT. While ECT is endorsed by NICE for treatment-resistant depression, there is less convincing evidence for its use with patients who have OCD.

There have been very few studies of ECT in OCD, and those that do exist are case reports, rather than RCTs. Maletzky, McFarland & Burt (1994) administered ECT to 34 patients with refractory OCD and reported improvements in OCD symptomatology that were maintained at a 1-year follow-up. However, this study did not include a control group who did not receive ECT, and consequently it is difficult to draw conclusions about the usefulness of ECT at treating OCD.

Repetitive Transcranial Magnetic Stimulation (rTMS)

Repetitive Transcranial Magnetic Stimulation (rTMS) is a non-invasive method for stimulating cortical regions. In rTMS, a pulse of electrical current is sent through a magnetic coil, which induces a magnetic field in the area beneath the coil. The electrical pulse is strong enough to depolarize neurons that are superficial (i.e., near the surface/the skull) in a local area (i.e., with precision). Repetitive pulses are required to maintain the effect of the electrical current on the neurons. Given that neurocircuitry abnormalities have been identified in patients with OCD (see Chapter 6) it was hypothesized that rTMS might help to 'correct' this circuitry. In their review, Blom, Figee, Vulink & Denys (2012) report that rTMS has been used in patients with OCD in the following ways: (i) stimulation of the dorsolateral prefrontal cortex; (ii) inhibition of the orbitofrontal cortex; (iii) inhibition of the supplementary motor area.

A Cochrane Review of the efficacy of rTMS in OCD was first published in 2003 (Rodriguez-Martin, Barbanoj, Pérez & Sacristan, 2003). The review reported the results from three trials, two of which contained data that allowed quantitative analysis to be conducted. Rodriguez-Martin et al. (2003) found no significant difference in OCD symptomatology as measured by the Yale-Brown Obsessive Compulsive Scale (YBOCS) between rTMS and sham TMS. The authors concluded that there is currently insufficient evidence from RCTs to draw conclusions about the efficacy of rTMS in the treatment of OCD. However, there were limitations of the studies included in this review such as asymmetric stimulation (to the right or left side of the brain, only), limited stimulation sites (to the dorsolateral prefrontal cortex, only), and different stimulation frequencies used in the studies (Khalsa, Schiffman & Bystritsky, 2011). More recent RCTs have shown more favourable results. For example, Mantovani, Simpson, Fallon, Rossi & Lisanby (2010) administered either rTMS or sham TMS to 18 individuals with treatment-resistant OCD over a four-week period. After four weeks, 67 per cent of the group who received rTMS met criteria for responding to the treatment (defined by Mantovani et al. as a reduction of 25% on the YBOCS) compared to 22 per cent of the group who received sham rTMS. Furthermore, in a RCT with a longer follow-up period of three months, favourable results were also found for rTMS (Gomes, Brasil-Neto, Allam & de Souza, 2012). In Gomes et al.'s (2012) double-blind RCT, they found an average reduction in YBOCS scores of 35 per cent for individuals who had received rTMS compared to an average reduction of 6.2 per cent for individuals in the sham treatment condition. Interestingly, both the Mantovani et al. (2010) RCT and the Gomes et al. (2012) RCT used stimulation of the supplementary motor area, rather than the dorsolateral prefrontal cortex, and this highlights the importance of identifying the regions of the brain that are most likely to respond favourably to rTMS. However, Khalsa et al. (2011) argue that rTMS will always be a limited therapeutic technique for OCD because of its inability to penetrate deeper brain regions involved in the OCD neurocircuitry, such as the thalamus and the caudate nucleus.

Deep brain stimulation (DBS)

In a similar vein to ablative neurosurgery, deep brain stimulation (DBS) involves inserting small electrodes stereotactically guided by MRI. However, the advantage of DBS over neurosurgery is that this method is reversible, and the amount of neurostimulation can be adjusted.

Greenberg et al. (2010) reviewed the DBS studies conducted by four different centres. They examined the long-term follow-up data of

26 patients treated at these four centres. At the last follow-up (which was more than 36 months post-insertion) 73 per cent of patients had at least a 25 per cent improvement in their YBOCS score, and for the majority this improvement was equal to or greater than 35 per cent. Greenberg et al. (2010) found that results are more favourable for patients who have undergone DBS more recently, which, they argue, reflects the improvements that the teams at the centres are making as they learn from each implantation. For example, Greenberg et al. (2010) report that electrodes are being inserted at increasingly posterior sites.

However, there are potentially *serious adverse events* (SAEs) that can occur with DBS. Greenberg et al. (2010) classified SAEs as (1) 'procedure related' (i.e., as a result of the surgery); (2) 'device related' (i.e., due to the implanted device); (3) 'therapy-related' (i.e., occurring because of stimulation, or cessation of stimulation in patients for whom DBS was associated with a clinical benefit). There were 23 SAEs reported in 11 patients (42.3%), which accounted for a period of time that was equal to 52 patient years of experience. Two patients (7.7%) had small intracerebral haemorrhages (procedure related), and 1 patient (3.8%) required the stimulation lead/extension wire to be replaced (device related). Regarding therapy-related SAEs, three patients (11.5%) experienced worsening depression/suicidal ideation. However, these patients had experienced periods of depression/suicidal ideation before the insertion of the electrodes, and may represent part of these individuals' natural course of OCD, rather than be a consequence of the DBS. Three patients (11.5%) experienced worsening OCD symptoms, there was one case of serious hypomania, and another patient experienced domestic problems/irritability associated with stimulation. Yet, despite these reported SAEs, overall, Greenberg et al. (2010) conclude that DBS was well-tolerated, and the SAEs were transient. Indeed, Khalsa et al. (2011) report that the side effects observed in DBS typically go away when the stimulation is altered.

We do not fully understand how DBS helps some individuals with OCD. The emerging research seems to support the biological models of OCD that we read about in Chapter 6, such as neurocircuitry and neurotransmitter abnormalities. For example, it has been suggested by Figee, Luigjes et al. (2013) that DBS reduces OCD symptoms by restoring frontostriatal network activity, in part by reducing excessive connectivity between the nucleus accumbens and the prefrontal cortex. It has also been found that DBS can lead to the release of dopamine in the striatum (Figee, de Koning et al., 2013).

While DBS has been approved by NICE for use in movement disorders, such as Parkinson's disease, it has not yet been recommended for use in OCD. Nonetheless, there is growing interest in exploring DBS in psychiatric conditions, such as OCD. However, Ashkan, Shotbolt, David and Samuel (2013) acknowledge that more research is required to determine the patients that are most likely to respond to DBS, the best sites to target in the brain during DBS, the most effective stimulation parameters (e.g., frequency and intensity of stimulation), and the extent that individuals can expect to experience post-operative improvement.

Chapter summary

In this chapter we have learnt about the biological treatments that are currently available for people with OCD. Generally, these treatments are only considered after the individual has undergone cognitive behavioural therapy with exposure and response prevention (see Chapter 7), although antidepressants remain a NICE-endorsed first-line treatment option. We have seen that antidepressant medications can be successful for about 40–60% of people with OCD. When they are not successful, adding an antipsychotic can help in some cases. For individuals who have not responded to psychological or pharmacological treatments, other options include repetitive transcranial magnetic stimulation and deep brain stimulation, although the evidence for these being effective treatments is not conclusive at this point in time. There is not very good evidence for electroconvulsive therapy. In very rare and severe cases, neurosurgery can help some people. With all biological treatments there are potentially negative side effects, and these must be weighed up against any potential benefit. The future of biological treatments will likely be informed by a better understanding of genetics, which may help us to understand which treatments are most likely to be effective for particular individuals.

Section Three Summary

In this final section we have examined treatment of OCD including psychological approaches to treatment and biological and pharmacological treatments. Chapter 7 examined different psychological approaches to the treatment of OCD. There is evidence suggesting that ERP is a useful tool in the treatment of OCD. However, ERP can be difficult and distressing for some people, which may mean that they drop out of treatment. Cognitive Therapy (CT) for OCD has also been found to be effective, although some evidence suggests that ERP shows greater therapeutic gains at a one year follow-up when compared to CT. The NICE guidelines currently recommend CBT that includes ERP as a treatment for OCD. Other psychological treatment approaches for OCD include Metacognitive therapy and E-Therapy. Both of these approaches are being assessed for their efficacy in the treatment of OCD. There are some published results that support both of these approaches in the treatment of OCD, but there is not yet enough evidence to indicate whether or not they are useful treatment approaches. The final part of Chapter 7 discussed Psychodynamic treatment approaches to OCD and concluded that there is no evidence that this approach can offer therapeutic gains for the treatment of OCD.

In Chapter 8 we looked at biological and pharmacological treatments of OCD. To decide whether or not a specific pharmacological agent is a useful treatment for OCD, a Randomised Control Trial (RCT) may be used to assess the effectiveness of the drug as compared to a placebo. NICE recommends antidepressant medication in the treatment of OCD and these medications can be useful for about 40–60 per cent of people. Other approaches include repetitive transcranial magnetic stimulation and deep brain stimulation, although the evidence for these being effective treatments is currently inconclusive. In some rare and very severe cases, neurosurgery can help some people, but as with all biological treatments there are potentially negative side effects, and these must be weighed up against any potential benefit.

Epilogue

Whether you are a student, a clinician, a researcher or an interested layperson, this book has attempted to provide you with an accessible insight into OCD, its symptoms, its causes and its treatment. Just as in other branches of science, we are continually finding new ways to understand OCD, and discovering more effective ways of treating it, and these endeavours will continue for many more years to come. These are significant and important endeavours because, for the individual with a diagnosis of OCD, their symptoms are distressing and disabling and we are still some way from developing interventions and treatments that will significantly benefit everyone with OCD symptoms.

In the most recent edition of the Diagnostic & Statistical Manual (DSM-5, 2013) the importance of OCD as a significant mental health problem was recognized with OCD being allocated its own chapter, elevating it to a status equivalent to anxiety disorders, depressive disorders and schizophrenia spectrum disorders. For many people OCD is a lifelong affliction, and one that will significantly affect that person's quality of life, their productivity and their relationships with others. In this respect, there is an urgency to understand more about the conditions that give rise to OCD symptoms, to help sufferers identify their problems at an early stage and receive prompt advice and support, and to develop interventions that sufferers feel happy to engage with and will enable them to make as full a recovery as possible.

There are many research questions that continue to be asked about OCD where answers will provide significant insights into OCD and its treatment. We reckon that some of these include the following: (1) why do OCD symptoms normally have such a gradual onset? (2) What role do life stressors play in the onset of OCD symptoms? (3) Are there certain conditions (e.g. autistic spectrum disorder) that make people specifically vulnerable to developing OCD? (4) Many OCD-related disorders have been identified (see Chapter 3), do these disorders have causal factors in common with OCD? (5) Various cognitive constructs have been developed to help understand how cognitive factors may influence the development of OCD symptoms (see Chapter 4), but how can these different constructs be integrated to form a single, coherent model of OCD? (6) Are those neurobiological factors that have been found to be associated with OCD symptoms (e.g. differences in brain neurotransmitter levels and brain functioning, see Chapter 6) causes of OCD, or merely consequences of having developed OCD symptoms? (7) Pharmacological treatments for OCD are largely ones that were developed either to treat depression or psychosis (Chapter 8) – is the development of an effective drug treatment specifically for OCD symptoms a possibility? And (8) One of the main psychological interventions for OCD is Exposure & Response Prevention (ERP, see Chapter 7), yet many people drop out of this treatment programme, can it be developed to improve retention?

OCD is complex and enduring, but significant progress has been made in understanding and treating the disorder over the past 30 years. This has provided us with an important springboard from which to further our knowledge of this disabling mental health problem.

Glossary

12-month prevalence The number of people in a statistical population that in the previous 12 months have experienced a particular condition, disease or disorder.

agonist A substance that binds to a receptor and enhances the normal cell activity level.

alleles Two or more different genes that may occupy the same locus on a specific chromosome.

anal stage of development In Freud's psychosexual stages of development, the second stage, from 18 months to 3 years in which the child obtains pleasure through expelling and withholding faeces.

animal hoarding Acquiring and keeping larger than usual numbers of animals as pets without having the ability to properly house or care for them.

anterior cingulate cortex The frontal part of the cingulate cortex resembling a 'collar' form around the corpus callosum, used for the relay of neural signals between the right and left hemispheres of the brain.

anterior cingulotomy A surgical procedure that involves creating a lesion in the anterior cingulate gyrus.

antidepressant drugs Drug treatments intended to treat symptoms of depression and mood disorder.

antipsychotic drugs Drug treatments intended to treat symptoms of psychosis and schizophrenia.

attentional biases The presence of differential responding towards threat and neutral stimuli

augmentation Adding a treatment to an existing treatment.

autogenous thoughts Thoughts that seem to come 'out of the blue'.

basal ganglia A series of structures located deep in the brain responsible for motor movements.
Behaviourism A theory of human and animal behaviour based on the idea that all behaviours are acquired through conditioning.
biochemistry Chemical processes within living organisms.
body dysmorphic disorder Preoccupation with assumed defects in physical appearance.
burr holes A surgical intervention in which holes are made in the skull using a drill.
candidate gene analysis The study of whether specific genes are associated with a phenotype, including psychological disorders.
cerebrospinal fluid (CSF) A clear bodily fluid produced, which fills the ventricles and cavities in the brain, as well as the spinal cord.
checking compulsions See compulsive checking.
classical conditioning The learning of an association between two stimuli, the first of which (the conditioned stimulus, CS) predicts the occurrence of the second (the unconditioned stimulus, UCS).
cleaning compulsions A manifestation of OCD in which a person excessively and repeatedly needs to confirm that they have removed possible sources of contamination.
cognitive behaviour therapy (CBT) An intervention for changing both thoughts and behaviour. CBT represents an umbrella term for many different therapies that share the common aim of changing both cognitions and behaviour.
comorbidity The co-occurrence of two or more distinct disorders.
compulsions Repetitive or ritualized behaviour patterns that the individual feels driven to perform in order to prevent a negative outcome.
compulsive checking The ritualised and persistent checking of items such as locks, switches and appliances to ensure they are secure and safe.
compulsive rituals Repetitive behaviour patterns that the individual feels driven to perform in order to prevent some negative outcome happening.
conceptual processing Processing based on the semantic meaning of the object.
contamination fear See Fear of contamination.
contamination-related OCD See Fear of contamination.
cost-effectiveness Economical in terms of the outcome obtained based on the money spent.
countertransference The response elicited in the recipient (the psychoanalyst) by the other's (patient's) unconscious transference communications.

deep brain stimulation (DBS) A form of treatment initially approved for Parkinson's disease, which uses a surgically implanted, battery-operated device called a neurostimulator to deliver electrical stimulation to cortical, midbrain or thalamic areas of the brain.

defence mechanism In psychoanalysis, the means by which individuals attempt to control conflict between the id, ego and superego and also reduce stress and conflict from external events.

Diagnostic & Statistical Manual (DSM) An American Psychiatric Association handbook for mental health professionals that lists different types of mental health problems and the criteria for diagnosing them.

dichotic listening task Presentation of a stimulus to one ear that differs in some respect from a stimulus presented to the other ear.

disgust A food-rejection emotion whose purpose is to prevent the transmission of illness and disease through the oral incorporation of contaminated item.

disgust sensitivity The perceived negative impact of experiencing disgust.

ecological validity The extent to which conditions simulated in the laboratory reflect real-life conditions.

ego In psychoanalysis, a rational part of the psyche that attempts to control the impulses of the id.

electrocardiogram A psychophysiological measurement technique used for measuring heart rate.

electroconvulsive therapy (ECT) A method of treatment for depression or psychosis, first devised in the 1930s, which involves applying 70–130 volts through the head of the patient for around half a second.

epidemiology The study of the patterns, frequencies and causes of health and health disorders in the population.

epigenetics The study of changes in gene expression, which do not alter the underlying DNA.

excoriation disorder (skin picking) A chronic and compulsive urge to pick skin and scabs that leads to tissue damage.

executive function Cognitive skill that involves problem-solving, planning and attentional control.

exposure and response prevention (ERP) A technique often used in cognitive behaviour therapy for OCD where the person with OCD confronts the thoughts or situation that makes them feel uncomfortable (exposure) without employing the accompanying compulsive behaviour that usually results in only short term anxiety reduction.

family studies Studies in which researchers have compared the probability with which offspring of an individual with symptoms indicative of a psychopathology also develop these symptoms in order to assess genetic contributions to that psychopathology.

fear hierarchy A list of situations that trigger anxiety graded from the least to the most anxiety provoking.

fear of contamination Fear of being exposed to germs, disease or other contaminating substances that may cause illness to oneself or others.

formulation A theoretically based conceptualization or explanation of the information that is given about a case during an assessment.

fractional anisotropy A value between zero and one that indicates the extent that water molecules are restricted in their movement.

functional abnormalities In studies of the brain, acting in a different way to a specific role usually performed by a brain region.

functional magnetic resonance imaging (fMRI) A development of MRI technology that allows the clinician or researcher to take brain images so quickly that tiny changes in brain metabolism can be detected and can provide minute-to-minute information about actual brain activity.

generalized anxiety disorder A pervasive condition in which the sufferer experiences continual apprehension and anxiety about future events, which leads to chronic and pathological worrying about those events.

genes A hereditary unit consisting of a sequence of DNA that occupies a particular location on a specific chromosome.

genetic polymorphisms The occurrence of different versions of a gene in different individuals.

genetics The branch of science that deals with heredity.

genome-wide complex trait analysis (GCTA) A method for examining the contribution to variation in a complex trait from SNPs on a chromosome or in the entire genome.

genome-wide linkage studies Analyses involving comparisons of the inheritance of characteristics for which gene location is known (e.g., eye colour) with the inheritance of symptoms of psychopathology.

glial cells Cells that support neurons and regulate the brain environment.

glutamate A major mediator of excitatory signals in the mammalian central nervous system that plays a role in many important brain processes, including cognition, learning, and memory.

GPs with a special interest in mental health A General Practitioner doctor who has undergone specialist training in supporting individuals with mental health problems.

gray matter Brain tissue containing neuronal cells, as well as glial cells, unmyelinated axons, dendrites and capillaries. Gray matter is part of the central nervous system.

habituation A decrease in response to a stimulus after repeated presentations.

heritable The proportion of a trait that is passed from one generation to another due to genetic and environmental factors.

hoarding disorder A pattern of behaviour that is associated with the excessive acquisition of and the inability or unwillingness to discard large quantities of objects that may cover living areas and create health problems.

hypnosis A therapeutic technique in which the patient is placed in a trance.

id In psychoanalysis, the concept used to describe innate instinctual needs – especially sexual needs.

immediate enhancement effect An increase in the frequency of a suppressed thought during a period of thought suppression.

implicit memory biases Non-conscious recollection of information that is either enhanced or impaired for example for emotional material.

inflated responsibility The belief that one has power to bring about or prevent subjectively crucial negative outcomes. These outcomes are perceived as essential to prevent. They may be actual, that is, having consequences in the real world, and/or at a moral level.

International List of Causes of Death (ICD) The international standard diagnostic classification developed by the World Health Organization (WHO).

interpretation biases Cognitive biases in which an individual interprets ambiguous events as threatening and evidence for potential negative outcomes.

intolerance of uncertainty A cognitive bias that affects how a person perceives, interprets, and responds to uncertain situations.

knockout mice Mice used for research purposes in which researchers have knocked out or inactivated a particular gene.

Learning Theory The body of knowledge encompassing principles of classical and operant conditioning (and which is frequently applied to explaining and treating psychopathology).

lesions A pathological change in bodily tissue that can be caused by wound or injury.

lifetime prevalence The number of people in a statistical population that at some point in their life have experienced a particular condition, disease or disorder.

longitudinal studies Research which takes measures from the same participants at two or more different times in order to specify the time relationships between variables. This may extend over many years or even over a participant's whole lifetime.

magnetic resonance imaging (MRI) A neuroimaging technique which involves the participant being placed inside a large circular magnet that causes the hydrogen atoms in the body to move. This produces an electromagnetic signal that is converted by the scanner's computer into visual pictures of the brain.

memory biases A cognitive bias that either enhances or impairs the recall of a memory.

meta-analyses Statistically accepted ways of assessing the strength of a particular finding across a number of different studies.

metacognitive model A hypothesis claiming that the way people think about their own mental processes can become biased and lead to emotional distress.

metacognitive therapy (MCT) Therapeutic approach for OCD that challenges people's metacognitive beliefs about the importance of intrusive thoughts.

mood-as-input model A hypothesis claiming that people use their concurrent mood as information about whether they have successfully completed a task or not.

muscle dysmorphia A disorder in which a person becomes obsessed with the idea that he or she is not muscular enough.

mutually exclusive When only one of two or more possibilities etc. can exist at any one time.

myelinated axons Nerve cells covered in myelin, a fatty insulating layer.

National Institute for Health and Clinical Excellence (NICE) An independent UK organization responsible for providing national guidance on promoting good health and preventing and treating ill health.

neutralizing behaviours An effortful cognitive or behavioural act aimed at removing or preventing an intrusive thought and discomfort caused by the thought.

not just right experiences An uncomfortable sensation of things being not right and a drive to perform an action until this uncomfortable sensation is reduced, or until a sense of perfection is achieved.

neurocircuitry The study of neural mapping.

neurons Excitable cells of the nervous system that can transmit information through chemical and electrical activity.

neurosurgery A medical specialty focusing on disorders affecting the nervous system. Interventions include brain operations.

neurotransmitters Chemicals that transmit messages from a neuron to a target cell in a vesicle across a synapse.

non-mendelian inheritance A pattern of genetic inheritance that does not conform to Mendel's laws of inheritance.

noradrenaline A neurotransmitter and a hormone. Also known as norepinephrine.

obsessions/obsessive thoughts Intrusive and recurring thoughts that an individual finds disturbing and uncontrollable.

obsessive-compulsive personality disorder (OCPD) A personality disorder in which individuals show exceptionally perfectionist tendencies including a preoccupation with orderliness and control at the expense of flexibility, efficiency and productivity.

onychophagia Compulsive nail biting.

operant conditioning The learning of a specific behaviour or response because that behaviour has certain consequence.

orbitofrontal cortex A region of the prefrontal cortex that is involved in decision-making.

paediatric autoimmune neuropsychiatric disorders associated with streptococcal infections (PANDAS) A proposed condition in which OCD symptoms develop in children who have been exposed to group A beta-hemolytic streptococcal infections.

parietal cortex Part of the parietal lobe, it plays a role in cognition, planning, sensory integration, and spatial orientation. It projects to the dorsolateral prefrontal cortex and the motor areas.

penetrance The proportion of individuals who have a particular allele and also display an associated trait.

perceptual processing Processing based on physical features of stimuli.

perfectionism The setting of excessively high standards for performance accompanied by overly critical self-evaluation.

placebo-controlled A methodological approach used in clinical trials that involves including a control condition to assess the effects of participant expectations.

point prevalence The proportion of a population that has a particular condition, disease or disorder at a specific point in time.

positron emission tomography (PET) A neuroimaging technique which scans to allow measurement of both brain structure and function by utilizing radiation emitted from the participant to develop images.

postsynaptic neuron A dendrite or cell body of a neuron to which a chemical message is transmitted from the presynaptic neuron in the form of a neurotransmitter across a synapse.

presynaptic neuron A neuron terminal axon which transmits a chemical message to the dendrite or cell body of a postsynaptic neuron in the form of a neurotransmitter across a synapse.

prevalence rate The proportion of a population found to have a particular disease, condition or disorder, computed by comparing the number of people with the condition with the total number of people studied.

proband In genetics, an individual exhibiting a condition that brings their family under study.

procedural memory Long term memory of how to perform different actions and skills.

psychiatrist A medical doctor who has undergone specialist training in mental disorders.

psychodynamic approach Theory which assumes that unconscious conflicts develop early in life. Part of the therapy is designed to identify life events that may have caused these unconscious conflicts.

psychosexual stages of development In psychoanalytic theory, five stages of development (oral, anal, phallic, latency, genital). Each stage is characterized by the erogenous zone that gives rise to the instinctual libido. It is proposed that fixation occurs at any stage where unresolved conflicts arise.

radiotracers A radioactive isotope (atoms of the same element with different masses and unstable nuclei) that can be tracked by measuring emitted radiation from the isotope in the form of alpha, beta or gamma rays.

randomized controlled trial (RCT) A procedure for assessing the effectiveness of therapies by comparing the effectiveness of the treatment being assessed (using objective measures) with a control condition, and with other forms of therapy or treatment (if necessary).

rebound effect An increase in frequency of a thought after a period of thought suppression.

receptors A protein molecule that typically exists on the surface of a cell and receives chemical signals from outside the cell.

replicable Results of research which have been collected under controlled conditions that will allow any other researcher to reproduce those exact conditions.

schema A cognitive framework or system that helps to organize and interpret information.

scrupulosity A form of OCD involving religious or moral obsessions.

semantic memory Part of the long-term memory responsible for storing meaning, such as meanings of words and general knowledge.

side effect profile The unintended, unexpected or adverse effects associated with a particular treatment. Usually in reference to drug treatments.

simple tics Abrupt, sudden, and brief movements, occurring in single and isolated fashion.

single-nucleotide polymorphisms (SNPs) In genetics, a difference between two genomes that is based on deletion, insertion, or exchange of a single nucleotide.

single-photon emission computer tomography (SPECT) An imaging technique in which radiotracers emitting gamma rays are administered and then detected using cameras rotated around the individual's body. The two-dimensional images of internal structures are combined to provide a three-dimensional image.

spontaneous remission The fact that many people who have psychological disorders will simply get better anyway over a period of time, even without therapy.

stepped care approach Stepped Care is a system of delivering and monitoring treatments, so that the most effective yet least resource intensive, treatment is delivered to patients first.

stepped-care model A treatment approach that emphasizes that the type of treatment provided should be tailored to the severity of an individual's symptoms and their personal and social circumstances.

stereotactically In neurosurgery, a method (usually guided by imaging techniques) for locating a precise position in the brain.

structural abnormalities In neuroanatomy, when a structure of the brain is altered.

Summary of Product Characteristics A document required by European Law before a medicine can be licensed detailing the drug's properties and clinical use.

superego In psychoanalysis, a development from both the id and ego which represents our attempts to integrate 'values' that we learn from our parents or society.

synaptic cleft A small space between two neurons, across which neurotransmitters travel.

the Rat Man A case history document by Sigmund Freud in which a young man develops rituals to prevent his fear that rats will burrow into the anus of his loved ones from occurring.

thought action fusion A dysfunctional assumption held by OCD sufferers that having a thought about an action is like performing it.

thought suppression A defence mechanism used by individuals with obsessive thoughts to actively suppress them (using either thought suppression or distraction techniques).

tic disorder Uncontrollable physical movements such as facial twitches, rapid blinking or twitches of the mouth.

Tourette's syndrome A disorder in which motor and vocal tics occur frequently throught the day for atleast 1 year.

transdiagnostic construct Psychological construct that is present across a number of psychological disorders.

transference A technique used in psychoanalysis where the analyst is used as a target for emotional responses: clients behave towards the analyst as they would have behaved towards an important person in their lives.

trichotillomania (hair-pulling disorder) An irresistible urge to pull out one's own hair.

tricyclic antidepressants Antidepressant drugs developed in the 1960s which have their effect by increasing the amount of noradrenaline and serotonin available for synaptic transmission.

twin studies Studies in which researchers have compared the probability with which monozygotic (MZ) and dizygotic (DZ) twins both develop symptoms indicative of a psychopathology in order to assess genetic contributions to that psychopathology.

undoing A psychoanalytic defence mechanism occurring when an individual is compelled to carry out a behaviour/thought with the goal of preventing/undoing the anticipated consequences.

vesicles In the synapse these store neurotransmitters, which are released into the synaptic cleft.

waitlist control The use of patients who are on a waiting list for treatment as a no treatment control condition in treatment outcome studies.

white matter Brain tissue consisting of glial cells and myelinated axons, which form part of the central nervous system.

References

Abramowitz, J. S. (2006). The psychological treatment of obsessive-compulsive disorder. *Canadian Journal of Psychiatry,* 51, 407–416.

Abramowitz, J. S., Deacon, B. J., Woods, C. M. & Tolin, D. F. (2004) Association between Protestant religiosity and obsessive-compulsive symptoms and cognitions. *Depression & Anxiety*, 20, 70–76.

Abramowitz, J. S., Huppert, J. D., Cohen, A. B., Tolin, D. F. & Cahill, S. P. (2002). Religious obsessions and compulsions in a non-clinical sample: The Penn Inventory of Scrupulosity (PIOS). *Behaviour Research and Therapy,* 40, 825–838.

Abramowitz, J. S., Tolin, D. F. & Street, G. P. (2001). Paradoxical effects of thought suppression: A meta-analysis of controlled studies. *Clinical Psychology Review,* 21, 683–703.

Abramowitz, J. S., Whiteside, S. P. & Deacon, B. J. (2005). The effectiveness of treatment for pediatric obsessive-compulsive disorder: A meta-analysis. *Behavior Therapy,* 36, 55–63.

Abramowitz, J. S., Whiteside, S. P., Lynam, D. & Kalsy, S. A. (2003). Is thought-action fusion specific to obsessive-compulsive disorder: A mediating role of negative affect. *Behaviour Research and Therapy*, 41, 1069–1079.

Ackerman, D. L. & Greenland, S. (2002). Multivariate meta-analysis of controlled drug studies for obsessive compulsive disorder. *Journal of Clinical Psychopharmacology*, 22, 309–317.

Albert, U., Maina, G., Forner, F. & Bogetto, F. (2004). DSM-IV obsessive-compulsive personality disorder: Prevalence in patients with anxiety disorders and in healthy comparison subjects. *Comprehensive Psychiatry*, 45(5), 325–332.

American Psychiatric Association. (2000). *Diagnostic and Statistical Manual of Mental Disorders: DSM-IV-TR®*. Washington, DC: Author.

American Psychiatric Association (2013) *Diagnostic & Statistical Manual of Mental Disorders*. Fifth Edition.

Amir, N., Najmi, S. & Morrison, A. (2009). Attenuation of attention bias in obsessive-compulsive disorder. *Behaviour Research and Therapy*, 47(2), 153–157.

Andersson, E., Ljótsson, B., Hedman, E., Kaldo, V., Paxling, B., Andersson, G., Lindefors, N. & Rück, C. (2011). Internet-based cognitive behavior therapy for obsessive compulsive disorder: A pilot study. *BMC Psychiatry*, 11, 125.

Andrews, G., Stewart, G., Allen, R. & Henderson, A. S. (1990). The genetics of six neurotic disorders: A twin study. *Journal of Affective Disorders*, 19, 23–29.

Aouizerate, B., Pujol, H., Grabot, D., Faytout, M., Suire, K., Braud, C., Auriacombe, M., Martin, D., Baudet, J. & Tignol, J. (2003) Body dysmorphic disorder in a sample of cosmetic surgery applicants. *European Psychiatry*, 18, 365–368.

Arnold, P. D., Rosenberg, D. R., Munds, E., Tharmalingam, S., Kennedy, J. L. & Richter, M. A. (2004). Association of a glutamate (NMDA) subunit receptor gene (GRIN2B) with obsessive-compulsive disorder: A preliminary study. *Psychopharmacology*, 174, 530–538.

Arnold, P. D., Sicard, T., Burroughs, E., Richter, M. A. & Kennedy, J. L. (2006). Glutamate transporter gene SLC1A1 associated with obsessive-compulsive disorder. *Arch Gen Psychiatry*, 63(7), 769–776.

Ashkan, K., Shotbolt, P., David, A. S. & Samuel, M. (2013). Deep brain stimulation: A return journey from psychiatry to neurology. *Postgraduate Medical Journal*, 89, 323–328.

Baxter, L. R., Saxena, S., Brody, A. L., Ackermann, R. F., Colgan, M., Schwartz, J. M., Allen-Martinez, Z., Fuster, J. M. & Phelps, M. E. (1996). Brain medication of obsessive-compulsive symptoms: Evidence from functional brain imaging studies in the human and nonhuman primate. *Semin Clin Neuropsychiatry*, 1, 32–47.

Bejerot, S. (2007) An autistic dimension: A proposed subtype of obsessive-compulsive disorder. *Autism*, 11, 101–110.

Belloch, A., Morillo, C., Lucero, M., Cabedo, E. & Carrio, C. (2004). Intrusive thoughts in non-clinical subjects: The role of frequency and unpleasantness on appraisal ratings and control strategies. *Clinical Psychology and Psychotherapy, 11*, 100–110.

Berry, L. M. & Laskey, B. (2012). A review of obsessive intrusive thoughts in the general population. *Journal of Obsessive-Compulsive and Related Disorders, 1*, 125–132.

Bickerton, D., Worrall, A. & Chaplain, R. (2009). Trends in the administration of electroconvulsive therapy in England. *The Psychiatrist,* 33, 61–63.

Blaya, C., Dornelles, M., Blaya, R., Kipper, L., Heldt, E., Isolan, L., Bond, M. & Manfro, G. G. (2006). Do defense mechanisms vary according to the psychiatric disorder? *Revista Brasileira de Psiquiatria*, 28(3), 179–183. Retrieved 8 August 2013, from http://www.scielo.br/scielo.php?script=sci_arttext&pid=S1516-44462006000300007&lng=en&tlng=en. 10.1590/S1516-44462006000300007.

Bloch, M. H., Green, C., Kichuk, S. A., Dombrowski, P. A., Wasylink, S., Billingslea, E., Landeros-Weisenberger, A., Kelmendi, B., Goodman, W. K., Leckman, J. F., Coric, V. & Pittenger, C. (2013) Long-term outcome in adults with obsessive-compulsive disorder. *Depression & Anxiety*, 30, 716–722.

Blom, R. M., Figee, M., Vulink, N. & Denys, D. (2012). Electroconvulsive therapy, transcranial magnetic stimulation in OCD. In J. Zohar (Ed.), *Obsessive-Compulsive Disorder: Current Science and Clinical Practice.* Chichester, UK: Wiles & Sons, Ltd.

Bohne, A., Wilhelm, S., Keuthen, N. J., Baer, L. & Jenike, M. A. (2002) Skin picking in German students: Prevalence, phenomenology, and associated characteristics. *Behavior Modification*, 26:320–339.

Boschen, M. J. & Vuksanovic, D. (2007). Deteriorating memory confidence, responsibility perceptions and repeated checking: Comparisons in OCD and control samples. *Behaviour Research and Therapy,* 45, 2098–2109.

Bouchard, C., Rhéaume, J. & Ladouceur, R. (1999). Responsibility and perfectionism in OCD: An experimental study. *Behaviour Research and Therapy,* 37, 239–248.

Bower, G. H., Monteiro, K. P. & Gilligan, S. G. (1978). Emotional mood as a contest for learning and recall, *Journal of Verbal Learning and Verbal Behavior,* 17, 573–585.

Bryant, C., Jackson, H. & Ames, D. (2008) The prevalence of anxiety in older adults: Methodological issues and a review of the literature. *Journal of Affective Disorders*, 109, 233–250.

Buhlmann, U., Glaesmer, H., Mewes, R., Fama, J. M., Bohne, A., Wilhelm, S., Keuthen, N. J., Baer, L. & Jenike, M. A. (2010) Updates on the prevalence of body dysmorphic disorder: A population-based survey. *Psychiatry Research*, 178, 171–175.

Burt, V. K. & Rudolph, M. (2000) Treating an Orthodox Jewish woman with obsessive-compulsive disorder: Maintaining reproductive and psychologic stability in the context of normative religious rituals. *American Journal of Psychiatry*, 157, 620–624.

Butler, A. C., Chapman, J. E., Forman, E. M. & Beck, A. T. (2006). The empirical status of cognitive-behavioral therapy: A review of meta-analyses. *Clinical Psychology Review*, 26(1), 17–31.

Butler, G. & Mathews, A. (1983). Cognitive processes in anxiety. *Advances in Behaviour Research and Therapy, 5*(1), 51–62.

Butler, G. & Mathews, A. (1987). Anticipatory anxiety and risk perception. *Cognitive Therapy and Research,* 11(5), 551–565.

Calamari, J. E., Pontarelli, N. K. & Armstrong, K. M. (2012) Obsessive-compulsive disorder in late life. *Cognitive & Behavioral Practice*, 19, 136–150.

Calikusu, C., Kucukgoncu, S., Tecer, Ö. & Bestepe, E. (2012) Skin picking in Turkish students: Prevalence, characteristics, and gender differences. *Behavior Modification*, 36, 49–66.

Carey, G. & Gottesman, I. I. (1981). Twin and family studies of anxiety, phobic and obsessive disorders. In D. F. Klein & J. Rabkin (Eds), *Anxiety: New Research and Changing Concepts*. New York: Raven Press, pp. 117–136.

Carleton, R. N., Mulvogue, M. K., Thibodeau, M. A., McCabe, R. E., Antony, M. M. & Asmundson, G. J. G. (2012). Increasingly certain about uncertainty: Intolerance of uncertainty across anxiety and depression. *Journal of Anxiety Disorders,* 26, 468–479.

Carleton, R. N., Norton, M. A. & Asmundson, G. J. G. (2007). Feeling the unknown: A short version of the intolerance of uncertainty scale. *Journal of Anxiety Disorders,* 21, 105–117.

Carleton, R. N., Weeks, J. W., Howell, A. N., Asmundson, G. J. G., Antony, M. M. & McCabe, R. E. (2012). Assessing the latent structure of the intolerance of uncertainty construct: An initial taxometric analysis. *Journal of Anxiety Disorders,* 26, 150–157.

Carmin, C. N., Calamari, J. E. & Ownby, R. L. (2013) OCD and spectrum conditions in older adults. In G. Steketee (Ed.) *Oxford Handbook of Obsessive Compulsive & Spectrum Disorders*. New York: Oxford University Press.

Carr, A. T. (1974). Compulsive neurosis: A review of the literature. *Psychological Bulletin,* 81, 311–318.

Chakrabarty, K., Bhattacharyya, S., Christopher, R. & Khanna, S. (2005). Glutamatergic dysfunction in OCD. *Neuropsychopharmacology,* 30, 1735–1740.

Christenson, G. A. & Crow, S. J. (1996) The characterization and treatment of trichotillomania. *Journal of Clinical Psychiatry*, 57, 42–49.

Christenson, G. A. & Mansueto, C. S. (1999) Trichotillomania: descriptive characteristics and phenomenology, in Stein, D. J., Christianson, G. A. & Hollander, E. (Eds) *Trichotillomania*. Washington, DC, American Psychiatric Press, pp 1–41.

Christenson, G. A., Mackenzie, T. B., Mitchell, J. E. (1991) Characteristics of 60 adult chronic hair pullers. *Am J Psychiatry* 148:365–370.

Christenson, G. A., Mackenzie, T. B. & Mitchell, J. E. (1994). Adult men and women with trichotillomania: A comparison of male and female characteristics. *Psychosomatics*, 35, 142–149.

Christenson, G. A., Ristvedt, S. L. & Mackenzie, T. B. (1993) Identification of trichotillomania cue profiles. *Behaviour Research & Therapy*, 31, 315–320.

Cisler, J. M. & Koster, E. H. W. (2010). Mechanisms of attentional biases towards threat in anxiety disorders: An integrative review. *Clinical Psychology Review*, 30, 203–216.

Cisler, J. M. & Olatunji, B. O. (2010). Components of attentional biases in contamination fear: Evidence for difficulty in disengagement. *Behaviour Research and Therapy*, 48, 74–78.

Clark, A., Kirkby, K. C., Daniels, B. A. & Marks, I. M. (1998). A pilot study of computer-aided vicarious exposure for obsessive-compulsive disorder. *Australian and New Zealand Journal of Psychiatry,* 32, 268–275.

Clark, D. A., Purdon, C. & Byers, E. S. (2000). Appraisal and control of sexual and non-sexual intrusive thoughts in university students. *Behaviour Research and Therapy*, 38, 439–455.

Coles, M. E. & Heimberg, R. G. (2002). Memory biases in the anxiety disorders: Current status. *Clinical Psychology Review,* 22, 587–627.

Coles, M. E., Frost, R. O., Heimberg, R. G. & Rheaume, J. (2003). Not just right experiences: Perfectionism, obsessive-compulsive features and general psychopathology. *Behaviour Research and Therapy,* 41, 681–700.

Cottraux, J., Bouvard, M. A. & Milliery, M. (2005). Combining pharmacotherapy with cognitive-behavioral interventions for obsessive-compulsive disorder. *Cognitive Behaviour Therapy,* 34(3), 185–192.

Cottraux, J., Note, I., Yao, S. N., Lafont, S., Note, B., Mollard, E., Bouvard, M., Sauteraud, A., Bourgeois, M. & Dartigues, J.-F. (2001). A randomized controlled trial of cognitive therapy versus intensive behaviour therapy in obsessive compulsive disorder. *Psychotherapy and Psychosomatics,* 70, 288–97.

Cougle, J. R., Lee, H.-J. & Salkovskis, P. M. (2007). Are responsibility beliefs inflated in non-checking OCD patients? *Journal of Anxiety Disorders*, 21(1), 153–159.

Coles, M. E., Pinto, A., Mancebo, M. C., Rasmussen, S. A. & Eisen, J. L. (2008). OCD with comorbid OCPD: A subtype of OCD? *Journal of Psychiatric Research*, 42, 289–296.

Cororve, M. B. & Gleaves, D. H. (2001) A review of conceptualizations, assessment, and treatment strategies. *Clinical Psychology Review*, 21, 949–970.

Costa, D. L. C., Assuncao, M. C., Ferrao, Y. A., Conrado, L. A., Gonzalez, C. H., Fontenelle, L. F., Fossaluza, V., Miguel, E. C., Torres, A. R. & Shavitt, R. G. (2012) Body Dysmorphic disorder in patients with obsessive-compulsive disorder: Prevalence and clinical correlates. *Depression & Anxiety*, 29, 966–975.

Coughtrey, A. E., Shafran, R., Knibbs, D. & Rachman, S. J. (2012) Mental contamination in obsessive-compulsive disorder. *Journal of Obsessive-Compulsive & Related Disorders*, 1, 244–250.

Coughtrey, A. E., Shafran, R. & Lee, M. (2013) The treatment of mental contamination: A case series. *Cognitive & Behavioral Practice*, 20, 221–231.

Cuijpers, P., Sijbrandij, M., Koole, S. L., Anderson, G., Beekman, A. T. & Reynolds, C. F. (2013). The efficacy of psychotherapy and pharmacotherapy in treating depressive and anxiety disorders: A meta-analysis of direct comparisons. *World Psychiatry,* 12(2), 137–148.

Davey, G. C. L. (1994). Self-reported fears to common indigenous animals in a UK population: The role of disgust sensitivity. *Br. J. Psychol.* 85, 541–554.

Davey, G. C. L. (2006). A mood-as-input account of perseverative worrying. In G. C. L. Davey & A. Wells (Eds), *Worry and Its Psychological Disorders*. Chichester, UK: Wiley.

Davey, G. C. L. (2008) *Psychopathology: Research, Assessment & Treatment in Clinical psychology*. BPS Wiley-Blackwell.

Davey, G. C. L. (2011). Disgust: The disease-avoidance emotion and its dysfunctions. *Philosophical Transactions of the Royal Society B*, 366, 3453–3465.

Davey, G. C. L. (2014). *Psychopathology: Research, Assessment & Treatment in Clinical Psychology*. BPS Wiley-Blackwell, 2nd Edition.

De Bruin, E. I., Ferdinand, R. F., Meester, S., de Nijs, P. F. & Verheij, F. (2007) High rates of psychiatric co-morbidity in PDD-NOS. *Journal of Autism & Developmental Disorders*, 37, 877–886.

Decloedt, E. H. & Stein, D. J. (2010). Current trends in drug treatment of obsessive-compulsive disorder. *Neuropsychiatric Disease and Treatment*, 6, 233–242.

de Oliveira, S. K. F. & Pelajo, C. F. (2010). Pediatric autoimmune neuropsychiatric disorders associated with streptococcal infection (PANDAS): A controversial diagnosis. *Curr Infect Dis Rep*, 12, 103–109.

Dold, M., Aigner, M., Lanzenberger, R. & Kasper, S. (2013). Antipsychotic augmentation of serotonin reuptake inhibitors in treatment-resistant obsessive-compulsive disorder: A meta-analysis of double-blind, randomized, placebo-controlled trials. *The International Journal of Neuropsychopharmacology*, 16(3), 557–574.

Dougherty, D. D., Baer, L., Cosgrove, G. R., Cassem, E. H., Price, B. H., Nierenberg, A. A., Jenike, M. A. & Rauch, S. L. (2002). Prospective long-term follow-up of 44 patients who received cingulotomy for treatment-refractory obsessive-compulsive disorder. *American Journal of Psychiatry*, 159, 269–275.

Dugas, M. J. & Robichaud, M. (2007). *Cognitive-Behavioral Treatment for Generalized Anxiety Disorder: From Science to Practice*. New York: Routledge.

Esman, A. H. (2001) Obsessive-compulsive disorder: Current views. *Psychoanalytic Inquiry*, 21, 145–156.

Evans, D. W., Leckman, J. F., Carter, A., Reznick, J. S., Henshaw, D., King, R. A. & Pauls, D. (1997). Ritual, habit, and perfectionism: The prevalence and development of compulsive-like behavior in normal young children. *Child Development*, 68, 58–68.

Fernandez, C. E. & Lopez-Ibor, J. J. (1967). Monochlorimipramine in the treatment of psychiatric patients resistant to other therapies. Actas *Luso-Españolas de Neurología Psíquiatría y Ciencias Afines*, 26, 119–147.

Figee, M., de Koning, P., Klaasen, S., Vulink, N., Mantione, M., van den Munckhof, P. Schuurman, R., van Wingen, G., van Amelsvoort, T., Booiji, J. & Denys, D. (2013). Deep brain stimulation induces striatal dopamine release in obsessive- compulsive disorder. *Biological Psychiatry,* doi:10.1016/j.biopsych.2013.06.021.

Figee, M., Luigjes, J., Smolders, R., Valencia-Alfonso, C-E., van Wingen, G. & de Kwaasteniet, B. (2013). Deep brain stimulation restores frontostriatal network activity in obsessive-compulsive disorder. *Nature Neuroscience,* 16, 386–387.

Fineberg, N. A. & Gale, T. M. (2005). Evidence-based pharmacotherapy of obsessive-compulsive disorder. *Int J Neuropsychopharmacol*, 8(1), 107–129.

Fischer, E. H., Dornelas, E. A. & Goethe, J. W. (2001) Characteristics of people lost to attrition in psychiatric follow-up studies. *Journal of Nervous & Mental Disease*, 189, 49–55.

Fisher, P. L. & Wells, A. (2005). Experimental modification of beliefs in obsessive compulsive disorder: A test of the metacognitive model. *Behaviour Research and Therapy*, 43, 821–829.

Fisher, P. L. & Wells, A. (2008). Metacognitive therapy for obsessive-compulsive disorder: A case series. *Journal of Behavior Therapy and Experimental Psychiatry*, 39, 117–132.

Foa, E. B. (2010). Cognitive behavioral therapy of obsessive-compulsive disorder. *Dialogues in Clinical Neurosceince,* 12, 199–207.

Foa, E. B., Amir, N., Gershuny, B, Molnar, C. & Kozak, M. J. (1997). Implicit and explicit memory in obsessive-compulsive disorder. *Journal of Anxiety Disorders,* 11, 119–129.

Foa, E. B., Huppert, J. D., Leiberg, S., Langner, R., Kichic, R., Hajcak, G. & Salkovskis, P. M. (2002). The obsessive-compulsive inventory: Development and validation of a short version. *Psychological Assessment*, 14, 485–496.

Foa, E. B., Kozak, M. J., Goodman, W. K., Hollander, E., Jenike, M. & Rasmussen, S. A. . (1995). DSM-IV field trial: obsessive compulsive disorder. *American Journal of Psychiatry,* 152, 90–6.

Foa, E. B., Liebowitz, M. R., Kozak, M. J., Davies, S., Campeas, R., Franklin, M. E., Huppert, J. D., Kjernisted, K., Rowan, V., Schmidt, A. B. & Simpson, B. (2005). Treatment of obsessive-compulsive disorder by exposure and ritual prevention, clomipramine, and their combination: A randomized, placebo controlled trial. *American Journal of Psychiatry,* 162, 151–161.

Foa, E. B. & McNally, R. J. (1986). Sensitivity to feared stimuli in obsessive-compulsives: A dichotic listening analysis. *Cognitive Therapy and Research,* 10, 477–485.

Foa, E. B., Sacks, M. B., Tolin, D. F., Prezworski, A. & Amir, N. (2002). Inflated perception of responsibility for harm in OCD patients with and without checking compulsions: A replication and extension. *Journal of Anxiety Disorders,* 16, 443 – 453.

Fontenelle, L. F., Mendlowicz, M. V., Marques, C. & Versiani, M. (2004) Trans-cultural aspects of obsessive-compulsive disorder: A description of a Brazilian sample and a systematic review of international clinical studies. *Journal of Psychiatric Research*, 38, 403–411.

Franklin, M. E. & Foa, E. B. (1998). Cognitive-behavioral treatment of Obsessive-Compulsive Disorder. In P. Nathan & J. Gorman (Eds), *A Guide to Treatments that Work*. Oxford, England: Oxford University Press, pp. 339–357.

Franklin, M. E., Kozak, M. J., Cashman, L., Coles, M., Rheingold, A. & Foa, E. (1998) Cognitive-behavioral treatment of pediatric obsessive-compulsive disorder: An open clinical trial. *Journal of the American Academy of Child & Adolescent Psychiatry*, 37, 412–419.

Frare, F., Perugi, G., Ruffalo, G. & Toni, C. (2004) Obsessive-compulsive disorder and body dysmorphic disorder: A comparison of clinical features. *European Psychiatry, 19*, 292–298.

Freeston, M. H. & Ladouceur, R. (1997). What do patients do with their obsessive thoughts? *Behaviour Research and Therapy*, 35, 335–348.

Freud, A. (1937). *The Ego and the Mechanisms of Defense.* London: Hogarth.

Freud, S. (1909). Notes upon a case of obsessional neurosis. In J. Strachey (ed.) *The Standard Edition of the Complete Psychological Works of Sigmund Freud, Volume X*. London: Hogarth Press, pp. 151–318.

Freud, S. (1990). *Case Histories 2: The 'Rat Man', Schreber, the 'Wolf Man', and a Case of Female Homosexuality*. A. Richards (Ed.). London: Penguin Books.

Frost, R. O., Marten, P., Lahart, C. & Rosenblate, R. (1990). The dimensions of perfectionism. *Cognitive Therapy and Research*, 14, 449–468.

Frost, R. O. & Steketee, G. (1997). Perfectionism in Obsessive–Compulsive Disorder patients. *Behaviour Research and Therapy*, 35, 291–296.

Frost, R. O., Patronek, G. & Rosenfield, E. (2011) Comparison of object and animal hoarding. *Depression & Anxiety*, 28, 885–891.

Frost, R. O., Steketee, G. & Tolin, D. F. (2011) Comorbidity in hoarding disorder. *Depression & Anxiety*, 28, 876–884.

Frost, R. O., Steketee, G. & Tolin, D. F. (2012) Diagnosis and assessment of hoarding disorder. *Annual Review of Clinical Psychology*, 8, 219–242.

Fullana, M. A., Vilagut, G., Rojas-Farreras, S., Mataix-Cols, D., de Graaf, R., Demyttenaere, K., Haro, J. M., de Girolamo, G., Lépine, J. P., Matschinger, H. & Alonso, J. (2010) Obsessive-compulsive symptom dimensions in the general population: Results from an epidemiological study in six European countries. *Journal of Affective Disorders*, 124, 291–299.

Garcia, A. M., Freeman, J. B., Himle, M. B., Berman, N. C., Ogata, A. K., Ng, J., Choate-Summers, M. L. & Leonard, H. (2009) Phenomenology of early childhood onset obsessive compulsive disorder. *Journal of Psychopathology & Behavioral Assessment*, 31, 104–111.

García-Soriano, G., Belloch, A., Morillo, C. & Clark, D. A. (2011). Symptom dimensions in obsessive-compulsive disorder: From normal cognitive intrusions to clinical obsessions. *Journal of Anxiety Disorders*, 25, 474–482.

Garyfallos, G., Katsigiannopoulos, K., Adamopoulou, A., Papazisis, G., Karastergiou, A. & Bozikas, V. P. (2010). Comorbidity of obsessive-compulsive disorder with obsessive compulsive personality disorder: Does it imply a specific subtype of obsessive compulsive disorder? *Psychiatry Research*, 177(1–2), 156–160.

Geller, D., Biederman, J., Griffin, S., Jones, J. & Lefkowitz, T. R. (1996) Comorbidity of juvenile obsessive-compulsive disorder with disruptive behaviour disorders: A review and report. *Journal of the American Academy of Child & Adolescent Psychiatry*, 35, 1637–1646.

Geller, D. A., Biederman, J., Faraone, S., Agranat, A., Cradock, K. & Hagermoser, L. (2001). Developmental aspects of obsessive compulsive disorder: Findings in children, adolescents, and adults. *Journal of Nervous & Mental Diseases*, 189, 471–477.

Gentile, S. (2011). Efficacy of antidepressant medications in children and adolescents with obsessive-compulsive disorder: A systematic appraisal. *Journal of Clinical Psychopharmacology*, 31(5), 625–632.

Gillihan, S., Williams, M. T. Malcoun, E., Yadin, E., Foa, E. B. (2012). Common pitfalls in exposure and response prevention (EX/RP) for

OCD. *Journal of Obsessive-compulsive and Related Disorders*. 1(4), 251–257.

Goodman, W. K., Price, L. H., Rasmussen, S. A., Mazure, C., Delgado, P., Heninger, G. R. & Charney, D. S. (1989). The Yale-Brown obsessive compulsive scale. 1. Development, use, and reliability. *Archives of General Psychiatry*, 46, 1006–1011.

Gomes, P. V. O., Brasil-Neto, J. P., Allam, N. & de Souza, E. R. (2012). A randomized, double-blind trial of repetitive transcranial magnetic stimulation in obsessive-compulsive disorder with three-month follow-up. *The Journal of Neuropsychiatry and Clinical Neurosciences*, 24(4), 437–443.

Goodman, W. K., Price, L. H., Rasmussen, S. A., Mazure, C., Fleischmann, R. L., Hill, C. L. & Charney, D. S. (1989). The Yale-Brown obsessive compulsive scale: I. Development, use, and reliability. *Archives of General Psychiatry*, 46(11), 1006.

Gordon, O. M., Slakovskis, P. M., Oldfield, V. B. & Carter, N. (2013) The association between obsessive compulsive disorder and obsessive compulsive personality disorder prevalence and clinical presentation. *British Journal of Clinical Psychology*, 52, 300–315.

Graber, J. & Arndt, W. B. (1993) Trichotillomania. *Comprehensive Psychiatry*, 34, 340–346.

Grant, J. E., Mancebo, M., Pinto, A., Williams, K. A., Eisen, J. L. & Rasmussen, S. A. (2007) Late-onset obsessive-compulsive disorder: Clinical characteristics and psychiatric comorbidity. *Psychiatry Research*, 152, 21–27.

Grant, J. E., Mooney, M. E. & Kushner, M. G. (2012) Prevalence correlates and comorbidity of DSM-IV obsessive-compulsive personality disorder: Results from the National Epidemiologic Survey on Alcohol and Related Conditions. *Journal of Psychiatric Research*, 46, 469–475.

Grant, J. E., Odlaug, B. L., Chamberlain, S. R., Keuthen, N. J. Lochner, C. & Stein, D. J. (2012) Skin picking disorder. *American Journal of Psychiatry*, 169, 1143–1149.

Greenberg, B. D., Gabriels, L. A., Malone, D. A. Jr., Rezai, A. R., Friehs, G. M., Okun, M. S., Shapira, N. A., Foote, K. D., Cosyns, P. R., Kubu, C. S., Malloy, P. F., Salloway, S. P., Giftakis, J. E., Rise, M. T., Machado, A. G., Baker, K. B., Stypulkowski, P. H., Goodman, W. K., Rasmussen, S. A. & Nuttin, B. J. (2010). Deep brain stimulation of the ventral internal capsule/ventral stimulation for obsessive-compulsive disorder: Worldwide experience. *Molecular Psychiatry*, 15(1), 64–79.

Greenberg, B. D., Rauch, S. L. & Haber, S. N. (2010). Invasive circuitry-based neurotherapeutics: stereotactic ablation and deep brain stimulation for OCD. *Neuropsychopharmacology*, 35, 317–336.

Greenberg, D. & Witztum, E. (1991). Problems in the treatment of religious patients. *American Journal of Psychotherapy*, 45, 554–565.

Greenwald, A. G., McGhee, D. E. & Schwartz, J. L. K. (1998). Measuring individual differences in implicit cognition: The implicit association test. *Journal of Personality and Social Psychology*, 74(6), 1464–1480.

Greist, J. H., Marks, I. M., Baer, L., Kobak, K. A., Wenzel, K. W., Hirsch, M. J., Mantle, J. R. & Clary, C. M. (2002). Behaviour therapy for obsessive compulsive disorder guided by a computer or a clinician compared with relaxation as a control. *Journal of Clinical Psychiatry*, 63, 2.

Guisinger, S. (2003). Adapted to flee famine: Adding an evolutionary perspective on anorexia nervosa. *Psychological Review*, 110(4), 745–761.

Hamilton, W. D. (1964). The genetical evolution of social behaviour I & II. *Journal of Theoretical Biology*, 7, 1–52.

Hanna, G. L., Veenstra-VanderWeele, J., Cox, N. J., Boehnke, M., Himle, J. A., Curtis, G. C., Leventhal, B. L. & Cook, E. H., Jr. (2002). Genome-wide linkage analysis of families with obsessive-compulsive disorder ascertained through pediatric probands. *Am J Med Genet*, 114, 541–552.

Haslam, N. (2003). Categorical versus dimensional models of mental disorder: The taxometric evidence. *Australian and New Zealand Journal of Psychiatry*, 37, 696–704.

Haslam, N., Williams, B. J., Kyrios, M., McKay, D. & Taylor, S. (2005). Subtyping obsessive-compulsive disorder: A taxometric analysis. *Behavior Therapy*, 36, 381–391.

Hasselbalch, S. G., Hansen, E. S., Jakobsen, T. B., Pinborg, L. H., Lonborg, J. H. & Bolwig, T. G. (2007). Reduced midbrain-pons serotonin transporter binding in patients with obsessive-compulsive disorder. *Acta Psychiatr. Scand.*, 115, 388–394.

Helgadottir, F. D., Menzies, R. & Einstein, D. (2012). Magical thinking and obsessive compulsive disorder in Australia and Iceland: A cross-cultural comparison. *Journal of Obsessive-Compulsive and Related Disorders*, 1, 216–219.

Hemmings, S. M. J., Kinnear, C. J., Lochner, C., Niehaus, D. J. H., Knowles, J. A., Moolman-Smook, J. C., Corfield, V. A. & Stein, D. J. (2004). Early- versus late-onset obsessive-compulsive disorder: investigating genetic and clinical correlates. *Psychiatry Research,* 128, 175–182.

Hesse, S., Muller, U., Lincke, T., Barthel, H., Villmann, T., Angermeyer, M. C., Sabri, O. & Stengler-Wenzke, K. (2005). Serotonin and dopamine transporter imaging in patients with obsessive-compulsive disorder. *Psychiatry Res.,* 140, 63–72.

Himle, M. B. & Franklin, M. E. (2009). The more you do it, the easier it gets: Exposure and response prevention for OCD. *Cognitive and Behavioral Practice,* 16, 29–39.

Hodgson, R. & Rachman, S. (1972). The effects of contamination and washing in obsessional patients. *Behaviour Research and Therapy,* 10, 111–117.

Hoehn-Saric, R. & Greenberg, B. D. (1997). Psychobiology of obsessive-compulsive disorder: Anatomical and physiological considerations. *Int Rev Psychiatry,* 9, 15–30.

Holaway, R. M., Heimberg, R. G. & Coles, M. E. (2006). A comparison of intolerance of uncertainty in analogue obsessive-compulsive disorder and generalized anxiety disorder. *Journal of Anxiety Disorders,* 20(2), 158–174.

Horowitz, M. J. (1998). Psychoanalysis. In H. Friedman (Ed.). Assessment and therapy specialty articles. *Encyclopedia of Mental Health,* 2, 261–275.

Huppert, J. D., Siev, J. & Kushner, E. S. (2007) When religion and obsessive-compulsive disorder collide: Treating scrupulosity in ultra-orthodox Jews. *Journal of Clinical Psychology*, 63, 925–941.

Inozu, M., Clark, D. A. & Karanci, A. N. (2012). Scrupulosity in Muslins and Christians: A Comparative Study of Turkish and Canadian Students, *Behavior Therapy*, 43, 190–202.

Inozu, M., Karanci, A. N. & Clark, D. A. (2012) Why are religious individuals more obsessional? The role of mental control beliefs in Muslims and Christians. *Journal of Behavior Therapy & Experimental Psychiatry*, 43, 959–966.

Insel, T. R., Hamilton, J. A., Guttmacher, L. B. & Murphy, D. L. (1983). D-amphetamine in obsessive-compulsive disorder. *Psychopharmacology (Berl)*, 80, 231–235.

Inyoue, E. (1965). Similar and dissimilar manifestations of obsessive-compulsive neurosis in monozygotic twins. *Am J Psych,* 121, 1171–1175.

Janeck, A. S. & Calamari, J. E. (1999). Thought suppression in obsessive-compulsive disorder. *Cognitive Therapy and Research*, 23, 497–509.

Janet, P. (1903). *Les Obsessions et la Psychasthénie*. Paris: Alcan.

Jenike, M. A., Baer, L., Minichiello, W. E., Rauch, S. L. & Buttolph, M. L. (1997) Placebo-controlled trial of fluoxetine and phenelzine for obsessive-compulsive disorder. *American Journal of Psychiatry*, 154, 1261–1264.

Junginger, J., Phelan, E., Cherry, K. & Levy, J. (1993) Prevalence of psychopathology in elderly persons in nursing homes and in the community. *Hospital & Community Psychiatry*, 44, 381–383.

Julien, D., O'Connor, K. & Aardema, F. (2009). Intrusions related to obsessive-compulsive disorder: A question of content or context? *Journal of Clinical Psychology,* 65, 709–722.

Karno, M., Golding, J. M., Sorenson, S. B. & Burnam, M. A. (1988) The epidemiology of obsessive-compulsive disorder in five US communities. *Archives of General Psychiatry*, 45, 1094–1099.

Kenwright, M., Marks, I. M., Graham, C., Franses, A. & Mataix-Cols, D. (2005). Brief scheduled phone support from a clinician to enhance computer-aided self-help for obsessive-compulsive disorder: Randomized controlled trial. *Journal of Clinical Psychology,* 61(12), 1499–1508.

Kessler, R., Berglund, P., Demler, O., Jin, R., Merikangas, K. R. & Walters, E. E. (2005) Lifetime prevalence and age-of-onset distributions of DSM-IV disorders in the National Comorbidity Survey Replication. *Archives of General Psychiatry*, 62, 593–602.

Keuthen, N. J., Koran, L. M., Aboujaoude, E., Large, M. D., Serpe, R. T. (2010) The prevalence of pathologic skin picking in US adults. *Compr Psychiatry* 51:183–1.

Khanna, S. & Channabasavanna, S. M. (1988) Phenomenology of obsessions in obsessive-compulsive neurosis. *Psychopathology*, 20, 23–28.

Khalsa, S. S., Schiffman, J. E. & Bystrtsky, A. (2011). Treatment-resistant OCD: Options beyond first-line medications. *Current Psychiatry,* 10(11), 45–52.

Kim, C. H., Koo, M. S., Cheon, K. A., Ryu, Y. H., Lee, J. D. & Lee, H. S. (2003). Dopamine transporter density of basal ganglia assessed with [(123)I]IPT SPET in obsessive-compulsive disorder. *Eur J Nucl Med Mol Imaging*, 30, 1637–1643.

Kim, H., Steketee, G. & Frost, R. O. (2001) Hoarding by elderly people. *Health & Social Work*, 26, 176–184.

Kirsch, I., Scoboria, A. & Moore, T. J. (2002). Antidepressants and placebos: Secrets, revelations, and unanswered questions. *Prevention & Treatment*, 5(1), Jul 2002, No Pagination Specified Article 33.

Knight, T., Steeves, T., Day, L., Lowerison, M., Jette, N. & Pringsheim, T. (2012) Prevalence of tic disorders: A systematic review and meta-analysis. *Pediatric Neurology*, 47, 77–90.

Kobori, O., Salkovskis, P. M., Read, J., Lounes, N. & Wong, V., 2012. A qualitative study of the investigation of reassurance seeking in obsessive-compulsive disorder. *Journal of Obsessive-Compulsive and Related Disorders*, 1 (1), 25–32.

Kozak, M., Foa, E. & McCarty, P. (1987). Assessment of obsessive-compulsive disorder. In C. Last & M. Hersen (Eds), *Handbook of Anxiety Disorders*. New York: Pergamon.

Kozak, M. J. & Foa, E. B. (1997). *Mastery of Obsessive Compulsive Disorder: A Cognitive Behavioral Approach. Therapist Guide*. San Antonio: The Psychological Corporation.

Krockmalik, A. & Menzies, R. G. (2003). The classification and diagnosis of OCD. In R. G. Menzies & P. deSilva (eds), *Obsessive-Compulsive Disorder: Theory, Research and Treatment*. UK: John Wiley & Sons, pp. 3–20.

Kyrios, M., Sanavio, E., Bhar, S. & Liguori, L. (2001). Associations between obsessive-compulsive phenomena, affect and beliefs: Cross-cultural comparisons of Australian and Italian data. *Behavioral & Cognitive Psychotherapy*, 29(4), 409–422.

Lane, R. C., Quintar, B. & Goeltz, W. B. (1998). Directions in psychoanalysis. *Clinical Psychology Review*, 18, 857–883.

Laplane, D., Levasseur, M., Pillon, B., Dubois, B., Baulac, M., Mazoyer, B., Tran Dinh, S., Sette, G., Danze, F. & Baron, J. C. (1989). Obsessive-compulsive and other behavioural changes with bilateral basal ganglia lesions. *Brain*, 112, 699–725.

Lavy, E. H. & Van den Hout, M. (1990). Thought suppression induces intrusions. *Behavioural Psychotherapy*, 18, 251–258.

Leckman, J. F. (1993) Tourette's syndrome. In E. Hollander (Ed.) *Obsessive-compulsive related disorders*. Washington DC: American psychiatric Press.

Leckman, J. F. & Bloch, M. H. (2008). A developmental and evolutionary perspective on obsessive-compulsive disorder: Whence and whither compulsive hoarding? *Am J Psychiatry,* 165(10), 1229–1233.

Leckman, J. F., Grice, D. E., Barr, L. C., de Vries, A. L. C., Martin, C., Cohen, D. J., McDougle, C. J., Goodman, W. K. & Rasmussen , S. A. (1995) Tic-related vs. non-tic related obsessive-compulsive disorder. *Anxiety*, 1, 208–215.

Leckman, J. F., Mayes, L. C., Feldman, R., Evans, D. W., King, R. A. & Cohen, D. J. (1999). Early parental preoccupations and behaviours and their possible relationship to the symptoms of obsessive-compulsive disorder. *Acta Psychiatrica Scandinavica,* 100, S396, 1–26.

Lee, H. J. & Kwon, S. M. (2003). Two different types of obsession: Autogenous obsessions and reactive obsessions. *Behaviour Research and Therapy,* 41, 11–29.

Lee, H. J., Kwon, S. M., Kwon, J. S. & Telch, M. J. (2005). Testing the autogenous–reactive model of obsessions. *Depression and Anxiety*, 21, 118–129.

Lehmkuhl, H. D., Storch, E. A., Bodfish, J. W. & Geffken, G. R. (2008) Brief report: exposure and response prevention for obsessive-compulsive disorder in a 12-year-old with autism. *Journal of Autism Development Disorders*, 38, 977–981.

Leonard, H. L., Lenane, M. C., Swedo, S. E., Rettew, D. C., Gershon, E. S. & Rapoport, J. L.(1992) Tics and Tourette's disorder: A 2 to 7 year follow up of 54 obsessive-compulsive children. *American Journal of Psychiatry*, 149, 1244–1251.

Lesch, K. P., Hoh, A., Sselkamp-Tietze, J., Wiesmann, M., Osterheider, M. & Schulte, H. M. (1991). 5-Hydroxytryptamine1A receptor responsivity in obsessive-compulsive disorder. Comparison of patients and controls. *Arch. Gen. Psychiatry,* 48, 540–547.

Lewin, A. B., Chang, S., McCracken, J., McQueen, M. & Piacentini J. (2010) Comparison of clinical features among youth with tic disorders, obsessive-compulsive disorder (OCD) and both conditions. *Psychiatry Research*, 178, 317–322.

Leyfer, O. T., Folstein, S. E., Bacalman, S., Davis, N. O., Dinh, E., Morgan, J., Tager-Flusberg, H. & Lainhart, J. E. (2006) Comorbid psychiatric disorders in children with autism: Interview development and rates of disorders. *Journal of Autism & Developmental Disorders*, 36, 849–861.

Lind, C. & Boschen, M. J. (2009). Intolerance of uncertainty mediates the relationship between responsibility beliefs and compulsive checking. *Journal of Anxiety Disorders*, 23, 1047–1052.

Lochner, C., Serebro, P., der Merwe, L. V., Hemmings, S., Kinnear, C., Seedat, S. & Steina, D. J. (2011). Comorbid obsessive compulsive personality in obsessive compulsive disorder (OCD): A marker of severity. *Progress in Neuro-Psychopharmacology and Biological Psychiatry*, 35, 1087–1092.

MacDonald, C. B. & Davey, G. C. L. (2005). Inflated responsibility and perseverative checking: The effect of negative mood. *Journal of Abnormal Psychology*, 114, 76–82.

MacLeod, A. K., Williams, M. J. & Bekerian, D. A. (1991). Worry is reasonable: The role of explanations in pessimism about future personal events. *Journal of Abnormal Psychology*, 100(4), 478–486.

Mahoney, A. E. J. & McEvoy, P. M. (2012). A transdiagnostic examination of intolerance of uncertainty across anxiety and depressive disorders. *Cognitive Behaviour Therapy*, 41, 212–222.

Mahony, P. (1986). *Freud and the Rat Man*. New Haven: Yale University Press.

Malan, D. (1979) *Individual Psychotherapy and the Science of Psychodynamics*. London: Butterworth.

Maletzky, B., McFarland, B. & Burt, A. (1994). Refractory obsessive compulsive disorder and ECT. *Convulsive Therapy*, 10(1), 34–42.

Mallinger, A. E. (1984). The obsessive's myth of control. *Journal of the American Academy of Psychoanalysis*, 12, 147–165.

Mansueto, C. S., Townsley-Stemberger, R. M., McCombs-Thomas, A. & Goldfinger-Golomb, R. (1997). Trichotillomania: A comprehensive behavioral model. *Clinical Psychology Review*, 17, 567–577.

Mantovani, A., Simpson, H. B., Fallon, B. A., Rossi, S. & Lisanby, S. H. (2010). Randomized sham-controlled trial of repetitive transcranial magnetic stimulation in treatment-resistant obsessive-compulsive disorder. *The International Journal of Neuropsychopharmacology*, 13(2), 217–227.

Marazziti, D., Akiskal, H. S., Rossi, A. & Cassano, G. B. (1999). Alteration of the platelet serotonin transporter in romantic love. *Psychological Medicine, 29*(3), 741–745.

Marks, I. M,. Baer, L., Greist, J. H., Park, J. M., Bachofen, M., Nakagawa, A., Wensel, K. W., Parkin, J. R., Manzo, P. A., Dottl., S. L. & Mantle, J. M. (1998) Home self-assessment of obsessive-compulsive disorder: Use of a manual and a computer-conducted telephone interview: two UK-US studies. *British Journal of Psychiatry,* 172, 406–412.

Massler, M. & Malone, A. J. (1950) Nailbiting. A review. *J Pediatr*, 36, 523–31.

Mataix-Cols, D., Nakatani, E., Micali, N. & Heyman, I. (2008) Structure of obsessive-compulsive symptoms in pediatric OCD. *Journal of the American Academy of Child & Adolescent Psychiatry*, 47, 773–778.

Mataix-Cols, D., Rosario-Campos, M. C. & Leckman, J. F. (2005) A multidimensional model of obsessive-compulsive disorder. *American Journal of Psychiatry*, 162, 228–238.

Mathews, C. A., Badner, J. A., Andresen, J. M., Sheppard, B., Himle, J. A. Grant, J. E. , Williams, K. A., Chavira, D. A., Azzam, A., Schwartz, M., Reus, V. I., Km, S. W., Cook, E. H., Hanna, G. L. (2012). Genome-wide linkage analysis of obsessive-compulsive disorder implicates chromosome 1p36. *Biological Psychiatry,* 72(8), 629–636.

Matsunaga, H., Nagata, T., Hayashida, K., Ohya, K., Kiriike, N. & Stein, D. J. (2009). A long-term trial of the effectiveness and safety of atypical antipsychotic agents in augmenting SSRI-refractory obsessive compulsive disorder. *The Journal of Clinical Psychiatry,* 70(6), 863–868.

McDougle, C. J., Kresch, L. E., Goodman, W. K., Naylor, S. T., Volkmar, F. R., Cohen, D. J. & Price, L. H. (1995) A case-controlled study of repetitive thoughts and behavior in adults with autistic disorder and obsessive-compulsive disorder. *The American Journal of Psychiatry*, 152, 772–777.

McEvoy, P. M. & Mahoney, A. E. J. (2011). Achieving certainty about the structure of intolerance of uncertainty in a treatment-seeking sample with anxiety and depression. *Journal of Anxiety Disorders*, 25, 112–122.

McGuire, W. (1974) *The Freud/Jung Letters*, trans. R. Manheim and R. F. C. Hull. Princeton, NJ: Princeton University Press.

Meeten, F. & Davey, G. C. L. (2011). Mood-as-input hypothesis and perseverative psychopathologies. *Clinical Psychology Review,* 31 (8), 1259–1275.

Menzies, L., Chamberlain, S. R., Laird, A. R., Thelen, S. M., Sahakian, B. J. & Bullmore, E. T. (2008). Integrating evidence from neuroimaging and neuropsychological studies of obsessive-compulsive disorder: the orbitofronto-striatal model revisited. *Neurosci Biobehav Rev*, 32, 525–549.

Menzies, L., Williams, G. B., Chamberlain, S. R., Ooi, C., Fineberg, N. A., Suckling, J., Sahakian, B. J., Robbins, T. W. & Bullmore, E. T. (2008). White matter abnormalities in patients with obsessive-compulsive disorder and their first-degree relatives. *Am J Psychiatry*, 165, 1308–1315.

Meyer, V. (1966). Modification of expectations in cases with obsessional rituals. *Behaviour Research and Therapy*, 196, 273–280.

Moritz, S., Fischer, B., Hottenrott, B., Kellner, M., Fricke, S., Randjbar, S. & Jelinek, L. (2008). Words may not be enough! No increased emotional Stroop effect in obsessive-compulsive disorder. *Behaviour Research and Therapy*, 46, 1101–1104.

Moritz, S., Kempke, S., Luyten, P., Randjbar, S. & Jelinek, L. (2011). Was Freud partly right on obsessive-compulsive disorder (OCD)? Investigation of latent aggression in OCD. *Psychiatry Research*, 187, 180–184.

Moritz, S. & von Muhlenen, A. (2008) Investigation of an attentional bias for fear-related materials in obsessive-compulsive checkers. *Depression and Anxiety*, 25, 225–229.

Moritz, S., Ruhe, C., Jelinek, L., Naber, D. (2009). No deficits in nonverbal memory, metamemory and internal as well as external source memory in obsessive-compulsive disorder (OCD). *Behaviour Research and Therapy*, 47, 308–315.

Morris, D. R., Meighen, K. G. & McDougle, C. J. (2005) Acute onset of obsessive-compulsive disorder in an adolescent with acute lymphoblastic leukemia *PSYCHOSOMATICS* 46 (5): 458–460.

Moses, L. J. & Baird, J. A. (1999). Metacognition. In R. A. Wilson & F. C. Keil (Eds), *The MIT Encyclopedia of the Cognitive Sciences*. Cambridge, USA: The MIT Press.

Mowrer, O. H. (1939). A stimulus-response analysis of anxiety and its role as a reinforcing agent. *Psychological Review*, 46, 553–565.

Mulken, S. & Jansen, A. (2009). Mirror gazing increases attractiveness in satisfied, but not in dissatisfied women: A model for body dysmorphic disorder? *Journal of Behavior Therapy and Experimental Psychiatry*, 40, 211–218.

Muller, J. & Roberts, J. E. (2005). Memory and attention in Obsessive-Compulsive Disorder: A review. *Journal of Anxiety Disorders*, 19, 1–28.

Myers, S. G., Fisher, P. L. & Wells, A. (2009). An empirical test of the metacognitive model of obsessive-compulsive symptoms: Fusion beliefs, beliefs about rituals, and stop signals. *Journal of Anxiety Disorders*, 23, 436–442.

Najmi, S., Riemann, B. C. & Wegner, D. M. (2009). Managing unwanted intrusive thoughts in obsessive compulsive disorder: Relative effectiveness of suppression, distraction, and acceptance. *Behaviour Research and Therapy, 47,* 494–503.

Nakagawa, A., Marks, I. M., Park, J. M., Bachofen, M., Baer, L., Dottl, S. L. & Greist, J. H., (2000). Self-treatment of obsessive-compulsive disorder guided by manual and computer conducted telephone interview. *Journal of Telemedicine and Telecare,* 6, 22–26.

Narrow, W. E., Rae, D. S., Robins, L. N. & Regier, D. A. (2002) Revised prevalence estimates of mental disorders in the United States – Using a clinical significance criterion to reconcile 2 survey estimates. *Archives of General Psychiatry*, 59, 115–123.

National Institute of Clinical Excellence National Clinical Practice Guideline (2006) *Obsessive-compulsive Disorder: Core Interventions in the Treatment of Obsessive-compulsive Disorder and Body Dysmorphic Disorder*. [CG31]. Published by the British Psychological Society and the Royal College of Psychiatrists. http://www.nice.org.uk/nicemedia/live/10976/29948/29948.pdf

Nelson, E., Abramowitz, J. S., Whiteside, S. P. & Deacon, B. J. (2006). Scrupulosity in patients with obsessive-compulsive disorder: Relationship to clinical and cognitive phenomena. *Journal of Anxiety Disorders,* 20, 1071–1086.

Nestadt, G., Grados, M. & Samuels, J. F. (2010). Genetics of OCD. *Psychiatry Clin North Am,* 33(1), 141–158.

Obsessive Compulsive Cognitions Working Group (OCCWG). (2005). Psychometric validation of the obsessive belief questionnaire and interpretation of intrusions inventory. Part 2:Factor analyses and testing of a brief version. *Behaviour Research and Therapy,* 43, 1527–1542.

Ohashi, J. & Tokunaga, K. (2002). The expected power of genome-wide linkage disequilibrium testing using single nucleotide polymorphism markers for detecting a low-frequency disease variant. *Ann Hum Genet,* 66(4), 297–306.

Olatunji, B. O. (2010). Changes in disgust correspond with changes in symptoms of contamination-based OCD: A prospective examination of specificity. *J. Anxiety Disord.* 24, 313–317.

Olatunji, B. O. & Armstrong, T. (2009). Contamination fear and effects of disgust on distress in a public restroom. *Emotion* 9, 592–597.

Olatunji, B. O., Tart, C., Ciesielski, B., McGrath, P. M. & Smits, J. A. J. (2011). Specificity of disgust vulnerability in the discrimination and treatment of OCD. *Journal of Psychiatric Research,* 45, 1236–1242.

Olatunji, B. O., Williams, B. J., Haslam, N., Abramowitz, J. S. & Tolin, D. F. (2008). The latent structure of obsessive-compulsive symptoms: A taxometric study. *Depression and Anxiety,* 25, 956–968.

Olivardia, R., Pope, H. G., Hudson, J. I. (2000) Muscle dysmorphia in male weightlifters: A case-control study. *American Journal of Psychiatry*, 157 (8): 1291–1296.

Ozonoff, S., Pennington, B. F. & Rogers, S. J. (1991) Executive function deficits in high-functioning autistic individuals: Relationship to theory of mind. *Journal of Child Psychology & Psychiatry*, 32, 1107–1122.

Pacan, P., Grzesiak, M., Reich, A. & Szepietowski, J. C. (2009) Onychophagia as a spectrum of obsessive-compulsive disorder. *Acta Dermato-Venereologica*, 89, 278–280.

Pallanti, S. & Querciolo, L. (2006). Treatment-refractory obsessive-compulsive disorder: Methodological issues, operational definitions and therapeutic lines. *Progress in Neuro-Psychopharmacology,* 30(3), 400–412.

Parrish, C. L. & Radomsky, A. S. (2010). Why do people seek reassurance and check repeatedly? An investigation of factors involved in compulsive behavior in OCD and Depression. *Journal of Anxiety Disorders,* 24(2), 211–222.

Patronek, G. J. (1999) Hoarding of animals: An unrecognized public health problem in a difficult to study population. *Public Health Reports*, 114, 81–87.

Pauls, D. L. (2008). The genetics of obsessive compulsive disorder: A review of the evidence. *American Journal of Medical Genetics Part C (Seminars in Medical Genetics)*, 148C, 133–139.

Pauls, D. L., Alsobrook, J. P., Goodman, W., Rasmussen, S. & Leckman, J. F. (1995) A family study of obsessive-compulsive disorder. *American Journal of Psychiatry*, 152, 76–84.

Pennington, L. A. (1945) Incidence of nail biting among adults. *Am J Psychiatry*, 102, 241–4.

Perse, T. (1988). Obsessive-compulsive disorder: A treatment review. *Journal of Clinical Psychiatry,* 49, 48–55.

Pertusa, A., Frost, R. O., Fullana, M. A., Samuels, J., Steketee, G., Tolin, D., Saxena, S., Leckman, J. F. & Mataix-Cols, D. (2010) Refining the diagnostic boundaries of compulsive hoarding: A critical review. *Clinical Psychology Review*, 30, 371–386.

Phillips, K. A. (2001) *Somatoform and Factitious Disorders: Review of Psychiatry*. (Vol 20). Washington DC: American Psychiatric Association.

Phillips, K. A., Didie, E. R., Menard, W., Pagano, M. E., Fay, C. & Weisberg, R. B. (2006) Clinical features of body dysmorphic disorder in adolescents and adults. *Psychiatry Research,* 141, 305–314.

Pinto, A., Mancebo, M. C., Eisen, J. L., Pagano, M. E. & Rasmussen, S. A. (2006) Brown Longitudinal Obsessive-Compulsive Study – Clinical features and symptoms of the sample at intake. *Journal of Clinical Psychiatry*, 67, 703–711.

Pogarell, O., Hamann, C., Popperl, G., Juckel, G., Chouker, M., Zaudig, M., Riedel, M., Moeller, H. J., Hegerl, U. & Tatsch, K. (2003). Elevated brain serotonin transporter availability in patients with obsessive-compulsive disorder. *Biol Psychiatry,* 54, 1406–1413.

Purdon, C., Rowa, K. & Antony, M. M. (2005). Thought suppression and its effects on thought frequency, appraisal and mood state in individuals with obsessive-compulsive disorder. *Behaviour Research and Therapy,* 43, 93–108.

Rachman, J., Shafran, R., Radomsky, A. & Zysk, E. (2011) Reducing contamination by exposure plus safety behaviour. *Journal of Behavior Therapy and Experimental Psychiatry,* 42(3), 397–404.

Rachman, S. (1993). Obsessions, responsibility and guilt. *Behaviour Research and Therapy*, 31, 149–154.

Rachman, S. (1994). Pollution of the mind. *Behaviour Research and Therapy,* 32, 311–314.

Rachman, S. (1997). A cognitive theory of obsessions. *Behaviour Research and Therapy*, 35, 793–802.

Rachman, S. (1998). A cognitive theory of obsessions: Elaborations. *Behaviour Research and Therapy*, 36, 385–401.

Rachman, S. (2002). A cognitive theory of compulsive checking. *Behaviour Research and Therapy,* 40, 625–639.

Rachman, S. (2004). Fear of contamination. *Behaviour Research and Therapy, 42*, 1227–1255.

Rachman, S. (2006). *The Fear of Contamination: Assessment and Treatment* (Cognitive Behaviour Therapy: Science and Practice). Oxford.

Rachman, S. & de Silva, P. (1978). Abnormal and normal obsessions. *Behaviour Research and Therapy* 16, 233–248.

Rachman, S., Radomsky, A. S. & Shafran, R. (2008) Safety behaviour: Reconsideration. *Behaviour Research and Therapy,* 46(2), 163–173.

Radomsky, A. S., Shafran, R., Coughtrey, A. E. & Rachman, S. (2010) *Cognitive-behavior therapy for compulsive checking in OCD. Cognitive and Behavioral Practice,* 17(2), 119–131.

Rachman, S., Shafran, R., Mitchell, D., Trant, J. & Teachman, B. (1996). How to remain neutral: An experimental analysis of neutralization. *Behaviour Research and Therapy*, 34, 889–898.

Rachman, S. J. (2003). Compulsive checking. In R. G. Menzies & P. de Silva (Eds), *Obsessive Compulsive Disorder: Theory, Research and Treatment* (The Wiley Series in Clinical Psychology edn). West Sussex: Wiley, pp. 138–180.

Rachman, S. J. (2004). Fear of contamination. *Behaviour Research and Therapy*, 42, 1227–1255.

Rachman, S. J. (2006). *The fear of contamination: Assessment and treatment*. Oxford: Oxford University Press.

Rachman, S. J. (2010) Betrayal: A psychological analysis. *Behaviour Research and Therapy*, 48, 304–311.

Radomsky, A. S. & Alcolado, G. M. (2010). Don't even think about checking: Mental checking causes memory distrust. *Journal of Behavior Therapy & Experimental Psychiatry*, 41, 345-351.

Radomsky, A. S., Gilchrist, P. T. & Dussault, D. D. (2006). Repeated checking really does cause memory distrust. *Behaviour Research and Therapy*, 44, 305–316.

Radomsky, A. S. & Rachman, S. (1999). Memory bias in obsessive-compulsive disorder (OCD). *Behaviour Research and Therapy* , 37(7), 605–618.

Radomsky, A. S. & Rachman, S. (2004). The importance of importance in OCD memory research. *Invited paper in the Journal of Behavior Therapy and Experimental Psychiatry,* 35(2), 137–151.

Radomsky, A. S. & Rachman, S. (2004). Symmetry, ordering and arranging compulsive behaviour. *Behaviour Research & Therapy*, 42, 893–913.

Rasmussen, S. A. & Eisen, J. L. (1989). Clinical Features of Obsessive Compulsive Disorder. *Psychiatric Annals,* 19, 67–73.

Rasmussen, S. A. & Tsang, M. T. (1986) Clinical characteristics and family history in DSM-III obsessive-compulsive disorder. *American Journal of Psychiatry*, 143, 317–322.

Rassin, E., Merckelbach, H., Muris, P. & Schmidt, H. (2001). The thought action fusion scale: Further evidence for its reliability and validity. *Behaviour Research and Therapy,* 39, 537–544.

Rassin, E., Merckelbach, H., Muris, P. & Spaan, V. (1999). Thought-action fusion as a causal factor in the development of intrusions. *Behaviour Research and Therapy*, 37, 231–237.

Rauch, S. L. & Jenike, M. A. (1993). Neurobiological models of obsessive-compulsive disorder. *Psychosomatics,* 34, 20–32.

Rees, C. S. & van Koesveld, K. E. (2008). An open trial of group metacognitive therapy for obsessive-compulsive disorder. *Journal of Behavior Therapy and Experimental Psychiatry,* 39, 451–458.

Regier, D. A., Farmer, M. E., Rae, D. S., Myers, J. K., Kramer, M., Robins, L. N., George, L. K., Karno, M. & Locke, B. Z. (1993) One-month prevalence of mental-disorders in the United States and sociodemographic characteristics – the Epidemiologic Catchment-Area Study. *Acta Psychiatrica Scandinavica*, 88, 35–47.

Regier, D. A., Myers, J. K., Kramer, M., Robins, L. N., Blazer, D. G., Hough, R. L., Eaton, W. W. & Locke, B. Z. (1984) The NIMH Epidemiologic Catchment-Area Program – Historical context, major objectives, and study population characteristics. *Archives of General Psychiatry, 41*, 934–941.

Reimold, M., Smolka, M. N., Zimmer, A., Batra, A., Knobel, A., Solbach, C., Mundt, A., Smoltczyk, H. U., Goldman, D., Mann, K., Reischl, G., Machulla, H. J., Bares, R. & Heinz, (2007). Reduced availability of serotonin transporters in obsessive-compulsive disorder correlates with symptom severity – a [11C]DASB PET study. *J Neural Transm.*, 114, 1603–1609.

Reinisch, A. I. (2009) Characteristics of six recent animal hoarding cases in Manitoba. *Canadian Veterinary Journal*, 50, 1069–1073.

Rheaume, J., Freeston, M. H., Dugas, M. J., Letarte, H. & Ladouceur, R. (1995). Perfectionism, responsibility and obsessive–compulsive symptoms. *Behaviour Research and Therapy*, 33, 785–794.

Rheaume, J., Ladouceur, R., Freeston, M. H. & Letarte, H. (1994). Inflated responsibility and its role in OCD. II. Psychometric studies of a semi-idiographic measure. *Journal of Psychopathology and Behavioral Assessment*, 16, 265–276.

Richter, M. A., Summerfeldt, L. J., Antony, M. M. & Swinson, R. P. (2003) Obsessive- compulsive spectrum conditions in obsessive-compulsive disorder and other anxiety disorders. *Depress Anxiety* 18, 118–127.

Rodriguez-Martin, J. L., Barbanoj, J. M., Perez, V. & Sacristan, M. (2003). Transcranial magnetic stimulation for the treatment of obsessive-compulsive disorder. *Cochrane Database of Systematic Reviews*, 2.

Roper, G., Rachman, S. & Hodgson, R. (1973). An experiment on obsessional checking. *Behaviour Research and Therapy*,11, 271–277.

Rosa-Alcázar, A. I., Sánchez-Meca, J., Gómez-Conesa, A. & Marín-Martínez, F. (2008). Psychological treatment of obsessive-compulsive disorder: A meta-analysis. *Clinical Psychology Review*, 28, 1310–1325.

Rosenberg, D. R., Mirza, Y., Russell, A., Tang, J., Smith, J. M., Preeya-Banerjee, S., Bhandari, R., Rose, M., Ivey, J., Boyd, C. & Moore, G. J. (2004). Reduced anterior cingulate glutamatergic concentrations in childhood OCD and major depression versus healthy controls. *Journal of the American Academy of Child & Adolescent Psychiatry*, 43(9), 1146–1153.

Ross, J., Badner, J., Garrido, H., Sheppard, B., Chavira, D. A., Grados, M., Woo, J. M., Doo, P., Umaña, P.. Fournier, E., Murray, S. S., Mathews, C. A. (2011). Genomewide linkage analysis in Costa Rican families implicates chromosome 15q14 as a candidate region for OCD. *Human Genet*, 130, 795–805.

Rousseau, F., Bonaventure, J., Legeai-Mallet, L., Pelet, A., Rozet, J-M., Maroteaux, P., Le Merrer, M. & Munnich, A. (1994). Mutations in the gene encoding fibroblast growth factor receptor-3 in achondroplasia. *Nature*, 371, 252–254.

Rowa, K. & Purdon, C. (2005).Why are certain intrusive thoughts more upsetting than others? *Behavioural and Cognitive Psychotherapy*, 31, 1–11.

Ruffolo, J. S., Phillips, K. A., Menard, W., Fay, C. & Weisberg, R. B. (2006) Comorbidity of body dysmorphic disorder and eating disorders: Severity of psychopathology and body image disturbance. *International Journal of Eating Disorders*, 39, 11–19.

Ruscio, A. M., Stein, D. J., Chiu, W. T. & Kessler, R. C. (2010) The epidemiology of obsessive-compulsive disorder in the National Comorbidity Survey Replication. *Molecular Psychiatry*, 15, 53–63.

Ruta, L., Mugno, D., D'Arrigo, V. G., Vitiello, B. & Mazzone, L. (2010) Obsessive-compulsive traits in children and adolescents with Asperger syndrome. *European Childs & Adolescent Psychiatry*, 19, 17–24.

Saad, G. (2006). Sex differences in OCD symptomatology: An evolutionary hypothesis. *Medical Hypotheses*, 67, 1455–1459.

Sackeim, H. A., Prudic, J., Fuller, R., Keilp, J., Lavori, P. W. & Olfson, M. (2007). The cognitive effects of electroconvulsive therapy in community settings. *Neuropsychopharmacology*, 32, 244–254.

Salkovskis, P. M. (1985). Obsessional-compulsive problems: A cognitive-behavioural analysis. *Behaviour Research and Therapy*, 23, 571–583.

Salkovskis, P. M. (1996). Cognitive-behavioral approaches to understanding obsessional problems. In R. M. Rapee (Ed.), *Current Controversies in the Anxiety Disorders.* New York: Guilford, pp. 103–133.

Salkovskis, P. M. & Campbell, P. (1994). Thought suppression in naturally occurring negative intrusive thoughts. *Behaviour Research and Therapy*, 32, 1–8.

Salkovskis, P. M., Shafran, R., Rachman, S. J. & Freeston, M. H. (1999). Multiple pathways to inflated responsibility beliefs in obsessional problems: Possible origins and implications for therapy and research. *Behaviour Research and Therapy*, 37, 1055–1072.

Salkovskis, P. M., Wroe, A., Gledhill, A., Morrison, N., Forrester, E., Richards, C., Reynolds, M. & Thorpe, S. (2000). Responsibility attitudes and interpretations are characteristic of obsessive compulsive disorder. *Behaviour Research and Therapy*, 38(4), 347–372.

Salzman, L. (1983) Psychoanalytic therapy of the obsessional patient. *Current Psychiatric Therapies*, 22, 53–59.

Samuels, J. F., Bienvenu, O. J., Grados, M. A., Cullen, B., Riddle, M. A., Liang, K., Eaton, W. W. & Nestadt, G. (2008) Prevalence and correlates of hoarding behavior in a community-based sample. *Behaviour Research & Therapy*, 46, 836–844.

Sassouni, V. & Forrest, E. J. (1971) *Orthodontics in Dental Practice*. St Louis: C. V. Mosby.

Satel, S. L. & McDougle, C. J. (1991). Obsessions and compulsions associated with cocaine abuse [letter]. *Am J Psychiatry*, 148, 947.

Savage, C. R., Baer, L. & Keuthen, N. J. (1999) Organizational strategies mediate nonverbal memory impairment in obsessive-compulsive disorder. *Biological Psychiatry*, 45, 905–916.

Saxena, S., Bota, R. G. & Brody, A. L. (2001). Brain-behavior relationships in obsessive-compulsive disorder. *Semin Clin Neuropsychiatry*, 6, 82–101.

Schmidt, N. B. & Harrington, P. (1995) Cognitive-behavioral treatment of body dysmorphic disorder: A case report. *Journal of Behavior Therapy & Experimental Psychiatry*, 26, 161–167.

Sealey, A. (2011). The strange case of the Freudian case history: The role of long case histories in the development of psychoanalysis. *History of the Human Sciences,* 24(1), 36–50.

Sensky, T., Turkington, D., Kingdon, D., Scott, J. L., Scott, J., Siddle, R. & Barnes, T. R. (2000). A randomized controlled trial of cognitive-behavioral therapy for persistent symptoms in schizophrenia resistant to medication. *Archives of General Psychiatry*, 57(2), 165.

Sexton, K. A. & Dugas, M. J. (2009). Defining distinct negative beliefs about uncertainty: Validating the factor structure of the Intolerance of Uncertainty Scale. *Psychological Assessment*, 21, 176–186.

Shabanpour, R., Zahiroddin, A. R., Janbozorgi, M. & Ghaeli, P. (2012). Assessment of defense styles and mechanisms in Iranian patients suffering from obsessive compulsive or panic disorders versus normal controls using Persian version of Defense Style Questionnaire-40. *Iranian J Psychiatry,* 7(1), 31–35.

Shafran, R., Cooper, Z. & Fairburn, C. G. (2002). Clinical perfectionism: A cognitive-behavioural analysis. *Behaviour Research and Therapy,* 40(7), 773–791.

Shafran, R. & Rachman, S. (2004). Though-Action Fusion: A review. *Journal of Behaviour Therapy and Experimental Psychiatry,* 35, 87–107.

Shafran, R., Thordarson, D. S. & Rachman, S. (1996). Thought-action fusion in obsessive compulsive disorder. *Journal of Anxiety Disorders*, 10, 379–391.

Shafran, R., Watkins, E. & Charman, T. (1996). Guilt in obsessive-compulsive disorder. *Journal of Anxiety Disorders,* 10, 509–516.

Sher, K. J., Frost, R. O., Kushner, M., Crews, T. M. & Alexander, J. E. (1989). Memory deficits in compulsive checkers: Replication and extension in a clinical sample. *Behaviour Research and Therapy,* 27, 65–69.

Sher, K. J., Mann, B. & Frost, R. O. (1984). Cognitive dysfunction in compulsive checkers: further explorations. *Behaviour Research and Therapy,* 22, 493–502.

Shih, R. A., Belmonte, P. L. & Zandi, P. P. (2004). A review of the evidence from family, twin and adoption studies for a genetic contribution to adult psychiatric disorders. *International Review of Psychiatry,* 16(4), 260–283.

Shugart, Y. Y., Samuels, J., Willour, V. L., Grados, M. A., Greenberg, B. D., Knowles, J. A. , McCracken, J. T., Rauch, S. L., Murphy, D. L., Wang, Y., Pinto, A., Fyer, A. J., Piacentini, J., Pauls, D. L., Cullen, B.,

Page, J., Rasmussen, S. A., Bienvenu, O. J., Hoehn-Saric, R., Valle, D., Liano, K. Y., Riddle, M. A. & Nestadt, G. (2006). Genome-wide linkage scan for obsessive compulsive disorder: Evidence for susceptibility loci on chromosomes 3q, 7p, 1q, 15q, and 6q. *Molecular Psychiatry*, 11, 763–770.

Sibbald, B. & Roland, M. (1998). Understanding controlled trials: Why are randomised controlled trials important? *British Medical Journal*, 316, 201–202.

Sica, C., Novara, C., Sanavio, E., Dorz, S. & Coradeschi, D. (2002). Obsessive compulsive disorder cognitions across cultures. In R. O. Frost & G. Steketee (eds), *Cognitive Approaches to Obsession and Compulsions: Theory Assessment and Treatment*. Pergamon Press, pp. 371–384.

Sieg, J. & Scholz, O. B. (2001). Subjektives Gefü hls- und Kö rpererleben bei Wasch- und Kontrollzwangshandlungen [Subjective emotional and physical experience during compulsive washing and checking.]. *Verhaltenstherapie*, 11, 288–296.

Siev, J. & Cohen, A. B. (2007) Is thought-action fusion related to religiosity? Differences between Christians and Jews. *Behaviour Research & Therapy*, 45, 829–837.

de Silva, P. (2006). Culture and obsessive compulsive disorder. *Psychiatry*, 12, 402–404.

Simpson, H. B., Lombardo, I., Slifstein, M., Huang, H. Y., Hwang, D. R., bi-Dargham, A., Liebowitz, M. R. & Laruelle, M. (2003). Serotonin transporters in obsessive-compulsive disorder: A positron emission tomography study with [(11)C]McN 5652. *Biological Psychiatry*, 23, 1079–1099.

Soomro, G. M., Altman, D. G., Rajagopal, S. & Oakley Browne, M. O. (2008). Selective serotonin re-uptake inhibitors (SSRIs) versus placebo for obsessive-compulsive disorder (OCD). *Cochrane Database of Systematic Reviews, Issue 1.*

Starcevic, V., Berle, D., Brakoulias, V., Sammut, P., Moses, K., Milicevic, D., Hannan, A. (2011). The nature and correlates of avoidance in obsessive-compulsive disorder.. *Australian and New Zealand Journal of Psychiatry*, 45, 871–9.

Steketee, G. & Frost, R. O. (2007). *Compulsive Hoarding and Acquiring: Therapist Guide*. New York: Oxford University Press.

Steketee, G., Frost, R. O. & Kyrios, M. (2003). Cognitive aspects of compulsive hoarding. *Cognitive Therapy & Research*, 27, 463–479.

Steketee, G., Quay, S. & White, K. (1991) Religion and guilt in OCD patients. *Journal of Anxiety Disorders*, 5, 359–367.

Stengler-Wenzke, K., Muller, U., Angermeyer, M. C., Sabri, O. & Hesse, S. (2004). Reduced serotonin transporter-availability in obsessive-compulsive disorder (OCD). *Eur. Arch. Psychiatry Clin. Neurosci.*, 254, 252–255.

Stobie, B., Taylor, T., Quigley, A., Ewing, S. & Salkovskis, P. M. (2007) 'Contents may vary': A pilot study of treatment histories of OCD patients. *Behavioural and Cognitive Psychotherapy*, 35(3), 273–282.

Storch, E. A., Ledley, D. R., Lewin, A. B., Murphy, T. K., Johns, N. B., Goodman, W. K. & Geffken, G. R. (2006) Peer victimization in children with obsessive-compulsive disorder: Relations with symptoms of psychopathology. *Journal of Clinical Child and Adolescent Psychology,* 35 (3), 446–455.

Szesko, P. R., Christian, C., MacMaster, F., Lencz, T., Mirza, Y., Taormina, S. P., Easter, P., Rose, M., Michalopoulou, G. A. & Rosenberg, D. R. (2008). Gray matter structural alterations in psychotropic drug-naive paediatric obsessive-compulsive disorder: An optimized voxel-based morphometry study. *Am J Psychiatry,* 165, 1299–1307.

Swedo, S. E. & Leonard, H. L. (1994) Childhood movement disorders and obsessive-compulsive disorder. *Journal of Clinical Psychiatry*, 55, 32–37.

Swedo, S. E., Leonard, H. L., Garvey, M., Mittleman, B., Allen, A. J., Perlmutter, S. , Lougee, L., Dow, S., Zamkoff, J. & Dubbert, B. K. (1998). Pediatric autoimmune neuropsychiatric disorders associated with streptococcal infections: clinical description of the first 50 cases. *Am J Psychiatry,* 155, 264–271.

Swedo, S. E., Rapoport, J. L., Leonard, H. L., Lenane, M. & Cheslow, D. (1989) Obsessive-compulsive disorder in children and adolescents: Clinical phenomenology of 70 consecutive cases. *Archives of General Psychiatry*, 46, 335–341.

Tallis, F. (1996). Compulsive washing in the absence of phobic illness and anxiety. *Behaviour Research and Therapy,* 34, 361–362.

Tallis, F., Pratt, P. & Jamani, N. (1999). Obsessive compulsive disorder, checking, and non-verbal memory: A neuropsychological investigation. *Behaviour Research and Therapy*, 37, 161–166.

Tata, P., Leibowitz, J., Prunty, M. J., Cameron, M. & Pickering, A. D. (1996). Attentional bias in obsessional compulsive disorder. *Behaviour Research and Therapy,* 34, 53–60.

Timpano, K. R., Exner, C., Glaesmer, H., Rief , W., Keshaviah, A., Brähler, E. & Wilhelm, S. (2011) The epidemiology of the proposed DSM-5 hoarding disorder: Exploration of acquisition specifier, associated features, and distress. *Journal of Clinical Psychiatry*, 72, 780–786.

Tolin, D., Frost, R. & Steketee, G. (2007). An open trial of cognitive-behavioral therapy for compulsive hoarding. *Behaviour Research and Therapy*, 45(7), 1461–1470.

Tolin, D. F., Abramowitz, J. S., Bartholomew, D. B., Amir, N., Street, G. P. & Foa, E. B. (2001). Memory and memory confidence in obsessive–compulsive disorder. *Behaviour Research and Therapy*, 39, 913–927.

Tolin, D. F., Abramowitz, J. S., Brigidi, B. & Foa, E. B. (2003). Intolerance of uncertainty in obsessive-compulsive disorder. *Journal of Anxiety Disorders, 17*, 233–242.

Tolin, D. F., Hamlin, C. & Foa, E. B. (2002). Directed forgetting in obsessive-compulsive disorder: Replication and extension. *Behaviour Research and Therapy,* 40, 793–803.

Tolin, D. F., Woods, C. M. & Abramowitz, J. S. (2006). Disgust sensitivity and obsessive-compulsive symptoms in a non-clinical sample. *Journal of Behavior Therapy and Experimental Psychiatry,* 37, 30–40.

Trinder, H. & Salkovskis, P. M. (1994). Personally relevant intrusions outside the laboratory: Long-term suppression increases intrusion. *Behaviour Research and Therapy*, 32, 833–842.

Tolin, D. F. & Villavicencio, A. (2011) Inattention, but not OCD, predicts the core features of hoarding disorder. *Behaviour Research & Therapy*, 49, 120–125.

Torres, A. R., Prince, M. J., Bebbington, P. E., Bhugra, D., Brugha, T. S., Farrell, M., Jenkins, R., Lewis, G., Meltzer, H. & Singleton, N. (2006) Obsessive-compulsive disorder: Prevalence, comorbidity, impact, and help-seeking in the British National Psychiatric Morbidity Survey of 2000. *American Journal of Psychiatry*, 163, 1978–1985.

Turner, C. M. (2006) Cognitive-behavioural theory and therapy for obsessive-compulsive disorder in children and adolescents: Current status and future directions. *Clinical Psychology Review*, 26, 912–938.

Van den Hout, M. & Kindt, M. (2003) Repeated checking causes memory distrust. *Behaviour Research & Therapy*, 41, 301–316.

van den Hout, M. A., Engelhard, I. M., Toffolo, M. B. J., van Uijen, S. L. (2011). Exposure plus response prevention versus exposure plus safety behaviours in reducing feelings of contamination, fear, danger and disgust: An extended replication of Rachman, Shafran, Radomsky & Zysk (2011). *Journal of Behavior Therapy and Experimental Psychiatry*, 42, 364–370.

van der Wee, N., Stevens, H., Hardeman, H., Denys, D., van Megen, H. J., Kahn, R. S. & Westenberg, H. G. (2001). Enhanced densities of dopamine but not of serotonin transporters in psychotropic-naïve patients with obsessive-compulsive disorder. *J Nucl Med*, 42, 238P.

Van Dijk, A., Klompmakers, A. & Denys, D. (2010). The serotonergic system in obsessive-compulsive disorder. In C. Müller and B. Jacobs (Eds) *Handbook of Behavioral Neurobiology of Serotonin.* London: Academic Press.

Van Grootheest, D. S., Cath, D. C., Beekman, A. T. & Boomsma, D. I. (2005). Twin studies on obsessive-compulsive disorder: A review. *Twin Research and Human Genetics,* 8(5), 450–458.

Veale, D. (2007) Psychopathology of obsessive compulsive disorder. *Psychiatry* 6(6), 225–228.

Veale, D. & Riley, S. (2001). Mirror, mirror on the wall, who is the ugliest of them all? The psychopathology of mirror gazing in body dysmorphic disorder. *Behaviour Research and Therapy*, 39, 1381–1393.

Verdellen, C. W. J., Keijsers, G. P. J., Cath, D. C., Hoogduin, C. A. L. (2004) Exposure with response prevention versus habit reversal in Tourettes's syndrome: A controlled study. *Behaviour Research and Therapy*, 42 (5): 501–511.

Wakabayashi, A., Baron-Cohen, S. & Ashwin, C. (2012) Do the traits of autism-spectrum overlap with those of schizophrenia or obsessive-compulsive disorder in the general population? *Research in Autism Spectrum Disorders*, 6, 717–725.

Warnock-Parkes, E., Salkovskis, P. M. & Rachman, J. (2012) When the problem is beneath the surface in OCD: The cognitive treatment of a case of pure mental contamination. *Behavioural & Cognitive Psychotherapy*, 40, 383–399.

Washington, C. S., Norton, P. J. & Temple, S. (2008) Obsessive-compulsive symptoms and obsessive-compulsive disorder. *Journal of Nervous & Mental Disease*, 196, 456–461.

Wegner, D. M., Schneider, D. J., Carter, S. R. & White, T. L. (1987). Paradoxical effects of thought suppression. *Journal of Personality and Social Psychology,* 53, 5–13.

Wegner, D. M. & Zanakos, S. (1994). Chronic thought suppression. *Journal of Personality,* 62, 615–640.

Weissman, M. M., Bland, R. C., Canino, G. J., Greenwald, S., Hwu, H. G., Lee, C. K., Newman, S. C., Oakley-Browne, M. A., Rubio-Stipec, M., Wickramaratne, P. J., Wittchen, H.-U. & Yeh, E.-K. (1994) The cross national epidemiology of obsessive-compulsive disorder. *Journal of Clinical Psychiatry*, 55, 5–10.

Wells, A. (1997). *Cognitive Therapy of Anxiety Disorders: A Practice Manual and Conceptual Guide*. Chichester, UK: Wiley.

Wells, A. (2000). *Emotional Disorders and Metacognition: Innovative Cognitive Therapy*. Chichester, UK: Wiley.

Wells, A. & Matthews, G. (1994). *Attention and Emotion: A Clinical Perspective*. Hove, UK: Erlbaum.

Wells, M. C. (1990) Treating obsessive-compulsive personalities in psychodynamic/ interpersonal group therapy. *Psychotherapy: Theory, Research, Practice, Training*, 27, 366–379.

Wenzlaff, R. M. & Wegner, D. M. (2000). Thought suppression. *Annual Review of Psychology,* 51, 59–91.

Westbrook, D., Kennerley, H. & Kirk, J. (2007). *An Introduction to Cognitive Behaviour Therapy: Skills and Applications*. London: Sage.

Westenberg, H. G. M., Fineberg, N. A. & Denys, D. (2007). Neurobiology of obsessive-compulsive disorder: Serotonin and beyond. *CNS Spectr,* 12(2, Suppl 3), 14–27.

Whittal, M. L., **Thordarson, D. S.** & McLean, P. D. (2005). Treatment of obsessive-compulsive disorder: Cognitive behavior therapy vs exposure and response prevention. *Behaviour Research & Therapy,* 43(12), 1559–76.

Wilhelm, S., McNally, R. J., Baer, L. & Florin, I. (1996). Directed forgetting in obsessive-compulsive disorder. *Behaviour Research and Therapy,* 34, 633–641.

Willour, V. L., Shugart, Y. Y., Samuels, J., Grado, M., Cullen, B., Bienvenu 3rd, O. J. , Wang, Y., Liang, K-Y., Valle, D., Hoehn-Saric, R., Riddle, M. & Nestadt, G. (2004). Replication study supports evidence for linkage to 9p24 in obsessive-compulsive disorder. *Am J Hum Genet,* 75, 508–513.

Wilson K. A. & Chambless D. L. (1999). Inflated perceptions of responsibility and obsessive-compulsive symptoms. *Behaviour Research & Therapy,* 37, 325–335.

Windheim, K., Veale, D. & Anson, M. (2011) Mirror gazing in body dysmorphic disorder and healthy controls: Effects of duration of gazing. *Behaviour Research & Therapy*, 49, 555–564.

Winnicott, D. (1958). Primary maternal preoccupation. In D.Winnicott (Eds), *Collected Papers: Through Pediatrics to Psychoanalysis*. New York: Basic Books, pp. 300–305.

Woods, D. W. & Miltenberger, R. G. (1996) Are persons with nervous habits nervous? A preliminary examination of habit function in a nonreferred population. *Journal of Applied Behavior Analysis*, 29, 259–261.

Wootton, B. M., Titov, N., Dear, B. F., Spence, J. & Kemp, A. (2011). The acceptability of internet-based treatment and characteristics of an adult sample with obsessive compulsive disorder. *PLoS One*, 6, e20548.

Yang, J., Lee, S. H., Goddard, M. E. & Visscher, P. M. (2011). GCTA: A tool for genome-wide complex trait analysis. *Am J Hum Genet*, 88(1), 76–82.

Yorulmaz, O., Gençöz, T. & Woody, S. (2009). OCD cognitions and symptoms in different religious contexts. *Journal of Anxiety Disorders*, 23, 401–406.

Yorulmaz, O., Gençöz, T. & Woody, S. (2010). Vulnerability factors in OCD symptoms: Cross-cultural comparisons between Turkish and Canadian Samples. *Clinical Psychology and Psychotherapy*, 17, 110–121.

Zhong, C. B. & Liljenquist, K. (2006) Washing away your sins: Threatened morality and physical cleansing. *Science*, 314, 254–254.

Zohar, J., Greenberg, B. & Denys, D. (2012). Obsessive-compulsive disorder. In T. E. Schlaepfer and C. B. Nemeroff (Eds), *Handbook of Clinical Neurology, Vol 106* (3rd Series), *Neurobiology of Psychiatric Disorders*. CITY: Elsevier.

Zohar, J., Mueller, E. A., Insel, T. R., Zohar-Kadouch, R. C. & Murphy, D. L. (1987). Serotongeric responsivity in obsessive-compulsive disorder: Comparison of patients and healthy controls. *Arch. Gen. Psychiatry*, 44(11), 946–951.

Index